REVISITING MARXISM

A Bourgeois Reassessment

Tibor R. Machan

Hamilton Books
A member of
The Rowman & Littlefield Publishing Group
Lanham · Boulder · New York · Toronto · Oxford

Copyright © 2006 by
Hamilton Books
4501 Forbes Boulevard
Suite 200
Lanham, Maryland 20706
Hamilton Books Acquisitions Department (301) 459-3366

PO Box 317
Oxford
OX2 9RU, UK

Library of Congress Control Number: 2005934028
ISBN 0-7618-3295-5 (paperback : alk. ppr.)

Table of Contents

Acknowledgements

J. Roger Lee has helped me focus some of my ideas on Marx throughout our many discussions of Marxism and I wish to thank him for this, as well as for his reading and making suggestions on the final draft of the manuscript. I have also benefited from many hours of discussion with Dr. Sidney Hook—some of it related in the Appendix to this work—who would very likely have disagreed with many of my interpretations and views but had been extremely patient with me as he tried to get me to see Marxism in a way he considered most appropriate. John C. O'Brien, editor of *IJSE/IREE*, has been helpful with my work on this project, which I appreciate a great deal. And David M. Brown read the manuscript and provided much help with its final configuration. Chapman University, the Hoover Institution, and Freedom Communications, Inc., gave me much support with this and other projects. Thanks to all.

Preface

Why Bother with Karl Marx Again?

For quite a long time there was no direct criticism of Marx's ideas from those who value the position he most harshly attacked, bourgeois capitalism. The few who did criticize Marx were economists such as Thomas Sowell and, much earlier, Eugen Böhm-Bawerk and Ludwig von Mises. Others attacked Marx's ideas but did not actually defend capitalism itself. And some tried to discredit Marx on the basis of his alleged bad behavior.

In 1987, shortly before the fall of the Soviet Empire, David Conway published his *A Farewell to Marx*, a very well-written outline and sustained philosophical criticism of Marx. But it is advanced in part from a position that uncritically embraces what I call economism—the *homo economicus* conception of human life. (For example, Conway says all parties must benefit from voluntary exchange. This assumes a subjective theory of value. My own view is that a classical individualist or egoist theory backs free exchange without Conway's implausible position. I find Conway's positive theory inadequate as an alternative to Marxism and I understand he has by now actually changed his thinking on this and many other issues.)

This work, which draws a good deal from my long essay in the *International Journal of Social Economics* (1988), aims to be an exposition and a novel *individualist* criticism of Marxism. In many of my works I have argued for and championed bourgeois capitalism, a position Marx despised and found much fault with, at least as a general system of political economy. My basic stance is that each person is by nature a human individual, which doesn't preclude a significant social attribute. This "classical" individualism sees the free society and capitalism as morally proper [Machan, 1998]. (It is *classical* because it doesn't construe the individual as being utterly unique, without a human nature; thus this position owes more to Aristotle than to Thomas Hobbes, albeit with certain modifications taken from John Locke and other classical liberals.)

Now, to begin with, the title of the work may seem paradoxical. The idea of the bourgeoisie is central in Marxist thought. It means roughly what some today designate the "middle class"—people who make their living by utilizing their property, including capitalists, entrepreneurs, manufacturers, merchants, business owners, and professionals (doctors, lawyers, etc.) who own their skills and labor. Used in this way, doesn't the term suggest concurrence with crucial aspects of Marx's system? Wasn't Marx himself the "inventor of the bourgeoisie"?

Yet Marx did not create the bourgeoisie, he merely isolated it for special focus and analysis. Some people could always have been usefully designated by that term or its cognates, Marx or no Marx. Such individuals merely became a good deal more numerous under a largely capitalist political economy, worthy of special study. Indeed, in a capitalist society arguably everyone is a member of the bourgeoisie. That political economic system gives legal recognition and protection to every individual's right to person and property. Proprietors—of whatever may be traded in markets by owners and their agents—are the bourgeoisie. This certainly suggests that membership in the bourgeoisie could be open to anyone, contrary to what Marx believed.

Marx saw the bourgeoisie as a reasonably fixed class, from which only a few people could extricate themselves, "subjectively." This class had a limited but determinate function in human history. Looked at in a different way, however, the bourgeois form of life is optional, a way in which most people might and maybe even ought to live.

This form of life is, moreover, *morally* defensible. Unlike Marxism, this kind of life is in no need of eventual liquidation, even by some allegedly inevitable force of history. But the bourgeoisie needs a moral defense. In this publication I will first criticize Marx's views and then offer some clear clues as to why bourgeois individualism is a better social, political and economic idea. In my concluding section I will briefly explain why the capitalist economy is justified as a byproduct of the political system of individual rights.

I address my work to the general reader who is only cursorily familiar with Karl Marx and the political movement he unleashed. Most of these potential readers have an impression of Marx marred by suspicion. Others carry around a puzzled view of Marx. For many, Karl Marx represents someone to be feared. These readers may have heard that the former Soviet Union had professed commitment to Marx's philosophy, or that terrorists in the Middle East, Europe, or Central and South America have been Marxists or neo-Marxists. They may be vaguely aware that some of the fiercest critics of the United States government, as well as American culture as a whole, at least admire Marx. They may know of some contemporary Marxist and neo-Marxist thinkers—the late Michael Harrington and Sidney Hook, Jürgen Habermas, Robert Heilbroner, Robert Lekachman and Robert Kuttner—as well as of Marxist social movements. They all drew heavily on Marx's ideas in their vehement reproach of capitalism and bourgeois values, although some bring in other anti-bourgeois sources, of which there are many.

I will be drawing heavily on Marx's *Grundrisse* [Marx, 1971]— with added reference to earlier and later quasi-humanistic and more dialectical materialist Marxist works. It is fruitful to approach Marx via *Grundrisse*. He was following a fairly steady path throughout his life's works and expressed all of his ideas in this very rich, albeit unpublished project.

Marx's main concern was to ameliorate humanity's suffering and misfortune. He seemed to think both could be eradicated. And, while there is much in this objective one can admire, it is a purely negative approach to human life and fails to take into account the inherently diverse character of human existence, not only regarding starting points but also achievements. Marx, I think, did not wish to admit that people can be morally good, bad, or mediocre. He wouldn't consider that this fact produces much that is lamentable in human life, despite the fact that in his own personal relations he freely blamed many people close to him for various ills of which he was aware. He was, in short, a utopian theorist with a scientistic confidence in the realization of his utopia. His arguments are interesting and worth looking at and scrutinizing by those who find it vital to address the issues he confronts.

I wanted to produce a rather plainspoken discussion of Marx. Marx himself meant to move people, to lead them to action, to raise their consciousness. I too wish to convince and influence.

The points I will raise are especially relevant now that even though the Soviet Union has collapsed, innumerable Marxists yet remain supportive of various Marxian notions, claiming, among other things, that the USSR never actually represented Marx's ideas at all. Seeing the central ideas of Marxism and just how flexible that doctrine is, we will be able to tell, for example, whether the much discussed and hailed *glasnost* (i.e. openness), *á la* Mikhail S. Gorbachev's leadership of the USSR just prior to its demise could be squared with Marxism or was a radical departure.

I aim to explain, also, what there is about Marxism that one needs to understand, so that its appeal may be appreciated. This is, accordingly, not yet another work that attempts to revamp Marxism. Many Marxist scholars have in fact largely revised Marx beyond recognition by now, removing from it any taint of support for its Stalinist, even Leninist versions. So I will not be dwelling on the innumerable varieties of Marxism forged by the likes of Marcuse, Althusser, Lukacs, Gramsci, Habermas, Cohen, Wood, Elster and others. I share the late Sidney Hook's view that if Marx were alive today, he would repeat what he said shortly before he died, namely, "I am not a Marxist."

Although there may be value in knowing about the works of all of those who wish to capture for themselves the label "true Marxist," in my view it is more important for us all to familiarize ourselves with Marx's views. Unlike other major thinkers of the

West, Marx hasn't been dead so long that we should now pay more attention to neo-Marxists than to him. This seems to be especially true when it comes to non-scholarly, lay discussions of his ideas.

Throughout this work I try to give a fair but uncomplicated rendition of Marx's views. I also explore the flaws of Marxism. I end by arguing that individualism, rightly understood, rather than Marxist collectivism, is a better way of understanding human life.

Marx tried to build a foundation for a way of life that takes human beings to be intelligent tribal animals. For him we lack any real individuality and, therefore, any individual rights. In this respect the Soviets followed Marxism quite faithfully. For Marxism the diversity of values in capitalist or in quasi-capitalist society is a frivolity, a sign of decadence. The view that communism is the last and most mature stage of humanity's development through history already hints at the main problem of Marxism. It is the notion that human beings are only important as bits of an "organic body," not as human individuals. The global commune is heaven on earth and the projects of individuals must be made, forcibly if need be, to conform to it.

Yet, in fact, human beings are by nature not just members of a species but also essentially individuals. Their individuality—thus their uniqueness and distinctiveness as individuals—is as significant about them as their collective selves or, as Marx put it, their species-being, perhaps for certain purposes even more so. This explains why the capitalist or free market economic system, with its legal foundation in constitutional natural rights theory, is the best economic arrangement for them. But then why does Marx's collectivist—socialist and communist—vision have such wide appeal to so many people?

One reason is that traditionally, the great human family has been offered up as some kind of wonderful image for us to anticipate, not to mention attempt to implement. The idea that somehow all humanity could turn out to be a wonderful family, living in harmony, peace and prosperity, is perennial. Marx's contribution to this idea is that it is actually attainable here on earth, sometime in the future. He thought the laws of nature were driving humanity to that state.

Then there is also Marx's view that human physical labor is the most important aspect of human living. This view may be regarded as radical enough, though Marx did not invent it. The idea certainly holds out promise to millions of people whose fives have been consigned to insignificance by different philosophies. These philosophies have tended to put the spiritual life ahead of everything else. The worker was thus left to take part in something menial and lowly. Yet this would appear to be quite unjust and cruel, given the evident hardship of most laborers. To promise these men and women that their kind of life will ultimately be rewarded, not after death but in the lives of at least most of their future brethren, can invite a considerable welcome from the masses of humankind. And compassionate intellectuals, religious leaders, politicians, and other social trendsetters would be expected to give their support to this vision as well. Finally, there is the idea that Karl Marx placed all this on a scientific basis. This would be important to all intelligent people who have great respect for science and what it can do and has done for humanity.

Sometimes the status quo is seen as unavoidable, as a necessary burden, and only vague moralistic hopes are offered to overcome it: the rich ought to be more generous, helpful, but will they be, really? This kind of utopian thinking will get the poor nowhere, nor those who would wish to come to their aid. It is more serious—is it not?—to rest one's confidence on science, on the laws of nature, which Marx argued will drive the working class toward its deserved salvation. With this idea there can now be some serious expectation, not just hope, of improvement.

There is another, more important reason why Marx needs to be understood by most people who take part in the life of a democratic political system. Marxism opposes certain objective values. These need to be defended: e.g. Marxism rejects the institution of private property rights. It advocates abolishing it, if not by way of violent revolution then by way of the ballot box. Measures such as rent control laws, forcing companies not to relocate when that means losing profits, limiting the authority individuals have even over their private homes—all this and many related developments on the contemporary intellectual and political front is a kind of creeping Marxism. It can lead to the eventual abolition of private property and, thereby, of private, individual responsibility, the foundation of liberal democratic republics.

But isn't Marxism itself the height of democracy? Despite the oft-heard claim that it is, Marxism rejects the independent decisions of individuals and prefers people to be made to do the right thing, be it their choice or not! The democracy in Marxism is of the kind that is "for the people" but not "by the people." It ushers in communal life forcibly, which will wipe out the personal domain. In this monograph I will argue that knowing something about Marxism and its antagonism to individualism is a vital prerequisite for making the right choice between the two. And such acknowledgement will also be vital to saving individualism—which, at any rate, I will defend as a worthy goal in its own right!

Most supporters of individualist capitalism, the system that Marxism is designed to erase and overcome by way of socialism and then communism, defend it on grounds of its practical value. They argue that capitalism works well, is efficient for producing a lot of what we like to have, makes us all free to boot. What they will not add is the crucial fact that such a system is philosophically and morally pre-eminent. Individualist capitalism is indeed morally superior to all other five options. It is not a phony panacea, not an approach that pretends to guarantee or promise success for all, regardless of personal effort, regardless of some good fortune. But nonetheless it is the best political idea around.

Communism, in contrast, despite Marx's protests, is a utopia, a vision with no substance behind it. Such visions often manage to be appealing to desperate as well as ambitious people who are looking for some release from hardship, if not for themselves personally, then at least for those for whom they have strong feelings of affinity. When one defends the better alternative, however, for it efficiency, practicality, but no moral superiority, then one is sure to lose the argument and, eventually, the actual political fight.

It is necessary, in connection with human affairs, to demonstrate that a system or policy is ultimately morally justified, superior to those with which it stands in competition. Human beings require some sense of being on the right side, not just of managing to be expedient and practical. They want to know that they have lived well, even nobly, not just "gotten by." Self-esteem, the knowledge of one's own worth—including the worth of the kind of system one believes to be just—is vital to everyone. As Adam Smith [Smith, 1939] noted:

> It is not the love of our neighbor, it is not the love of mankind, which upon many occasions prompts us to the practice of... the virtues. It is a stronger love, a more powerful love, which generally takes place upon such occasions: the love of what is honourable and noble, of the grandeur, and dignity, and superiority of our own character.

Marxism is wrong but alluring. It seems more inspiring than the "bourgeois" idea of a society of free and politically equal people who must, however, seek personal salvation on their own. Yet that kind of community is ultimately both more noble and practical. The free society makes ample room for human virtue and excellence in all the spheres of concern to us—commerce, science, leisure, art and the like. What it does not pretend to guarantee is that one will necessarily do well at one's life. It is honest. And yet it is fully gratifying from the moral point of view and indeed holds out the best hope for the very workers on whose behalf Marxism has been defended.

As I've suggested, I find the posthumously published *Grundrisse* the most measured yet clear expression of Marx's ideas. It was written while Marx was involved in numerous political and intellectual activities, and he mentioned writing it in several of his letters to Engels. It is not primarily a book addressed to economists but rather one in which Marx draws on all manner of ideas to make his points, historical, philosophical and economic.

Incidentally, I have no intention of attacking Marx personally. Even if justified, that would not show that his ideas are wrong—some very unpleasant people have good ideas! What is important is how good Marx's ideas are and whether they deserve our loyalty or disdain.

So we must do justice to the ideas, not lambaste their author or cast his views in a form that makes them unappealing from the start. Marx would not have caught on to the extent that he has if his ideas could be rendered honestly in a wholly unfavorable light. If entirely unappealing ideas really became popular with human beings, we would be in deep trouble indeed

Chapter 1. Essentials of Marxism: Philosophy and Political Economy

Is Marx a Dialectical Materialist?

As with all prominent thinkers, Marx too is indebted to several predecessors, most notably to the dialectical idealist philosopher G.W.F. Hegel (1770-1831) and to the materialist Ludwig Feuerbach (1804-72). Although Marx never applied to himself the characterization of dialectical materialist, he freely noted that "I am a materialist." And he tells us that "Hegel's dialectic is the basis of all dialectic, but only after it has been stripped of its mystical form, and this precisely is what differentiates my method" [Marx, 1977, p. 244]. Although, as many have noted, he rejected Hegel's particular version of the dialectic, he declared that "it must be turned right side up again, if you should discover the rational kernel within the mystical shell" [Marx, 1977, p. 420]. Thus it is perfectly accurate to designate Marx a dialectical materialist. He fashioned Hegelian dialectics to the materialism he learned from Feuerbach. Hegel's dialectics is idealist. That is, he saw reality mainly as spiritual and the principle of conflict roughly one that obtains between some spiritual and some material forces.

In Marx no clear-cut metaphysical basis for the dialectic can be found. Marx seems sometimes to accept the dialectical approach on the basis of its usefulness. At other times he seems to endorse it as a necessary part of a whole world view and something that explains everything that is puzzling about nature. It was Friedrich Engels who argued explicitly for a dialectical materialist metaphysics (in his *The Dialectics of Nature* [5]), but it is risky to hold Karl Marx responsible for this. True, he never openly protested Engels's doctrine. But this could very well have more to do with Marx's tolerance of his benefactor's ideas than with his full agreement with them. In the main, the basis of dialectical method in Marx has to he seen as ambivalent.

At the risk of complicating things too much, let me just give a very sketchy statement of the Hegelian origin of the dialectic. In Hegel this principle of constant basic conflict in reality is tied to the view that existence is constituted by the interaction of the Idea of Being with the Actuality. This produces, once the interaction occurs, Becoming. Hegel claimed that this is the actual meaning symbolically expressed in the Christian story of the nature of reality, i.e. the creation of the material universe by means of a spiritual being or pure consciousness. For Hegel it is Idea that ultimately accounts for Actuality. These produce an ongoing contrast or contradiction out of which a process of Becoming commences.

In less complex fashion one might imagine the story along the lines of the relationship of an architect's idea and the actual stuff that idea shapes. Through their interaction what results is the development of the actual structure that will be built. But of course in Hegel the relationship is not between some person's ideas but Idea as such—or Mind, Spirit, or Reason—and actual existence.

The dialectical process appeared to Hegel to solve the problem of change versus stability. How can things be both stable as well as changing or becoming? This is a problem everyone thinks of now and then: how is it that there are things, definite entities, and yet they are transformed from what they are to something else? This makes it appear that things can be both what they are and at once not what they are but something else. Those who worry about these matters—philosophers, cosmologists, and the like—seek, as Hegel did, solutions. The dialectic seemed like a good one to him.

Feuerbach, however, convinced Marx when he argued against Hegel's dialectical idealism. He pointed out, in essence, that for ideas to exist there must he actual beings who think these ideas! Brains must precede thoughts. It is from Feuerbach that we have inherited that now famous phrase, that quintessentially materialist slogan, "Der Mensch ist was er isst" or "Man is what he eats."

Feuerbach was, among other things, an atheist and the founder of modern humanism. He powerfully argued that God is created—i.e. imagined—by human beings, not the other way round. He contended that, if one considers the matter carefully, it is evident that God is an idea human beings thought up as a sort of perfect version of themselves. To wit, God knows everything, whereas we know only some things; God is eternal, whereas we live only for a while; God is omnipotent, whereas we can do only a limited number of things; and God is all good, whereas we are capable merely of being decent enough. Feuerbach proposed that instead of embarking on theology (the study of God) we should embark on anthropology (the study of man). And he also proposed that, instead of loving God, we should learn to love man— which is the central theme of humanism. He was also largely responsible for a central idea in Marx, namely, alienation—self-estrangement. Feuerbach thought God was the result of human beings producing something that is not only part of themselves but also alien to, i.e. far apart from, them.

Feuerbach, however, rejected dialectics. But with this Marx disagreed. For him there was sufficient evidence for the usefulness of dialectics, either as a way to look at history or as an actual process. Whether this shows that he was, after all, in agreement with Engels's dialectical materialist metaphysics, it certainly affected how he approached the analysis of political economy.

In essence, Marx, unlike traditional natural and social scientists, proposed to study not by first gathering unorganized, dispersed evidence but, instead, by first forming an understanding of what a completion of some process of development would produce. Only with this understanding could the processes leading to the completed result be understood. As Marx put it [Marx, 1971, p. 34]:

It seems to be the correct procedure to commence with the real and the concrete, the actual prerequisites; in the case of political economy, to commence with population, which is the basis and the author of the entire productive activity of society. Yet on closer consideration it proves to be wrong.... If we start out...with population, we do so with a chaotic conception of the whole, and by closer analysis we will gradually arrive at simpler ideas; thus we shall proceed from the imaginary concrete to less and less complex abstractions, until we arrive at the simplest determinations. This once attained, we might start on our return journey until we finally came back to population, but this time not as a chaotic notion of an integral whole, but as a rich aggregate of many determinations and relations. The former method is the one which political economy had adopted in the past as its inception. The economists of the seventeenth century, for example, always started out with the living aggregate: population, nation, state, several states, etc., but in the end they invariably arrived by means of analysis at certain leading abstract general principles such as division of labor, money, value, etc.

In contrast, Marx holds that "in the employment of the theoretical method in political economy, the subject, society, must constantly be kept in mind as the premise from which we start."

Marxist dialectical materialism functions as the (heuristic?) method by which the determination of the fully realized aspects of human reality can be understood. It can also be made use of for purposes of understanding actual, current and past, human history. As in attempting to understand a child or a sapling, one needs to keep in mind the adult or the fully-grown tree. Otherwise one cannot understand the fact that a child is in development toward adulthood, the sapling toward becoming a tree. So, in trying to understand (pre-)human history, one needs to keep in mind the subject, society, as it will be in its fullest development (i.e. at the communist stage).

Dialectical materialism sees the development of the central concept of the human sciences, namely, humanity or society, proceeding along lines of constant schism, struggle, conflict, contradiction. But otherwise dialectical materialism sees humanity as a kind of growing person going through infancy, childhood, adolescence, eventually reaching maturity. And when Marx complains about the hardships of the various stages, he might best be conceived of as a "natural historian" who observes what a given growing, developing being is still lacking and will need in its full maturity. Along this line of analysis, Marxism sees capitalism, for example, as the adolescent stage of (pre-)human history, with ample energy or productivity being spent on trivia, awaiting the emergence of socialism and communism, which will make rational use of this energy once it has fully matured.

Let me explain here why I wrote "(pre-)human" above. Marx takes humanity to be an "organic body" [Marx, 1971, p. 33]. When he talks about humanity, he has in mind a kind of being consisting of elements which include the individual people who comprise the human race. This organic whole, humanity, is not yet fully grown—that is, not quite human yet. What most of us call human history, then, for Marx is actually not the history of a fully mature humanity but of the pre-adult stages of history, pre-human history.

For the present I wish merely to sketch the overall picture of Marxism. To get at one of the crucial points in that system, a somewhat difficult issue needs to be considered. Marx undertakes, in a way, to solve one of the thorniest problems some of the greatest thinkers have tried to solve. This is the topic of reconciling a scientific approach to understanding human life with a concern for values, for what is important. In the way we think, usually, there appears to be a conflict between taking a scientific perspective and taking an ethical one. That is why many social scientists insist on the value-free status of their disciplines. Yet it is also clear that we all make value judgments—about how women should be treated, about prejudice, about war, about sexual harassment, about abortion, and so forth. We clearly do, often, blame and praise people—friends, mates, colleagues, political leaders, business executives, foreign heads of state, and so forth.

If the value-free approach were the right one, these activities of ours would be all beside the point—mere biases. If the way many of us think of science were the only sensible way to think about things, there would appear to be no room for values except as the likes and dislikes of people, neither right nor wrong. But when someone opposes, for example, the U.S. military invasion of Iraq, that person would not regard his or her stance as merely a matter of taste. Somehow values are more important, better grounded, than a mere taste or bias.

Marx tried to show that these two apparently mutually exclusive perspectives could be reconciled. And he also wanted to show that while human beings were made by (pre-)human history, they were also making it, not just experiencing it passively. Here again a major philosophical problem is being tackled. Do forces outside us move us, or do we move things on our own? Marx believed we do both. He seemed to agree with Engels that "Men make their history, however it may turn out ... It all depends on what the many individuals will" [quoted in Marx, 1971, p.87]. But he also seems to share the opposite view, also advanced most succinctly by Engels: "Individual wills will as they are driven to by their corporeal constitution and by external, in the last instance economic, circumstances (either their own personal circumstances or general social ones)" [quoted in Marx, 1971, p.112]. But it seems decisive that, when Marx discusses how human beings gain knowledge, he endorses the view, the reflective theory of perceptions [Marx, 1977, p. 164], that Vladimir Lenin would most clearly elaborate in his *Materialism and Empirio-Criticism*.

> The phantoms formed in the human brain are also, necessarily, sublimates of their material life-process, which is empirically verifiable and bound to material premises. Morality, religion, metaphysics, all the rest of ideology and their corresponding forms of consciousness, thus no longer retain the semblance of independence.

This means that independent human thought, in such areas as ethics, religion, philosophy and even science, is, according to Marx, impossible. Here is where Marx's famous economic determinism is most fundamentally grounded—in his epistemology.

Because human beings are naturally involved first of all in the material world, and because this material world impinges on their consciousness and will, what human beings do is entirely a function of the content of the material world that impinges on their minds. Different classes are involved in typically different kinds of material worlds—the propertied with a world of plenty, the proletariat with a world of extreme need.

But this theory is wrong—it fails to account for creative thinking. It even eliminates the possibility of independent thinking for Marx himself. On this view, everyone's behavior, mental or otherwise, is produced by the economic forces that prevail in his or her environment. This is a vital portion of Marxism, even though in their later years both Marx and Engels expressed some dismay about having insisted on it too strongly. But it is vital because it is the way that Marx can make sense of class membership. One belongs inextricably to one's economic class and cannot escape because one's economic environment controls one's thinking and values. This is statistically true, although here and there, as with all statistical generalizations, particular exceptions occur. So just because a few workers become capitalists, a few salaried employees acquire great or considerable wealth, it is not refuted.

Whatever Marx believed, he did not give an account of self-determined human choice but of human behavior that is moved by dialectical and historical forces and laws. Accordingly, he regarded himself as a scientific, not a utopian socialist. While Marx said yes to both—an inevitable development in human history and a history-making role for individuals—his overall theory could only include one of these ideas. Our history-making role had to give way to our passive role as history's creation.

Yet, Marx tried to exempt communists from this historicist trap, claiming that their dialectical science made it possible for them to remain objective, unbiased and able to identify universal laws of history. He wrote:

> Theoretical communists, the only ones who have time to devote to the study of history, are distinguished precisely be-

cause they alone have discovered that throughout history the 'general interest' is created by individuals who are defined as 'private persons.' They know that this contradiction is only a seeming one because one side of it, the so-called 'general,' is constantly being produced by the other side, private interest, and by no means opposes the latter as an impendent force with an independent history—so that this contradiction is in practice always being destroyed and reproduced. [Marx, 1977, p. 183]

In short, unlike *all* other theorists, Marx, as a communist theoretician, isn't captive of a mere historically relative perspective on important matters of political economy and such! A very nice move, one must say—the ideas of others then cannot have the chance of success, only those of communists can!

Marx also advanced the very hopeful idea that science and values are by no means opposed to each other. Marx argued that the values of the working class are sound and that scientifically workers could definitely count on the success of their struggle. He believed that his system could successfully resolve the apparent dichotomy between facts and values, a dichotomy still widely accepted. This view holds that science deals with facts, which we can observe via our senses, but value-judgments are unfounded in any such facts and thus could only be expressions of sentiments or feelings, carrying no factual and objective force. Marx therefore seems to have solved one of the perennial intellectual problems faced by human beings. Has he proved, based on evidence and argument available to any human being who is not seriously incapacitated in his or her faculties, that a certain way of life is really better than others? Has he established that some institutions are indeed superior to others; that acting in certain ways is nobler than acting in others; that certain political regimes are in fact more advanced than others, and so forth?

The realm of values or matters of right and wrong has always puzzled human beings. Virtually every major thinker has tried to address it. And Marx tried to do so by dismissing neither the scientific nor the humanistic or value element of reality. Unlike other philosophers, such as Immanuel Kant, Marx did not introduce a supernatural realm to make sense of values. And, if his attempt were a success, it would certainly be one of the greatest of philosophical feats. And it would also address a very prominent human concern. Just the belief that he succeeded would earn Marx great admiration and a considerable following. How did Marx propose to do what no one is credited with accomplishing? Marx found the solution in the scheme of dialectical materialism.

Unlike earlier materialists, Marx did not make the unbelievable claim that all of reality is in fact just one thing. He did not argue that matter-in-motion is all. He allowed that our ordinary awareness of a multitude of important differences must, in the end, be accepted as very significant. The dialectic process made it possible to explain why reality is both material and genuinely diverse. It even allows the presence of values in some realms of existence. If the dialectical process does obtain in reality, this could serve to explain the emergence of qualitative differences in nature. Such differences are due to more than the mere rearrangements of the same stuff, as earlier materialists had thought.

Of course, materialism itself is extremely satisfactory to anyone desiring to make a difference in this world. If one wants to improve, change, or experiment with things—that is, from the point of view of science and technology—materialism offers hope. Matter is directly accessible and capable of being handled, rearranged, manipulated, etc. The gods may listen and even honor prayers, but they do so at their own caprice. It is we who are able to control nature, at least to some extent. And it need hardly be pointed out to members of contemporary civilization that this view has reaped enormous fruits. Some may be less pleasant than others, but all are very impressive as a testament to the power of human beings to improve the world around them. One need but think of medicine as an example, with life expectancy more than doubling in the last 150 years. Materialism undeniably offers up the goods. But is that all?

In Marx's dialectical materialism human nature is conceived as constituted by two related central elements, consciousness and production. For Marx human beings are by nature conscious producers. This must be understood in the light of his belief in the dialectic. Thus, humanity is composed at first not of fully mature, completely realized conscious producers but of what we would best consider infant versions of this ultimately-to-be-realized human species. Looking at Marx's view this way makes it possible to understand that, while he had an idea of human nature, he also believed that humanity was in the process of attaining the realization of itself. It will reach a stage when all human beings would be fully conscious producers, laboring people or workers who have a direct hand in the organization of their labor.

Marx explicitly suggests viewing humanity the way we view an individual human being. Humanity grows from birth, through several stages such as infancy, childhood, adolescence, to full maturity. In one place he discusses why we still like Greek art, even though by the *dialectic* we must also view it as primitive or at least childish [Marx, 1977, p. 359]:

> But the difficulty is not in grasping the idea that Greek art and epos are bound up with certain forms of social development. It lies rather in understanding why they still constitute for us a source of aesthetic enjoyment and in certain respects prevail as the standard and model beyond attainment.
>
> A man cannot become a child again unless he becomes childish. But does he not enjoy the artless ways of the child, and must he not strive to reproduce its truth on a higher plane? Is not the character of every epoch revived, perfectly true to nature, in the child's nature? Why should the childhood of human society, where it had obtained its most beautiful development, not exert an eternal charm as an age that will never return?
>
> There are ill-bred children and precocious children. Many of the ancient nations belong to the latter class. The Greeks were normal children....

This apparently casual metaphor, whereby humanity is conceived of as a person growing up from childhood, with the Greeks being the best aspect of that childhood, actually enables us to understand Marx exactly. He held to the view, which emerges here, from his earliest writings [Marx, 1968, p.39]:

> When we have chosen the vocation in which we can contribute most to humanity burdens cannot bend us because they are sacrifices for all. Then we experience no meagre, limited egoistic joy, but our happiness belongs to millions, our deeds live on quietly but eternally effective, and glowing tears of noble men will fall on our ashes.

Evidently Marx saw humanity as one "organic body" from the start! But he wasn't alone. There are today, as there have always been, prominent advocates of the view that the idea of the independent autonomous human individual is a myth and that we are all, instead, part of a larger whole. Marx, however, believed two related and vital points: he believed that humanity is developing, and that this development went through a series of dialectical convulsions or upheavals pertaining to the way humanity confronts its material or economic circumstance

Marx believed that the basis of value judgment is collective human nature. If we have an idea about what humanity will be at its most mature stage of development, we can begin to assess earlier stages. We can ascertain contributes to and what hinders the growing process. Marx's famous labor definition of value—for he never offered what people refer to as a labor *theory* of value (i.e. some explanation of why value is supposed to consist of socially necessary labor power)—is one feature of this theory.

When completely developed, human beings are conscious social producers working not for the benefits to be reaped apart from work but for the love of work itself. Then their nature will have been fully realized. In a communist society, which is the highest stage of humanity's development, the ingredients of alienation—i.e., self-estrangement or the divorce of every indi-

vidual from his or her essential nature as a conscious producer—
would vanish. There would be no private property and division
of labor. As Marx puts it [Marx, 1977, p.424]:

> In communist society...where nobody has an exclusive area
> of activity and each can train himself in any branch he wishes,
> society regulates the general production, making it possible
> for me to do one thing today and another tomorrow, to hunt
> in the morning, fish in the afternoon, breed cattle in the eve-
> ning, criticize after dinner, just as I like without ever becom-
> ing a hunter, a fisherman, a herdsman, or a critic.

Accordingly, this mature, fully humanized society is to be the
standard by which the past and present are to be judged. (That is
why Marxists are so willing to lambaste everything in our society.)

But this value judgment is not primarily a *moral* one. This is
true even though Marx and Marxism are about as closely associated with moralizing as any movement other than Christianity
has been. Marx, however, tells us explicitly that "The communists
do not preach morality at all" [11, p. 183]. The *value* system in
Marxism pertains to standards of well-being or social *health.*
"Communism is not for us a state of affairs still to be established,
not an ideal to which reality will have to adjust. We call communism the real movement which abolishes the present state of affairs" [Marx, 1977, p. 171].

Again the analogy of the individual person will help to understand this: adulthood is not some ideal to be established but,
rather, the real movement, which will supersede adolescence. Yet
adulthood is also used as a standard of development—how well
someone is doing depends, in large part, on how mature he or
she is. One concrete area where the standard is invoked is in the
identification of the working class as the segment of humanity
that embodies the element of maturity toward which humanity is
striving. Working is part of human nature. It is only a question of
how this work fits into the life of a society and its individuals that

separates pre-human historical stages from the fully mature, emancipated stage.

In communism, "society regulates the general production." When Bakunin, the anarchist critic of Marxism, asked him "Will, for example, all the forty million [Germans] be members of the government?" Marx replied, "Certainly! For the thing begins with the self-government of Commune" [Marx, 1977, p. 562]. (Just what Bakunin answered is not relevant here.)

This is where the term "the dictatorship of the proletariat" gets its clearest meaning: in communism there will be no separate government—everyone will be part of government, not as separate entities but as integrated social beings, with "the actual individual man [having] take[n] the abstract citizen back into himself and...become a species-being" [Marx, 1977, p. 57]—and self-government will mean collective government, not individualism, privacy, independence and all of what is meant by self-government in the tradition of political thinking familiar to Americans, for example, and the English.

This is why Marx finds promise in his definition of value in terms of socially necessary labor power: considering where humanity is headed, considering the mature character of human society, the standard of mature human social health must be work that is directed toward human development [Marx, 1977, p. 197].

> In a future society, in which class antagonism will have ceased, in which there will no longer be any classes, use will no longer be determined by the minimum time of production; but the time of production devoted to different articles will be determined by the degree of their social utility.

There are divergent lines of analysis in Marx on the question of how social utility will be determined in the future. Still, we can surmise that anything that contributes to maturation is good, while anything detracting from it is evil or reactionary. The true interests of human beings in the future will lie in diversified labor that conforms to human nature and thus feels natural. Chores will be handled by automation; thus industrial capitalism, which creates the enormous machinery that takes over menial and unnatural labor, is essential within the Marxist scheme of human history.

But does this mean that the Soviets betrayed Marxism? Not quite. Marx ultimately approved of the promised Russian revolution. But he approved of it only conditionally: "If the Russian revolution becomes the signal for a proletarian revolution in the West, so that both complement each other, the present Russian common ownership of land may serve as the starting-point for a communist development" [Marx, 1977, p. 584]. But this is a big "if" and it points the road to the ensuing necessary imperialism of the Soviet Union if it should remain true to Marx's idea of what the communist revolution entails.

Capitalism is the adolescence of humanity and it must be experienced for the adult stage to come about successfully. Lack of muscle for an adult means that many responsible tasks cannot be carried out. Lack of the capitalist period of enormous productivity—albeit anarchic, unorganized, yet fierce—will mean that socialism will have nothing to distribute, no surplus value with which to feed the people who are no longer supposed to be feverishly seeking profit but are to cooperate in peaceful, even joyful, working life. And if there are shortages in socialism, it cannot turn into communism since in a society with shortages some group must see to it that those who lack what they need or want do not mount an uprising—in short, in such a society a ruling class is necessary, whereas in communism, "in which there will no longer be any classes," no such ruling class exists.

Let me now conclude this introduction by noting why what the above refers to is not at all simply some impossible utopian dream. It refers to a realm of possibility if some crucial claims are true. First of all, if humanity is indeed a kind of living being in the process of development, the Marxist picture is clearly plausible. And it should always be remembered that Marx was by no means the first or the last to believe in that progressive character of human history. Many classical liberals, among them Mill and

Spencer, held that humanity pursues a kind of progressive goal and is on a path of constant improvement. Indeed this is a widely held view today, probably influenced by the clear improvement of human technology through the upsurge of scientific understanding that has occurred through the last three centuries.

But what kind of society would communism be anyway? It would be the implementation of the ancient idea of the brotherhood or family of human beings. Communism would be a huge non-voluntary commune, a little like a big and very friendly family gathering, a warm and gentle party, where no antagonisms, no competitiveness, no jealousies, no envy, no untoward feelings and actions in general prevail but all behave as compatriots, as comrades with a single goal. It would be humanity acting like a wonderfully co-coordinated orchestra, all the players knowing most of the instruments and playing them all gladly without a conductor (that is, without a government, which will have "withered away"), and without any thought of reward or personal gain or any kind of idiosyncratic individual projects.

The feeling one might recall to conjure up the state of communism is that of an intimate party where everything is really clicking well, where the "vibes" are excellent, where one feels thoroughly at home, in no real need of anything other than just to be there, to go with the flow, to work only for the love of work.

Surely humanity has always found itself confronted by this ideal, by one or another of its philosophers, religious leaders, or prophets. And, however cynical one might be, there seems to be little that can be said against this idea of humanity, at least as an ideal of a given scope. Of course there are those who find the picture rather dull, even insulting, since it has an element of petrifaction built into it and it stresses the herd instinct rather than individual creativity. Yet even this is unfair to Marx, since he thought that in communism the individual traits of all would mesh with the rest, that we would all accept each other's individuality in a spontaneous, generous fashion. Marx has actually been called an extreme individualist, by, of all people, one of his classical liberal critics—Acton.

We have now before us an outline of the Marxist viewpoint. It is naturalistic—there is no room for a supernatural realm; it is materialistic—there is no causal efficiency exhibited by anything other than matter and energy, governed by the laws of nature; but it is not reductionist—there is objective development moving from primitive toward more developed stages in humanity's history. Marxism involves an attempt, also, to resolve the dichotomy between a scientific and a value-laden conception of human existence. It does this by way of the dialectic. It tries to avoid the dichotomy between the free will and the determinist perspectives on human action. It presents large-scale, inevitable movements within which individuals still have choices they can make. And in the last analysis Marx has been shown to be anything but a revolutionary in his vision of the ultimately good human society. It is in essence the idea of paradise or of heaven brought into realistic reach, rather than left for the after-life.

Marx combines many desirable ideals—what one likes, getting along with everyone, not indulging in waste, not leaving anyone to miss out on the progress human beings have made in life, not behaving immoderately, imprudently, or recklessly—as a central objective for political organization. It is a utopia that aims at the political realization of some noble objectives. And from the model that it has so created, it serves as the severest critic of its nemesis, bourgeois capitalism.

Chapter 2. Further Vital Elements of Marxism

Where the Dialectic Counts

Marxism is like a yarn of wool, with the beginning as elusive as the end, yet the whole quite systematic. To begin to grasp it one just has to unravel it somehow. Indeed, part of what is appealing about Marxism is that it seems to be as complicated as the world it tries to explain. Since it lacks a fixed starting point of the sort one finds in Aristotle or Descartes, we can begin pretty much where we choose.

The dialectical approach is about as crucial as anything in Marxism. It involves the heuristic principle of understanding at least human reality to progress by means of the process of certain social circumstances (theses) giving rise to their opposite (antitheses), clashing, and thus producing a new situation (a synthesis) that combines the best of the former, while dropping what is worst in them.

Yet the dialectic is also what seems most incredible. It is clearly a violation of common sense. Would anyone suppose from ordinary observations that everything in nature, or at least in human history, develops by means of basic and relentless conflict? We seem to hold out peace as an attainable goal and the idea that it is but a mirage, with conflict being the necessary scheme of things, is offensive to most of us. But common sense should not be taken as the final testing ground of a theory, lest the flat-earthers carry the day in geology. Common sense is only an initial benchmark. What we need to consider is why a scheme such as the dialectic would become appealing to serious philosophers. It will show why dialectical materialism isn't such a wild idea, whatever the verdict of common sense.

The sixteenth and seventeenth centuries saw the rise of the influence of empirical science in Western culture. One byproduct was reductive materialism, the view that everything is composed of matter-in-motion. This was appealing, in part because, if true, the laws of mechanics would help us understand everything. In this approach it came to be believed that the sort of physics we now learn in high school might then rule the world, including human affairs. Marx was impressed with the rise and influence of materialist thought but ultimately concluded that it would not do. British and French reductive materialism was an advance, he thought, but it oversimplified reality.

Could we really explain the world as nothing but matter-in-motion, where everything that seems to be different—e.g. musical sounds, human emotions and thoughts—is the same and the apparent difference due merely to the variations of matter's shape, size, speed, etc.? When they turned to the human "sciences," these materialists held that human life and society itself operate in line with the principles of classical mechanics, the science that explained the behavior of matter-in-motion. They proposed that all human beings strive for the acquisition of power and wealth. And that everything about human life could be understood as the operation of this basic principle—as laid out so neatly by Thomas Hobbes in *Leviathan*.

Marx found such views interesting but wrong and argued that these materialist philosophers allowed their class interest to guide their thinking. He believed that their "idea is merely the theoretical expression of the material relationships that dominate individuals" [Marx, 1971, p. 73]. They couldn't really help doing this, of course. He believed that a "closer investigation of people's external circumstances and conditions shows, however, how impossible it is for the individuals forming part of a class, etc. to surmount them *en masse* without abolishing them" [Marx, 1971, p. 72]. The only way out of the trap is to abolish the social conditions involved.

Marx makes this observation in reference to the impossibility of overcoming economic class membership. But he intends to have the point apply to philosophical perspectives. And he continues by noting that, of course, "The individual may by chance be rid of them; but not the masses that are ruled by them, since their mere existence is an expression of the subordination to which individuals must necessarily submit" [Marx, 1971, p. 72]. In the same way, Marx held that the major political thinkers of the age, such as Adam Smith, David Ricardo and, by his lights, their less innovative followers like Frederic Bastiat, believed what they did as a matter of conscious or subconscious expression of their own class membership. In other words, he believed that the materialism that supposedly governs all of human reality is in reality not well founded but a doctrine produced by intellectuals because those who advocate it find it convenient for their class's economic-political purposes. Even in our time Marxist thinkers characterize such defenses of various political ideas, most notably individualism and capitalism, as mere apologetics or rationalizations—in short, *ideological* thinking.

Rejecting Hegel's Idealism for Materialism

Nevertheless, Marx also thought that materialism was a significant advance over previous (idealistic and religious) thinking. Yet he thought the early—sixteenth and seventeenth century—versions of it to be insufficient, especially for purposes of understanding human social life. He thought metaphysical reductive materialism was inadequate—it could not explain the great diversity of nature. And he also thought that applying such a limited materialism to understanding human social life leads to drastic distortions. For example, Marx criticized materialistically inclined economists, such as John Stuart Mill, for trying "to represent production in contradistinction to distribution...as subject to eternal laws independent of history, and then to substitute bourgeois relations, in an underhanded way, as immutable natural laws of society *in abstracto*" [Marx, 1971, p. 20]. Marx evidently believed that the economic principles of classical liberalism or capitalism were historically relative, not applicable to all human economic life. It did occur to him that this criticism could boomerang against his own reductive materialist and communist viewpoint.

He believed, however, that his own proper scientific methodology, combining materialism with the dialectical principle, exempted his views from the flaws he ascribed to classical liberal economics [Marx, 1977, p. 183].

Seeing the economic principles of the status quo as eternal—and reducing the principles of every other form of life, past, present and future, to them—is the method of reductive materialism and its offshoot, bourgeois economic science. One consequence of this that Marx found especially odious was *the cash nexus.* "The bourgeoisie has stripped of its halo every occupation hitherto honored and looked up to with reverent awe. It has converted the physician, the lawyer, the priest, the poet, the man of science into its paid wage-laborers" [Marx, 1977, p. 224]. In our own time many non-Marxist critics of the kind of society that is hospitable to commerce or business repeat this charge, claiming that the force of the exchange system of a capitalist economy sweeps away most or all other human relationships in society. This is referred to often as the commercialization of the professions, and one can appreciate its point when one considers how many crafts have become subject to merchandising, from child care to emergency blood transfusions.

While as a claim as to what must occur in bourgeois society this point is certainly contestable, ironically enough it does capture how many mainstream economists tend to view bourgeois life. Some of the pre-eminent contemporary neo-classical economists, who follow in the footsteps of Smith and Ricardo, such as the late George Stigler and Gary Becker, of the University of Chicago, exemplify this tendency. Becker [Becker, 1976] has argued, with much benefit to his professional reputation—even winning the Nobel Prize—for reducing all human endeavors to economic ones, including marriage, love, religion and, yes, even crime. He puts the general thesis as follows: "The combined assumptions of maximizing behavior, market equilibrium, and stable preferences, used relentlessly and unflinchingly, form the heart of the economic approach as I see it." The leader of the famous University of Chicago school, Professor Milton Friedman, an earlier Nobel

Prize winner, has put the point somewhat differently: "Every individual serves his own private interest.... The great Saints of history have served their 'private interest' just as the most money-grubbing miser has served his interest. The *private interest* is whatever it is that drives an individual" [Friedman, 1976]. And Stigler, another Nobel winner, expresses the point only slightly differently when he tells us that: "Man is eternally a utility-maximizer—in his home, in his office (be it public or private), in his church, in his scientific work—in short, everywhere" [Meyer 1967, p. 6].

In each case human life is explained by reference to one main motivation, namely, to seek self-satisfaction, to fulfill one's desires. This is just what is implied in the view that all nature is governed by just one set of laws, namely, those of Newtonian mechanics: human life is just a more complex version of the permutations of matter-in-motion. Even such an astute anti-Marxist as David Conway fell into the trap of the economic-man approach in his earlier book on Marxism, when he said: "Capitalism has the great virtue of allowing people to pursue their self-interest in ways that at the same time promote the interests of others. For the essence of exchange is that, where uncoerced, both parties are better off for having engaged in it" [Conway, 1987, p. 50]. This is too obviously false: many exchanges do not truly benefit both or even one of the parties—e.g. that between heroin addicts and their pushers, or that between a merchant selling dresses and a person who is buying a dress she has no use for and who could do much more worthwhile things with her money.

The thesis that "the essence of exchange is that...both parties are better off for having engaged in it" rests on a purely subjective theory of what is worthwhile—namely, whatever an uncoerced individual happens to want (or, rather, acts to gain). Even without a philosophical demonstration most people know clearly enough that they don't always choose what is right, even in a free marketplace.

Anti-reductionism, Dialectical Materialism

Marx was one of the first to criticize this kind of economic imperialist thinking. He saw that it fails to recognize the enormous diversity of human motivation and objectives and reduces all human behavior to commerce. Marx realized that only a framework that acknowledges variety, history, and development could rescue us from this false scientism. He also denied that values are subjective and claimed that there is a standard of judging things of value. But more on that later.

For Marx the solution lay in the Hegelian idea of the dialectic. As we have already discussed, this is a conception of the way change occurs in reality, change that has puzzled thinkers from time immemorial. Consider that when we have something like a book, in a few years it will change—its pages will get faded, its paper will become brittle, and so forth. But why should that be so? What *in general* explains the fact that things change? Something must, since it is unthinkable to us (and probably impossible, also) that something, say a change in color, would come from nothing at all, be accounted for by no fact or principle.

And what of much more major changes evident around us? When inanimate objects change into living things, as within a naturalist understanding of the world they surely must have at some point. When a caterpillar changes into a butterfly. When apes slowly change to human beings. Or when an embryo changes into a fetus. These are all more or less drastic changes—some involving fundamental developments in reality—and *the mere linear motion of matter would not seem to be able to make sense of them all.*

Hegel developed the idea of the dialectic as the best way to explain change. Via Plato's Socrates, this idea has been around for a while in connection with how we should seek the truth (namely, through the *clash* of ideas). Hegel proposed that reality itself, not just our search for knowledge of it, undergoes radical but orderly development by way of such clashes. Different aspects of reality clash and then undergo transformation into a new kind of thing, and the process goes on until the purest form has been reached of what lay there potentially in the first place. We are familiar enough with this idea in connection with scientific inquiry. We think of some explanation and then we kick it around—place it against criticism, tests, and alternative ideas concerning the same subject, only to arrive, we hope, at a fully satisfactory resolution of all this in a sound or true theory. Hegel thought that this was not all there was to the dialectic. Not only our ideas about things but things themselves undergo this kind of process of development.

We have already touched briefly on Hegel's own account of all this. It is very complicated when fully explained and it need not detain us here. One thing does need to be noted. This is that Hegel was not a materialist and his explanation of why the dialectics of reality begins in the first place is closely tied to his contrary philosophy of idealism in which not matter but the idea—or Spirit—has primary existence. Idealism is spiritualist and posits some great immaterial force behind the complex motion of reality. (Hegel took it that Christianity is the simple way of understanding this.)

Marx rejected this part of Hegel's thought. He believed that Hegel's view had been formulated upside-down: the correct position is to begin with material facts, not with ideas. It won't be necessary to expound on this at length but it is important to see why this dialectical materialism is plausible.

To make sense of changes in nature, we must have a scheme that accounts for both what something is at the onset of the change and what it is not at the outset but changes into later. The scheme must bring these elements, the existent and the not (yet) existent, together. And the dialectical solution suggests that this is just what could happen if things clash with something contrary to them—black with white, round with square, peaceful with aggressive, poor with rich, etc. What starts out then clashes with its opposite, and the result combines the vital element from the first with that of the second. To put it in familiar terms, *a thesis* clashes with its *antithesis* and from the clash *a synthesis* emerges.

For example, when a society is composed of tribes or clans of men and women who live in dire poverty, this eventually meets with its opposite. That would be a highly individualistic society that generates considerable abundance. And from the clash of these two arises a system of co-operative communities that enjoy ample abundance. From the first stage it is the communitarian element that is retained, from the second the element of abundance. And that is exactly how Marx saw the overall development of humanity from its beginning to its ultimately perfect end.

Metaphysical or Historical Dialectics?

Marx may have confined the dialectical materialist scheme in his philosophy to his understanding of human history. Political economy, especially, was clearly studied by Marx dialectically. Yet, as noted earlier, he never disavowed his mentor Engels's more generalized version of the doctrine. Marx himself wrote [Marx, 1977, p. 420]:

> My dialectical method is not only different from the Hegelian, but is its direct opposite. To Hegel, the life process of the human brain, i.e. the process of thinking, which, under the name of "the Idea," he even transforms into an independent subject, is the demiurge of the real world, and the real world is only the external, phenomenal form of "the Idea." With me, on the contrary, the ideal is nothing else than the material world reflected by the human mind, and translated into forms of thought.

For Marx, Hegel's *Phenomenology* presents [Sowell, 1985, p. 177] "the dialectic of negativity as the moving and generating principle."

In his writing Marx employs the dialectical mode of analysis mainly to an understanding of human (economic) history, not so much to other subjects—for example, nature. While he learned of the idea from Hegel, who made the dialectic a centerpiece of a grand metaphysical system, for Marx it appears to have been a matter of plain historical observation that the dialectic scheme is what governs the development of humanity.

But it must also be noted that in his earlier writings Marx applies the dialectical approach to an explanation of human nature. Without the dialectic it is not possible for him to escape from the reductive, mechanistic-materialist framework in which there is no room for the "conscious vital activity [that] differentiates man immediately from animal vital activity [and] that makes man a species-being" [Marx, 1977, p. 82]. This would indicate that in fact Marxist thought cannot be fragmented into the dialectical and the non-dialectical segments—e.g. plain old naturalism, along mechanistic materialist lines popular in the eighteenth and nineteenth centuries, and dialectical historical analysis, introduced by Marx based upon his appreciation (but not unchanged adoption) of the thought of Hegel.

Marx's Charge: Capitalist Economics is Ahistorical

We can set aside the issue of whether the dialectic is ultimately a full-blown metaphysical idea in Marx. For now we can take it that for Marx it has value only in understanding human history.

It is because Marx sees the dialectic scheme present throughout human social development that he chides so persistently the "economists who blot out all historical differences and see the bourgeois form in all forms of society" [Marx, 1971, p. 39]. And he is quite right to observe that for the economists—including the many contemporary economists we referred to earlier who work in what is called the neo-classical tradition—all human history conforms to one system of economic principles. As Marx characterizes the economists' viewpoint, "One can understand the nature of tribute, tithes, etc., after one has learned the nature of rent" [Marx, 1971, p. 39]. But they are mistaken to think that these are all the same thing, to think that the former can be reduced to the latter. Yet this is just what most neo-classical economists want to do. They insist on explaining the past as if it were just a distorted version of the present, a kind of primitive variation on a static mechanism which is called the system of economic laws and which does not vary from one historical epoch to another.

If, however, Marx is right and humanity is developing toward its full maturity through several distinct changes, then such a generalization of capitalist economics to other phases of humanity's development would be no less mistaken than would be the generalization of adolescent psychology to that of childhood, infancy and adulthood. In fact different forms of production characterize different epochs or stages of humanity's development. And, as Marx argues, "every form of production creates its own legal relations, forms of government, etc." [Marx, 1971, p. 21]. And he says [ibid]:

> The bourgeois economists have a vague notion that production is better carried out under the modern police than it was, for example, under club law. They forget that club law is also law, and that the right of the stronger continues to exist in other forms even under their "government of law."

There is no question, despite some protests from certain scholarly circles, that Marx accepted the dialectical scheme, at least heuristically, as the governing principle of human history.[1] We shall see that many elements of Marxism make eminently good sense once we keep this point in mind. And indeed, if the dialectic scheme is correct, that is, if reality is governed by it, then much of Marxism has to be accepted as also correct. Even if it is merely very helpful to view human history as governed by dialectical laws, that, too, would give considerable support to the Marxian understanding.

Marxism's Collectivism

But there are other fundamental aspects of Marxism of which we must now take note. Marx regarded humanity as an organic body or whole; a kind of individual being that comes into existence and then develops through various stages and eventually ends up a fully mature entity. We have already seen that Marx regards this analogy as quite apt. He uses the phrase "organic body (or whole)" and gives evidence in his earliest writings that he treats humanity as a kind of being-in-itself that will eventually reach full maturity.

---

[1] See, for example, Sidney Hook in the Appendix of this book.

Here, too, Marxism comes to what we often take to be common sense, although we may have no theory from which we derive this common-sense view. But one source could be our familiarity with the natural historian's evidence, gained from the works of archaeologists and anthropologists. Most of us have been to those museums in which the history of the human race is traced pictorially, and clearly we see a development from what is actually identified as the earliest version of *homo sapiens* to subsequent versions, all the way to our own phase. There is here, of course, no mention of some end that will be reached, but that need not be something that is unthinkable or wrong. It seems, at any rate, clear enough to regard humanity itself, the human species, as a kind of being with its own history, headed toward some goal, some ultimate stage of development, roughly as we now think of individual human beings growing from infancy, through childhood and adolescence, to adulthood or maturity.

Toward Humanity's Ultimate Realization

It may appear that to add the idea that humanity will reach some stage of full development or maturity is a considerable departure from common sense, but no more than most scientific perspectives are, once coherence and completeness have been introduced into them after they started from common sense.

Marx notes, for example, that "the intimations of a higher animal in lower ones can be understood only if the animal of the higher order is already known" [Marx, 1971, p. 391]. And this seems clear enough. Consider, in addition, that unless we knew adult human beings, we would not understand that a child is a child—the child might appear to us as a distinctive kind of being, somewhat as a pony is, which is not regarded as a foal. Or if we didn't know what an oak tree is, could we appreciate that its sapling is indeed not yet a fully developed tree?

So in order to understand human societies, especially once one accepts that there is a dialectical development going on, it would appear to be scientifically necessary to gain an understanding of what it will be at full maturity. But, unlike trees and animals and individual people, no one has direct knowledge of a fully developed human race. It can only be understood by making use of the dialectical method of analysis and through it inferring the ultimate result. Marx reminds us of this when he says that "bourgeois society is only a form resulting from the development of antagonistic elements" and that "some relations belonging to earlier forms of society are frequently to be found in it, though in a crippled state or as a travesty of their former self..." [Marx, 1971, pp. 39-40]. Such statements, made within passages that deal specifically with the alleged faults of earlier social philosophers, who did not employ dialectical thinking, show that Marx saw humanity as an organic body in the process of dialectical development. Having gained an understanding of the role of dialectical thinking in Marxism, we can now turn to Marx's materialism.

Material Human Being!

Marx believed that it is the peculiarly or uniquely human contact that individuals have with nature—namely, production—which most firmly influences their way of thinking and the institutions that will emerge from such thinking. Unlike Hegel, whose view is that ideas have—or Idea has—priority in nature, Marx starts with matter or nature that then is reflected in the human mind as ideas. The reflection is, actually, not a simple process at all, consisting of "phantoms formed in the human brain" alone. It is rather a dialectical process that accounts for creative thinking. For Marx it is the basis also of all scientific understanding. Yet before a truly scientific approach to nature could be taken by humanity, a long road needs to be traveled.

In all pre-communist societies, except perhaps for a few select individuals (e.g. Marx), "Life is not determined by consciousness, but consciousness by life" [Marx, 1977, p. 164]. Because for Marx "life involves, before everything else, eating, drinking, a habitation, clothing, and many other things," he makes clear that "men must be in a position to live in order to be able to 'make history' " [Marx, 1977, p. 165]. By this he means that, unless the problems of human survival and flourishing are solved, there can be no intelligible talk about freedom for human beings, not even a clear understanding of such issues.[2]

Notice, here, that this goes directly contrary to the tradition of American political individualism wherein individual liberty and the understanding of its supreme importance is supposed to be possible even in the midst of economic hardship and is indeed a prerequisite of even the most elementary human thriving.[3] We will see later what significance this contrast has. For now it is crucial to observe that for Marx human individuals and groups will be unfree and ruled by those who control property, unless all their necessities are provided for. Not even their minds can be free to think up alternatives for themselves!

The development of humanity is the history of ridding humanity of the dependence it has on basic necessities. It is again as it is with a child—who is unfree, in a crucial respect, to govern himself, to choose (just as the law accepts this now and treats children as dependants)—because a child has not obtained the necessities by which a mature person can act responsibly. Humanity, too, is unfree to be responsible, to "make history," when it is still unliberated from the oppression of nature and the ruling class.

The Macro-path of Humanity is Determined

Marx is often regarded as a determinist—one who believes that human beings do not really choose to do most of what they do but are moved to do as their environment, and for Marx especially their economic conditions, force them. We have already made reference to this when we discussed that Marx takes human thinking to be determined by the surrounding environment. But this is a bit too simple a statement, as is often the case when

---

[2] The belief that human thinking is prior to eating, drinking, etc., is taken by Marx as a form of idealism and is one of the fundamental differences between his view of human life and that of many others, including most bourgeois thinkers.

[3] This is what explains outside a Marxian analysis why bourgeois thinkers promote private property rights as a fundamental requirement for economic development—it secures the chance for free thought and action.

one tries to capture Marx's ideas without getting terribly complicated. Let me try to make matters clear nevertheless.

Marx holds that humanity is in a constant process of development and follows discernible laws as it makes its way through history (laws more akin to those governing biology than those governing mechanics).

At its early stages of development, humanity is like a youngster, driven by whims, untamed desires, temptations. This does not mean that all individual human beings are so driven. It means that in the main the various classes that make up human societies are not yet embarking on creative, free thinking. They are motivated to think of mere survival or subsistence or, alternatively, of enrichment or exploitation—keeping their advantageous position safe from possible reversals.

In capitalist societies these classes contain the bulk of the population and these people generally act in terms of immediate desires, needs, simple wants, etc. This "class consciousness"—a kind of thinking that comes from the socio-economic position one occupies in a culture—leaves little room for free thought. There may be some opportunity for the selection of different ways of satisfying needs. But in major issues, such as what political direction humanity should take, which institutions should be established, elements of culture and the like, the forces that are at work are not human individuals who think up answers on the basis of free, independent and objective thought. These matters are caused by material or economic conditions that determine people's ways of thought and their subsequent actions. (Recall that for Marx we are primarily natural or material beings, so the material factors in our lives—food, shelter, etc.—are decisive for us.)

Full Emancipation: Bliss through Social Production

Fortunately, Marx thinks, the main driving force in human history is production. And production does, even if not quite perfectly, express the essence of humanity and guide its progress toward full realization. The end result for Marx is not very different from what many have wished for humanity, a kind of carefree, creative, spontaneous community in which chores will be taken care of by machines and the only work left to do, and the amount of it needed, will be what individuals will wish to do for the love of it alone.

"From each according to his abilities, to each according to his needs" [Marx, 1977, p. 569]. That is the principle of a congenial commune or family. If one of the children needs a grand piano in order to excel, while another a simple harmonica, we do not insist that the former work much harder because the piano costs so much more. When a community is governed by mutual love and not by profit and the work ethic, the rules regulating who gets what are different from those we are familiar with in connection with many democratic capitalist societies. Such is a fully developed human community.

Marx argues that only in such a community will the conditions for both individuality and free choice be possible, and this because people will no longer be governed by their desire for more and more of the things that satisfy them. In pre-communist societies most of us are concerned, mainly, with making a living, with "eating, drinking, a habitation, clothing." This restricts the scope of our thinking, limits our range or freedom of action. But once capitalism, through its ferocious quest for profits, produces plenty for everyone to have a reasonable amount, and once human appetites are tamed and organized communally, this preoccupation with wealth acquisition will give way to free and creative thought and action.

Only in pre-communist society are society and the individual in some kind of conflict. That is because the conditions of life, mainly scarcity, make this inevitable, just as they make class conflict and, in consequence, revolution inevitable. But once the final revolution ushering in the collapse of capitalism has occurred and the restrictions of scarcity have vanished, human beings will be free. They will be able, finally, truly to choose their own existence and to do so in the best way possible.

Marx puts it as follows [Marx, 1977, p. 91]:

The individual and the species-life of man are not different, although, necessarily, the mode of existence of individual life is a more particular or a more general mode of species-life or the species-life is a more particular or more general individual life.

Or, to make the point more succinctly, Marx explains a few lines earlier that "The individual is the social being."

Human Freedom is Unboundedness by Nature

It has to be understood that for Marx, following many others, being free is not merely not being under the rule of another person or persons (what is called now *negative* liberty). Being free is, rather, a state of having the ability to strive for what is good, to flourish (now called *positive* liberty or enablement). A person is free in this sense when he can excel in his humanity, when he is not impeded in his progress toward who he ought to be.[4]

Many in the tradition of American or even Western liberal political life think that freedom has to do with casting off chains that others have wrongfully placed on us. For Marx that kind of freedom is rather insignificant, because it doesn't actually help to remove the main impediments to human flourishing unless one is also provided with the ability to flourish on one's own. Modern liberals now fully share this view.[5]

We will return to this matter later, but for now it is important to keep in mind that Marx believed in the value of positive freedom—in unfettered self-actualization—not in the value of negative freedom or liberty, i.e., in others' keeping their intrusive presence away from one. In Western democracies there is a lot of talk about freedom which to Marxists seems a fraud because simply refraining from intruding on another does not do that other any good. (A similar alleged misunderstanding obtains with regard

---

[4] For example, such political economists as Amartya Sen use "freedom" in both of its senses, often imperceptibly interchangeably, in works such as *Rationality and Freedom* (Cambridge, MA: Harvard University Press, 2002).

[5] See, for a good case in point, Cass Sunstein, *The Second Bill of Rights: FDR's Unfinished Revolution and Why We Need it More than Ever* (New York: Basic Books, 2004).

to the idea of "democracy," as we shall see.)

Capitalists Are Blameless Exploiters

Marx and Marxists take what they understand to be the conditions of utter deprivation of most people as their central focus. They regard those conditions as far more oppressive than any coercion which might have been perpetrated on people by the state or criminals, for example. The extensive talk about exploitation makes this a bit confusing, of course.

As most people understand it, exploitation is a kind of blameworthy mistreatment that the agent could choose to avoid or refrain from. And by using this term it seems ultimately what Marx is claiming is that people are deprived because they were intruded on, conquered, colonized. And this makes it appear that Marx is blaming someone for the conditions of the worker. Yet he also says [Marx, 1977, p. 417]:

> I paint the capitalist and landlord in no sense *couleur de rose.* But here individuals are dealt with only in so far as they are the personifications of economic categories, embodiments of particular class-relations and class-interests. My standpoint, from which the evolution of the economic formation of society is viewed as a process of natural history, can less than any other make the individual responsible for relations whose creature he socially remains, however much he may subjectively raise himself above them.

Clearly, then, Marx is actually exempting capitalists from moral appraisal. This despite some of the harsh language Marx uses in certain places—e.g., in *The Communist Manifesto*—which suggests that he held capitalists personally morally responsible for causing the hardship of the workers, thus ascribing to them a capacity for choosing *their* conduct and the responsibility for doing so quite badly. (The role that Marx *seems* to have for the use of moral exhortation is complicated, but apparently he sees in such exhortation an instrument or weapon of revolutionary change.)

Values Yes, Morality No

This is actually a very tricky matter, as most socialists of a Marxist bent realize. Marx hoped he would overcome the simple determinism of British and French materialism by adding to materialism a historical or *dialectic* dimension. This makes room for higher forms of being as scientifically admissible. That explains the stress he laid on the scientific character of his socialism. If historical or dialectical materialism is correct, then not everything is the same kind of thing, in any supposedly last analysis. There are objective differences of kinds and types in nature, although they are all tied to matter. There is no room for supernaturalism in historical or dialectical materialism, but there is room for consciousness, mind, theory and other aspects of reality that get lost in a simple materialist picture. And, most of all, there is room for values!

What is true enough is that there is no room for *moral* values—or morality—in Marxism, at least not in pre-communist eras. And by the time, in communism, human beings are supposed to be free to make responsible judgments, what they will choose to do will make little difference. In fact, by Marx's account communism will be a society in which a certain kind of choice (found mostly in the marketplace) is moot—everyone will automatically yet, paradoxically also freely, do the good and right thing. So once again morality will have no place. We will see that this is something like what flows from Marx's vision of the communist community. And during pre-human history or our own time—when humanity is in infancy, childhood, or, as now, in adolescence—morality cannot apply since human beings are not free, indeed are not yet quite *human* beings. Just as the law exempts minors from full responsibility now, so Marx exempts people from full responsibility for their actions prior to the onset of communist society. (We have already seen that he exempts capitalists from blame for exploiting the workers!)

Now this may seem outlandish to most people in our culture, but it really should not. Our own common-sense thinking often seems to gravitate toward this view.

Human beings vacillate between holding people responsible and explaining their behavior by reference to prior causes—upbringing, cultural influences, economic conditions, nutrition, and so forth. This is especially so when it comes to dealing with our own faults. Rarely, if ever, does someone simply admit outright that he or she has done the thing wrong that he or she could have done right. Even within the framework of most religious moralities, in which personal responsibility for one's actions is accepted, there is the familiar line, "Well, nobody is perfect," meaning that somehow it is built into the human condition to fail, by means of some device like original sin.

If that is the case, then full personal responsibility is not accorded to us here either. And of course within the frameworks of the many psychological schools of thought, not to mention the sociological and the economic, personal moral responsibility is almost completely missing. The attempt to make the social sciences scientific has had this consequence. Common sense may here and there rail against the spectacle but common sense often yields to "science," gradually. Decisions along these lines in the law which accept that someone is temporarily insane or has diminished capacities are not technical but made by juries composed of lay people, using their common sense to pass judgment over what has transpired in a court. So, again, Marx isn't off in some fantasy land here.

So while the belief in human freedom of the will is widespread enough, it is no more widespread than its opposite. Marx is actually more closely aligned with those who wish to make room for human freedom of the will in the face of science than most other social and political theorists have been. In fact, Marx has made the attempt to render the free will thesis compatible with the scientific picture. Others, such as followers of Kant and theologically minded people, accept some grand contradiction in nature to the effect that human beings are a bit unnatural or supernatural, so they have some freedom in a sea of irreversible, relentless causation. Marx found this unacceptable.

Marxism's Appeal: Scientific Humanism

Now let us consider a bit further why Marxism is appealing. Here is a viewpoint that combines, in plausible enough terms, the best of science with the most precious of the humanistic perspectives on reality. Marx argued that millions are helpless. And to people across the globe this seems quite true. Especially when they live in Guatemala, Iran, Argentina, Chile, India, Somalia or the Sudan, or the former Poland, Hungary, Bulgaria, and Albania. The bulk of these people can rarely just get on a plane and leave town for another job when they are laid off or meet with some natural setback. They are indeed captives of their economic conditions, to a large extent. At least the explanation that they are helpless seems reasonable to them.

And many of us, in Western cultures, are not so differently situated. Just to walk away from our neighborhood, say when we become unemployed, and find a new prosperous one seems hardly possible—one reason why the phenomenon of outsourcing is so widely lamented. But to a large extent that is what economic freedom demands of us, namely, to be ready and willing to change our situation at the drop of a hat. We are supposed to be doing this of our own free will. But can we, really?

The theory of the free society, with its economic system of capitalism, views workers as facing many options in the marketplace. Not, perhaps, at the initial stages of society's capitalist development, say right after feudalism, but clearly once the society has been transformed into a capitalist one. In such a system, when some options vanish, others remain to be selected. (This is the gist of the economic defense of outsourcing, exporting jobs to regions where labor costs are low—in no time there will be new, different jobs that are created from the savings that are now spent on new items and services.) But is this right?

Marxism answers that there is no such freedom in the lives of most workers, not in advanced capitalist societies nor in newly developed, early capitalist societies. We cannot calmly turn from one foreclosed opportunity just to grab another, without much trouble in the process.

This kind of individual liberty [of the so-called free market] is thus at the same time the most complete suppression of all individual liberty and total subjugation of individuality to social conditions which take the form of material forces—and even of all powerful objects that are independent of the individual relating to them. [Marx, 1971, p. 131]

This is what many of us take ourselves to be facing in our lives. This Marxist picture looks quite true, then, to many people, especially in underdeveloped countries. And Marx constructed a perspective of human life that at least promises that eventually a desperate situation will not face ordinary workers. Eventually, we will all be liberated from capitalism; and then labor dislocations will not occur merely because people change their tastes or someone invents a better mousetrap.

Now I have put matters rather simply here, though in essence this is what made and still makes Marxism such an appealing outlook to millions of people. *It offers a promise of worldly salvation*, if not to us then to our offspring.

Of course, Marxism is anything but simple. That is one reason why there are umpteen varieties of Marxism and why Marx has been rapidly annexed by Freudians, Pragmatists, Existentialists, deconstructionist, postmodernists, and so forth. Even more important, Marx's own beliefs are supposedly in constant flux by his very own account, in line with the dialectical principles of either nature or at least human thought; and this invites consideration of how his own views must alter with time.

When we believe that everything must change, it makes sense to anticipate modifications of even that thought itself. So followers and students of Marx have had nothing much to restrain them, within limits, when it comes to "updating" Marxism. This is one hazard of the kind of dialectical thinking that Hegel encouraged, to be sharply distinguished from Aristotelian dialectical thinking (as spelled out, for example, by Chris Sciabarra[6]).

---

[6] Chris Matthew Sciabarra, *Total Freedom: Toward a Dialectical Libertarianism* (University of Pennsylvania Press, 2000).

But, once we have become clear on some of the basics in Marx's thinking, we can begin to understand why the system has been widely admired and attracted so many followers, some of them passionate to the point where no element of existing values or morality serves to temper the urgency with which they promote change. Thus some revolutionary Marxists have had no compunction about violating ordinary rules of morality, such as that we ought to tell the truth, we ought to read opponents' views charitably, we ought to apply due process when dealing with those accused of crimes, we ought to represent the views of others accurately, and, in the case of Marxist terrorists, that none ought to kill or injure those wholly innocent of any wrongdoing. Such niceties are viewed as bourgeois prejudices, not actually moral or professional imperatives. Nor need these revolutionary Marxists ever admit to having made a mistake—since, after all, history is on their side—so that even support for Stalin and the former Soviet Union can be viewed by Marxists as perfectly excusable, in no need of apology (as a debate in the journal *Dissent* shortly after the fall of the Berlin Wall clearly illustrates).[7]

I have covered some of the broader themes in Marx's point of view. Now it will be useful to consider some of the details. Here too it is impossible to say that one item is more important than another. A totalist view, which tends to bear on everything we have an interest in (and more), is not easy to break down into essentials. Everything counts for something vital. Still, it is safe to claim that for Marx the fact that human reality is best understood as if it were governed by the principle of dialectics and by economic—or material—forces is most general and crucial. All else is infused with this feature of the system.

---

[7] See, for example, Jonathan Wolff, *Why Read Marx Today?* (New York: Oxford University Press, 2002), for an attempt to separate the failed from the successful Karl Marx, based on the contention that Marx's critical points against liberal capitalism are still sound, never mind that such critical points are in fact tied conceptually to Marx's positive case for the coming communist system. (This approach is comparable to admitting that the conception of health of modern medicine is quite unsound, yet all the recommended cures made by modern medical professionals make perfectly good sense.)

Marx's Radical Altruism

First of all, let us look at one of Marx's earliest important ideas, one that is not so much original as crucial from the point of view of Marx's values. The source of this idea and ideal was Marx's school-leaving examination. Here he states that the highest goal one can have is to "contribute most to humanity." This is, of course, a fairly widespread ideal, certainly given much lip service. One thing we noted it means is that Marx seems to believe in that humanity is a sort of being in itself, of which individual human beings are a part. The species is the thing, so to speak; at least while humanity is in the developmental process. But for the present this is the less important point. What is more important is that at this stage of his thinking, Marx still did not regard human beings as in total bondage. After all, he seems to have thought that we can choose what we should devote ourselves to. (Recall, "When we have chosen the vocation....")

Marx here is showing that he considered the highest goal to be a devotion to humanity, not to God. This is one of the main ideas in Feuerbach's philosophy. The early writings of Marx are thoroughly infused with humanism, the view that it is humanity that should be our object of complete love, not some supernatural being. And in an age when the success of the sciences as a means for improving understanding and the lot of human beings was beginning to be quite evident, the loss of faith in supernaturalism could be understood easily enough.

Marx's humanism never entirely left him. What he did give up on is the idea of human freedom, at least for most of those who are members of our civilization. This is the idea that still underlies the humanistic exhortation of his earliest writing. The ethical system, while Marx subscribed to any, that underlies a good deal of Marx's value judgments is a kind of utilitarianism, according to which the greatest happiness of the greatest number among human beings should be served by us all.

But the utilitarian regards each person as an individual and merely demands of everyone that the cause of widespread happiness be served because it is an intrinsic good. Marx seems to have regarded humanity as an entire being and it is the ultimate well-being of this entity that should be the goal of each person. This is a kind of collective egoism or "specie-ism" rather than utilitarianism. We human beings should strive to make the best of humanity, which is after all our own organism, identity and real nature—that is, what we really are. Our actual, real current self is not what counts, of course, because it may be viewed as a means to the ultimate end of humanity's improvement. All the moralities that reject using others as means toward some great end are condemned by Marx as mere ideology, codes used by the rulers to keep us from demanding our due.

So Marx believes that a person becomes a good human being to the extent he or she chooses to serve—that is to say be an integral productive part of—humanity. At least this is one of his earliest views. Now let us see what it comes to as a feature of Marxism and as a possibly true idea.

Marx and Morality

The concept of morality is bandied about pretty casually in many circles—we hear about the moral majority, moral corruption, moral responsibility, the morality of business, etc. The term "ethics" is also widely used, nearly interchangeably, meaning essentially the same to most people—medical ethics, legal ethics, business ethics, etc.

There are some general things that can be observed about morality and these are quite clear, despite a lot of confusion in this area. First, for morality to be applicable to human beings, it must be possible for them to make genuine choices, to really cause some of what they do instead of having it imposed on them from other sources over which they have no control. If it is true that people *should* tell the truth, it must be that they *can* do so or refrain from doing so. It must be up to them, which they will do. Otherwise, there could not be a point to the idea that they *ought to* do so. They will or they won't, period.[8]

---

[8] Some maintain a "compatibilist" view, by which they mean one can be both a determinist and in favor of moral responsibility. Yet by "responsibility" they tend to mean "have

The second point about morality is that if it does apply to human life then some (objective) standard for choosing between various courses of action can be identified. For if I say that you ought to do something and there is no standard by which what I claim can be shown to be true while saying the opposite to be false, then it cannot be true that someone ought (or ought not) to do it. "Ought to" and "ought not to" would be inherently ambiguous, unspecifiable as to what they mean in concrete terms. Whatever our moral stand turns out to be, *some* standard is presupposed by the meaningfulness of moral language. Here too we could embark on a very long discussion because none of these ideas without difficulties. But for our purposes we need not pursue the matter further.

Let us say simply that, had Marx remained a person with a *bona fide* moral point view, he would have had to accept that human beings are free to choose and there is a standard of right and wrong. In fact Marx gave up the first idea as premature but accepted the latter. Value judgments can be made, but they are the sorts one expects from natural historians, especially from people who appraise various forms of life. Is this specimen of oak better than the other? Is this horse healthier the other? Value judgments apply to all life, moral judgments only to the kind that is self-directed.

Actually, however, there is a problem with trying to retain the viewpoint of value judgment but giving up the moral viewpoint, denying human liberty to most people. It gets one into some difficulties and helps to see how Marx escapes these, if at all.

Marxism, Truth and Criticism

Let me quickly reiterate that I am concerned to see what is important in Marx and how close it comes to the truth. In short I am interested not only in whether Marx is right but how close to

---

a causal role in" rather than "being the cause of" the actions at issue. And so what they are actually willing to accept is that people are often crucially *involved* in bringing about states of affairs that may be good or bad but not that they could have either brought them about or not brought them about, that is, that they were free to do either, which is what *genuine* morality or ethics requires.

being right he is. After all, hardly any point of view throughout human history managed to be all true. Completeness may be a Platonic ideal but it is unattainable in a world that continues to be understood and may even seriously change. It is no great shame to be nearly right but wrong. One might venture to guess that that is probably the best fate for the most successful of us in the disciplines of philosophy, science, and so on.

At any rate, after he found it necessary to consider humanity's fate from what he understood to be a scientific perspective, Marx found that perspective by means of studying Hegel. Materialism by itself didn't suffice—it obscured evident distinctions in nature. However much it may appear so sometimes, human beings are really quite different from other animals and a good philosophical viewpoint must account for that.[9] Marx accounted for it by regarding the material universe in a state of development with lower and higher forms of being (at different times), all having a place within it. The uniqueness of the place human beings have concerns their being conscious producers, or so Marx believes.[10]

So, here is why Marxism has been such a success: For several centuries the world had abandoned looking for a grand philosophical system by which to make sense of reality and the role human beings have in it. With the emergence of science, religion no longer fulfilled that purpose, not for intellectuals at least. But Marx's dialectical materialism, which still proclaimed the same values as many religions, seemed to do so. Human beings need to understand reality in a general way, and they would rather embrace a big mistake than nothing at all to satisfy this need, especially

---

[9] This is often ridiculed. As Michael Wheeler says, "For if we point to some AI system of the future…and dare to answer in the affirmative ["Could an artifact (such as a robot) ever really be said to have a mind…in exactly the same sense as a human being?'], then that just about wraps it up for the comforting idea that human beings are, in some fundamental sense, special parts of the universe." See his "Minds, brains and gases," *The Philosophers' Magazine*, Issue 28, 4th Quarter (2004), p. 65. The issue is not whether this is comforting but whether it is true. Being different from other things is rather routine, after all—frogs are different from chicken and turtles from zebras. Is that comforting?

[10] "Conscious vital activity differentiates man immediately from animal vital activity." [Marx, 1977, p. 82]

when it looks quite promising.

Of course, whether Marxism proves to be a mistake can be assessed only after a thorough study of it. Yet it is crucial to know that this is the issue. And it is a complex issue. Like other major philosophical systems, Marxism its own conception of what counts as truth and it is, roughly, *historicist*.[11] And like other systems it is often immune to challenge until an independent competing conception of truth has been established. Yet, once we have established such an independent conception of truth, it is very likely that Marxism will not prove correct; for this conception of truth is already a challenge to part of Marxism, namely, its conception of truth.

Still, perhaps we can proceed without running up against this kind of problem from the start. We need to consider the various topics first of all from the perspective of our normal, everyday viewpoint. Any view that contradicts a good deal of our ordinary experiences must be suspect because this is where we begin the study of any viewpoint, even as complex a one as Marxism. If, for example, a viewpoint makes it impossible for us to make sense of the experience of reading it, of taking it up as a challenge, of discussing it critically, and so forth, then we are entitled to raise our eyebrows. As D. Bannister put the point, "...the [theorist] cannot present a picture of man which patently contradicts his behavior in presenting that picture."[12]

Marxism's idea of class-consciousness—that each of us is limited in our understanding of reality by our membership in a certain economic class—appears to violate this idea openly. As capitalists or members of the middle class, for example, we are supposedly guided in our understanding of reality by what would advance the vested interest of our class. Thus, if we are capitalists or members of the middle class, we would be likely to think about at least socio-economic affairs with certain preconceptions favoring the welfare of members of our class. Alternatively, as

---

[11] But its historicist nature will terminate at some point in the future.

[12] D. Bannister, in Borger & Cioffi/Bannister, eds., *Explanation in the Behavioural Sciences* (London: Cambridge University Press, 1970), p. 417.

working people we would be guided by a perspective imposed on us by way of our development as working people, impelling us to prefer laws, institutions, practices and the like that advance the welfare of working people.

This is a very important idea in Marxism. It gives rise to a powerful tool of understanding, explaining, and even forecasting socio-economic developments. The clash of the different perspectives of the classes renders co-operation impossible between the classes in economic and political matters. This then will lead to the only way to resolve the conflict between the classes; namely, to revolution (mostly violent but at times peaceful, when conditions are ripe). If we did not suffer the limitation of class-consciousness, then class conflict and revolution would not occur and progress would cease as well. Yet class-consciousness makes it difficult to trust our perceptions of reality, including our perception of what we should do about our economic and political troubles. In the end we cannot even trust our perception of whether such a philosophical system as Marxism is true.

The Adjustability of Marxist Principles

So it is clear that Marxism faces some apparent problems at the outset. Yet Marx has what he believes is a solution. He holds that *some* people can escape the limits of class-consciousness, although not enough of them to matter politically. Still, if we stick to the methods of historical materialist science, then we are able to consider things objectively.

True enough, few people are liberated enough now—and throughout history (prior to the onset of communism)—to embark on genuine scientific inquiry. As a matter of statistical averages, class-consciousness prevails in all societies. Marx makes clear that "the realm of freedom actually begins only where labor which is determined by necessity and mundane considerations ceases; thus in the very nature of things it lies beyond the sphere of actual material production." Freedom—meaning acting unimpeded by constraints—"can only consist in *socialized* man, the associated producers, rationally regulating their interchange with

Nature, bringing it under their common control, instead of being ruled by it as by the blind forces of Nature...." Yet, even if all this *must* be the case, even if it is inevitable, it must be the case in general. The laws of history are laws that identify statistical relationships: *in general* capital exploits labor (though not every capitalist exploits the laborers hired by him): *in general*, capital sees the world one way while labor sees it in another, which pits the two classes against each other (though some capitalists can see eye to eye with some laborers); *in general*, the two classes think ideologically, they are not capable of objective, scientific understanding (though some individuals are ahead of their time and do reach a level of freedom that enables them to transcend or overcome ideological limitations on their way of thinking).

We can see that this is not at all implausible. In the social sciences the laws we identify tend to be statistical.[13] Adolescent psychology applies to the bulk of adolescents, not all of them. Laws which govern the behavior of groups—WASPs, blacks, blue-collar workers, Central American Indians, Jews, or intellectuals—all these laws apply statistically and not every individual member of such groups is expected to conform to what the law predicates about the group at large.

When Marx conceived of his approach as scientific, this is largely what justifies his idea. And it is a very significant departure from earlier ways of thinking about political economy. He realized that there had been socialist and communist thinking before his own. He notes, for example [Marx, 1977, p. 239]:

Nothing is easier than to give Christian asceticism a Socialist tinge. Has not Christianity declaimed against private property, against marriage, against the State? Has it not preached in the place of these charity and poverty, celibacy and mortification of the flesh, monastic life and Mother Church?

---

[13] As we saw, Marx held that "Theoretical communists, the only ones who have time to devote to the study of history, are distinguished precisely because they alone have discovered that throughout history .... [etc.]" [Marx, 1977, p. 183]

Yet Marx also regards such socialism as ultimately impotent—"at times, by its bitter, witty, and incisive criticism, striking the bourgeoisie to the very heart's core, but always ludicrous in its effect, through total incapacity to comprehend the march of modem history" [Marx, 1977, p. 238]. In its place we have to substitute scientific socialism. So, if there is a significant development in Marx's ideas, it is most likely to be that he moved from being a heartfelt, incisive socialist critic of society to being a revolutionary, practical, scientifically motivated activist instrument of human history. We might say that Marx took on the role of a scientific prophet, replacing spiritualist-type political thinking with social-political science.

As I noted before, most of Marx's ideas are entirely interdependent and incapable of being made fully clear without first getting clear on other ideas. These early ideas are not free of confusion until they are more fully explored and understood. But they do suggest certain fundamental themes in Marxism, ones that seem more basic than others. We will see how Marx makes use of them in all of his other discussions—and how contemporary Marxist thinking invokes these ideas at crucial points. Indeed, one reason Marxism may have managed so well to survive the demise of the Soviet Union is precisely that there is such flexibility in its exact content—e.g., as to what constitutes a proper historical stage and what it presupposes (so that the USSR is now widely said by Marxists not to have met those criteria after all).

Chapter 3. Definitions, Human Nature, and Alienation

On Defining "Human Being"

With what should we contrast Marx's idea of a human being? Sometimes the way we ordinarily discuss this issue does not conform to the more technical character of a philosophical discussion. (Similarly, when one uses the word "demand" in economics, one does not mean the same thing as one means by "demands" in ordinary contexts.) A definition of the concept "human being" (or "person," or "man") would state what human nature is. Let me give a simple example.

If we ask the question "What is the nature of chicken?" what we are seeking is a definition of the concept "chicken." (A concept is generally the same thing as an idea.) We have formed the concept "chicken," not just the word, because in Italian, Hungarian, and German they use a very different word for the same idea. So it's not just words we are defining; we are defining ideas.

The very same idea means a very large and varied class of things—we use it to think, talk and write about them. Thus the idea "chicken" means all chickens. If I ask someone, "Please go over to the grocery store and get me a chicken," the person will know what to pick out because we know (however subliminally, however subconsciously, however little articulated) the definition of the idea of a chicken. That is to say, we are aware of those characteristics a thing must have in order to be a chicken, i.e., *the nature of a chicken.*

One might think the characteristic of being an animal is a defining characteristic of a chicken. But that's not true because lots of very *different* things are animals. Most of them are not even birds. For something to be a chicken, it would have to have certain characteristics that are best left for zoologists or biologists to state precisely. But if one wishes to state those characteristics, they would be those that make a chicken the sort of thing it is.

A definition, then, states certain—to the best of our most current knowledge—*indispensable characteristics.*[14] Some of the characteristics are entirely unique to the thing, event, situation, or institution being defined, in this case a chicken. It would be, say, certain characteristics of fowl, including those that distinguish them from other kinds of birds—winged, warm-blooded, feathered animals. Other parts of a definition would link chickens to the next broader class, say fowl—e.g. ducks. Now, to define the concept of human being, we would first identify and state characteristics that only human beings are known to have and the characteristics that human beings all have and share with their kin, animals.

According to the definition "Human beings are rational animals," every human being is indeed presumably capable of some measure of abstract thought. This is what "rational" means. That is, every human being—at least every mature and intact human being—has the capacity or capability of engaging in some degree of abstract thought, some degree of rational or conceptual (idea-laden) mental process (not that they necessarily exercise that capacity, or do so reliably or conscientiously).

The other characteristic this definition gives us is "being an animal," a characteristic human beings share biologically with a lot of other things, orangutans, horses, and so on. There is no reasonable evidence that any human being is not an animal, according to this definition. And every human being must be capable of some measure of complex thinking. Not just of intelligence, which involves calculation, but of a measure of choice or determination of goals. (The few who are not are recognized as somewhat defec-

---

[14] For a more detailed explication of these points, see 16, 18, and Tibor R. Machan, *Libertarianism Defended* (London, UK: Ashgate, 2005), especially Chapter 6, "The Principles of the Declaration: Here to Stay." And for a very sensitive discussion of the general issue, see Hillary Putnam, *Words and Life* (Cambridge: Harvard University Press, 1994), especially Chapter 9, "Pragmatism and Relativism: Universal Values and Traditional Ways of Life." See, also, for a consideration of various philosophical challenges, 18, especially Chapter 4, "Why Objective Ethical Claims Appear Subjective."

tive versions but are still classified with other human beings. And extremely young humans are known to be heading in that direction; they are understood to be emerging human beings, children.) To put this into more specialized terms; a definition has a species and a genus. Genus, i.e., a broad trait, classifies the thing being defined within a broad group, in this case animals. A genus is the larger class to which a definition links something. A species or differentia is, as the word suggests, what differentiates that particular subset of beings from this larger class. So, when one gives a definition, one usually states something by which one distinguishes the thing and something else which links it to a broad class of beings. In the case of defining the concept of chair one would refer to something that distinguishes the object as a chair and something else that links it with other furniture, to things it has in common with tables, sofas and so forth. Features it will not have in common with any other kind of furniture are the *differentiating* characteristics. Of course, with each class of things being so defined, there can be some variations that do not fit the definition perfectly, as when a chair is a museum piece and thus does not function to support a person the way normal chairs do. Yet it is still a chair with appropriate qualifications. So, when human beings are, say, incapacitated—for example, they are in a coma or are mere infants—they are still properly classified along with the mature healthy humans but with certain qualifications. (Animal rights proponents make a great deal of the fact that some humans do not fully fit the definition "rational animal" insofar as they are not actually fully capable of reasoning, of choosing to think. But in fact this is a spurious objection. Every kind of being has some instances that are ill fitting due to impairments or flaws or being at the early stage of their development in to the fully realized kind.[15])

When we talk about human nature, we are referring to those

---

[15] See the points raised by Tom Regan, *The Case for Animal Rights* (Berkley, CA: University of California Press, 1983) and John Hadley, "Using and Abusing Others: A Reply to Machan," *The Journal of Value Inquiry* XXX: 1–4, 2004. I discuss the issue in greater detail in 16, as well as in *Putting Humans First* (Rowman & Littlefield, 2004).

features given in a definition, among others. If one asks, "Well, what is human nature?" the answer will probably be: "It consists of being an animal and being rational. It consists of having characteristics which link human beings to the animal world and having characteristics which differentiate human beings from other animals, namely their capacity for engaging in rational thought." (Marx, of course, explicitly disagrees with this. For him "[Men] themselves begin to distinguish themselves from animals as soon as they begin to produce their means of subsistence, a step which is conditioned by their physical organisation. By producing their means of subsistence men are indirectly producing their actual material life" [Marx, 1977, p. 160].)

Human nature is usually summarized in a definition of the concept human being. This is a bit cumbersome but usually when somebody asks for a definition, what is implied is that one should state whatever makes the thing special and whatever links it to the next broader category of things. For example, we seek to define government or law or forests or oceans in the sciences and scholarly disciplines where it is important to make this kind of categorization, of picking out things that link things to other things and differentiating them from other things and then studying them accordingly. That's the way we come to know the world, by differentiating and integrating. Not perhaps permanently, perhaps only provisionally and for some long periods of time, but clearly very usefully. We integrate things with other things, that is, we show how they relate to other things. We also single them out as worthy of special notice.

Nominal Definitions and Human Nature

Most social and political theorists—indeed almost anyone who has ever thought about things relating to human beings in a theoretical and systematic way—will have an explicit definition of the concept of man or human being, or will have a theory of human nature. Marx is no exception. Yet there are enormous philosophical controversies about whether we can indeed arrive at definitions at all.

In short, do our definitions really state something about the way the world is, or do they merely impose a kind of arbitrary, perhaps culturally determined and loose structure on the world, a world that we really do not know well enough to categorize? Do we *impose* rather than *discover* the categories? That is a very important philosophical controversy.

The terms in which this controversy is usually noted are "nominalism" versus "realism." Realistic definitions are supposed to be definitions that pick out characteristics that *actually* distinguish things from other things. Nominal definitions, as the terms make clear, are definitions only in the fashion in which someone has his or her name—it was so decided by a parent, that is all. Nothing in the nature of things required it. In other words, nominalism is the view that there needn't be anything in reality that correctly corresponds to a concept and its definition. It is only a sort of convenient or widely accepted or useful "label," but at any rate clearly unnecessary one that we have given things. It is something that conforms to our purposes, our desired way of looking at things.

This view means that when we form a definition, we are grouping things in accordance with our particular interests, either as individuals or, more likely, as members of certain groups (a culture, a society, a science, a social class). There is nothing that need actually correspond to these labels. The labels are merely there for our convenience—they are conventional, nominal.

Suppose we were to call everybody who is under 32 "blah" and everyone over 32 "bluy." We are now using the terms "blah" and "bluy" only because they have some relevance to some special interest that we may have, say a fetish about age. But in fact there is no known difference in the nature of humans between people under 32 and over 32. Age happens to matter very little to humanness. So the definitions of "blah" and "bluy" would be purely nominal. They wouldn't actually pick out any differences. They would just be an imposed distinction. However, if there were some things significantly different between people under 32 and those over 32, if the ones under 32 had greater propensity for shouting and carrying on and those over 32 were calm and more studious, and this was a real, discoverable and lasting or stable enough characteristic, then being designated with a different definition might be warranted and useful.

This, roughly, is the difference between a nominalist and a realist conception of definitions and of human nature. Those who are realists and offer a definition or a characterization of human nature insist that such a characterization or definition derives from actual facts about people. Among them certain theoretical distinctions do obtain—there are *radical* and there are *moderate* realists—but this is not important for our purposes. Nominalists maintain that this definition or statement of human nature picks out some things that we happen to have become interested in, but it doesn't really signify anything involving vital and also actual, real differences. (There is an extremely firm linkage between a certain philosophical tradition against which Marx was doing a lot of arguing, namely, reductive materialism and "nominalism.")

Thomas Hobbes, who is the kind of materialist we have already mentioned and from whom Marx differentiated his own materialism, also advocated the doctrine of "nominalism." Yet, at the same time, in the history of political thought Hobbes was perhaps the first to stress the ultimate significance of individuals in political society, as well as in metaphysics. Prior to Hobbes, most, though not all, of ancient and mediaeval political theory took as the most significant unit such groups as the family, the clan, the tribe or the community, and regarded individuals as basically *parts* of these. And when they talked about the purposes of law, the analysis of economic relationships, they didn't talk about individuals as for example classical and neo-classical economists do. They talked about households, the family, etc.

Ancient economics mainly examined the relationship between households, not between individuals in the marketplace. Ancient economics mainly studied the relationship between cities and between communities for economic analysis, not between individuals. Hobbes was the first to give an entirely different formation to social analysis, to political science. In fact, he has been credited with being the philosophical inventor of political science. There was a non-philosophical inventor who came before Hobbes, namely Machiavelli, but, when one speaks of who took the most robust first step in the direction of social science and, in particular, political science, one is speaking of Hobbes.

Hobbes maintained, in effect, that in society we have a large numbers of entities—live, moving beings that we have come to call "human beings." We don't really know if they have anything in common as such or not. So we will do best to forget about talking about some realistic human nature; let's simply have a nominal definition, one that is definition in name only: let's *call* these things humans; it is in our interest to do so. But what we really have are isolated, separate individuals. [For more, see Machan, 1989.]

Now then, when one encounters objections against individualism in political-economic arguments in both serious and vulgar political literature—arguments that claim that individualism is wrong, pernicious, false, or in some way defective—very often one will read the phrase "atomistic individual." (Marx's criticism in his "On the Jewish Question" is a case in point, and more recently the neo-Hegelian philosopher Charles Taylor has followed suit.[16]) What this evokes is the Hobbesian picture of the (human) individual as an isolated entity, totally separate, and separable from all other entities; a picture that sometimes surfaces in technical neo-classical economic analysis. And the only thing allowing such an individual to be seen as part of human society is that in our concern about understanding our societies we have decided to link these beings together and to start forming theories pertaining to these individuals. Just so as to avoid having one think of one of the great British political philosophers as simply wrong, one ought to consider again the experiment that I suggested a little earlier. Look around and ask "What indeed unites all of us?" People do indeed vary a good deal. They are distinct beings and the idea that they may all be utterly unique is not such

---

16 Charles Taylor, "Atomism," in *Philosophy and the Human Sciences* (Cambridge: Cambridge University Press, 1985). Sadly, Taylor never bothers with any versions of individualism that do not fit his caricature—e.g., F. A. Hayek, Ayn Rand, et al.

a wild one.

One need only look around and notice this. Unless one has a preconception by virtue of which one unites us all together, it is a genuine question whether we are all *human* beings? We really look very different, we sound very different, we smell very different, and we feel very different. I'm sure there are some things we have in common, but then we have some things in common with chairs too. If one throws a chair out of a window, it will fall. If one throws a human being out of a window, it will also fall. But one doesn't therefore link them together as *the same kind of thing*. One cuts a chicken and it will bleed, and then one cuts a human being, and it will bleed. But one does not therefore say that chickens and human beings are the same kind of things. They share some attributes, but does that make them the same kind of thing? (All of this is offered in contrast to a doctrine of realism about essences that I treated earlier.)

Do we have the logical, scientific justification to go so far as to say that human beings are indeed part and parcel of the same natural species? On superficial inspection that's a fair statement. But what if we are very careful and wish to avoid becoming dogmatic about it?

These questions were asked in an age that was beginning to react critically to theology, with its vast amount of un-confirmable dogma. When scientists and social theorists began to retreat from theology, one of their objectives was to avoid dogmatism and faith. They wanted to rely only on what could be justified by the facts in evidence and by argument, and their contention was that if one avoids preconceptions, such as that "God created man in his own image," one could only arrive at the conclusion that what we've got is a bunch of disparate individuals whom we have, probably for convenience's sake, decided to call human beings.

It is ultimately in contrast with this fundamental perspective on the way human beings ought to be looked at that Marx developed his secular social theory. Throughout his works Marx actually rails against those who view human beings as isolated atomic individuals. The word "atomic" is important here. The atom was then seen as the one indestructible and separable unit of the universe. It was the particular bit of matter-in-motion thought to be the final, irreducible item out of which all other things are constructed. For Hobbes it is also only a matter of arbitrary convention that we have such groupings as family, states, governments and so forth. We have them for our purposes but those purposes are not somehow given, or grounded in right versus wrong. We just have them.

More contemporary nominalists would have to say that the various animal species exist basically as stipulated units by way of which we have chosen or otherwise come to construct our picture/theory of the world. Hobbesian individualism was basically a major thrust in the direction of reducing the significance of social units in political analyses, of starting with individuals as opposed to groups. Marx, in contrast, kept his focus on humanity. That is what for him is the most real being involving human beings. His definition of human being [Marx, 1977, p. 126] is that "The human essence is the true collectivity of man."

Marx's Idea of the Emergence of Human Nature

Although Marx did think there is, in theory at least, a real human nature, he held also that it will only be realized at the culmination of humanity's development, in communism. Just as we normally think that children do not fulfill their human nature but will do so eventually, so Marx believed that humanity will fulfill its nature at its maturity. This is usually referred to in Marxist language as reaching human emancipation, at which point the *new man* shall emerge. It is also the condition of the disappearance of alienation.

Marx believed that first human societies were characterized by the existence of communal organization and economic scarcity. One can still see such tribal stages in some parts of the world, in certain Amazonian, Australian, or African regions, with hardly any accumulation of wealth and certainly no formation of capital. Everything is consumed in such societies right away because it's so scarce. (Actually, in our time anthropological and archaeological evidence gives only partial support to this belief.)

For Marx, the antithesis of this stage in the dialectic of humanity's development comes about via the emergence of individualism, which is combined with abundance, stemming from increased productivity. Because of the enormous scarcity that exists in the communitarian setting, the only way that development will ensue is through the dispersal of the community. People must *for a while* have the incentive to produce and to keep what they produce and not share it with everyone. Sharing dissipates the wealth of individuals within the tribe, since no individual incentive exists to produce a surplus. Marx recognized this, claiming the antithesis of this overarching dialectical scheme to be individualism and abundance.

The first phase then is, roughly, prehistoric tribalism, communalism with utter scarcity. The second is basically the capitalist phase, the antithesis involving individualism and abundance, with its Hobbesian greedy atomic individual in the driver's seat. And the final synthesis brings together the two positive elements—communalism and economic abundance to a mature, rational society. For Marx the ultimate synthesis of this dialectical process is the combination of communalism and abundance. The two undesirables, scarcity and individualism, drop off, are "negated." The synthesis is then the ultimate development of human society, a combination of community with abundance—that is, communism. (Feudalism in this history is an intermediary stage.)

We know, based on common sense, that this is plausible enough. If people are living in a group/family and there is scarcity, they usually start squabbling, bickering, arguing and getting into little skirmishes. Anybody familiar with group—and family!—living knows shared ownership of scarce goods leads to conflict and the tragedy of the commons.[17]

Suppose one is interested in playing the guitar. It is a per-

---

[17] For more, see Tibor R. Machan, ed., *The Commons—Its Tragedy and Other Follies* (Stanford, CA: Hoover Institution Press, 2001). Although recognized by both Aristotle and Thucydides, it was Garrett Hardin who recovered the idea in his essay, "The Tragedy of the Commons," *Science*, 162 (1968):1243-1248.

fectly decent wish, not some greedy, nasty one. However, there is only one instrument available but three people in the group who want to play. Any time one gets a chance and others do not pay that much attention, one will play the guitar. One need not be mean-minded or unwilling to share. But one also acts on the view: "I'm justifiably trying to develop myself." Yet others simply cannot play while one is playing, and vice versa. Still, all three want to play as much as possible. So this leads to conflict. More guitars would be the best solution. (Capitalists offer another, the regime of private property rights, that accepts scarcity as an unavoidable part of human living on this earth but ameliorated by human creativity and entrepreneurship.)

Now if there is abundance in a community, then share-and-share-alike is, of course, easy. With plenty of guitars one can have as much time with one of them as one wishes. And there would not even be a point in saying: "This is my guitar, it's not yours, so let me play it," because they are in abundance—no one cares if one is taken! In a condition of plenty there is no point to private property. As even the simplest and oldest lessons of economics teach us, if there is a non-scarce good, private property does not develop. Marx himself knew this and explained that the division of labor and private property are those two elements that grow out of scarcity and the individual desire for more of a good thing. Since the Asiatic form of economy, tribalism, prevents this, tribalism must be superseded and after feudalism lead eventually to capitalism. But Marx believed that the laws of history would eventually lead to abundance and wipe out scarcity.

Humanity's Development via Capitalism

Marx has a very elaborate economic explanation for why, under capitalism, there is a development of an enormous amount of capital and a capacity for production. But we can probably make it clear without getting into all the complications. The central point is as suggested above: Pre-human[18] wants and scarcity, with the prospect of exclusive control over what one obtains, make for the

---

[18] Granting for now that at this stage no *bona fide* human beings exist.

steady motivation to produce and obtain more. Indeed, Marx is a sort of supply-sider, at heart, at least for the time that capitalism must be in place for humanity's sake. On this front the classical and neo-classical economists and Marx saw eye to eye. Marx just refused to generalize the idea over all of history.

Once capitalism has run its course—and I will have more to say on why that (supposedly) would come about—things change. In socialist society one does not engage in conspicuous production or consumption—demand slows down with the end of self-aggrandizing acquisition. In non-socialist systems there are people, for example, who want to have six Rolls-Royces. They are caught up in commodity fetishism. That, Marx claims, is natural in capitalism. However, though the system is enormously productive, it is also involved in considerable (but indispensable) wasteful consumption. Why does the late night entertainer Jay Leno have dozens of classic vehicles while some people don't even have sufficient food?

What Marx believes is that socialism and communism emerge only after the selfish motivation to produce and acquire has run its course in (pre-)human history. Most criticism of the excesses of capitalism have this as their basis: the belief that there is too much wasteful production and (conspicuous) consumption. And "wasteful" is a value judgment, signifying that some standard of what the proper measure of production and consumption is can be identified.[19] This standard is human need. Marx has a theory of human needs, based on his general theory of human nature—that is why it is important that in communism production and consumption follow "From each according to his ability, to each according to his needs."

Now, this grand dialectical scheme that I have been explaining is very long-range. It is just an overarching scheme of three big steps involving centuries. It embodies all sorts of detours, aberrations and anomalies. Roughly speaking, Marx maintains that

---

[19] This standard, though, is akin to how we judge children as immature, fully aware they couldn't be otherwise—capitalism is what it must be, though it'll be overcome and that will be better.

as one looks at human history as a dialectical development, first one will find mainly communal existence with enormous scarcity. But there are exceptions—some chieftains were obviously wealthy. The contrasting stage is capital-producing individualism, where people firmly develop private industry, private enterprise, division of labor, and specialization. People are always engaged in looking out for how to make another buck. This is, roughly, the engine that will eventually produce what in the last historical stage can be distributed throughout the whole community and will be administered in accordance with the Marxist communist principle cited above.

We may surmise that, according to Marx, in capitalism what we have is "From each according to his luck, to each according to his power," which sounds more like feudalism, not the free society hailed by capitalism's defenders. It is certainly not to each according to his needs. Because of the private ownership of the means and results of production, there is a distribution unsuitable to actual needs in society. But this is all necessary so as to *forcefully* usher in later developments.

Marxist Revolution Need Not Be Violent

Often in the contemporary world, especially the mid-20th century, when one has Marxism in mind, one also has in mind the violent revolutions, terrorism, and the Soviet tyranny of the 20th century. Why then do some people still go to the barricades about Marxism, especially in the post-Soviet era? Because it still makes an appealing pitch: Some people are accumulating a disproportionately larger amount of goods than do others, which seems to be unfair to most.[20] Marx places this theme of inequality and equality in a broad secular theoretical framework, where previously it had gained its theoretical footing by reference to various religious precepts about, for example, just price and usury.

The system of capitalism is, however, necessary for a certain period of time because of its enormous productive capacity. But

---

[20] Whether this is really the case isn't the issue here. On that point, see Tibor R. Machan, *Wealth Care* (forthcoming).

once it has run its course and produced enough to go around for all, it is replaced. Capitalism itself replaced a system where people basically survived at a bare subsistence level and many of them didn't survive at all until mass production and industry came into existence. Prior to that, for example, very few newborn children survived. Only 150 years ago in most of the world, including Western Europe and the United States of America, life expectancy was in the 40s and 50s. Today, it is up to 82 for women, and around 76 for men. Marx himself says that capitalism, with its enormous productivity, makes this possible, only at the cost of alienation and enormous inequality.[21]

Marx also sees an enormous price paid for this success by way, also, of the loss of community. "Atomic" individuals, isolated and alienated from one another, characterize the conditions of capitalism. In the older political theories of Plato and Aristotle, the community, the polis, the social whole, was the focus. Individuals were only adjacent parts. The *polis* was, as many who follow Marx claim, the unit of central importance.[22]

Many conservatives—reactionaries as Marx saw them—were also loyal to community and family (e.g., Edmund Burke). For example, why are many of today's conservatives against abortion? Partly because they have family as their main unit of value, of what is important in society. The freedom to cut short on family, to terminate a pregnancy, goes against the grain for those who see family as the natural development of human life, the basic unit of human community life.

If one keeps this large dialectic in mind, one notices that in order to bring about abundance the primacy of community must be rejected. If Marx is right that there is a real emerging human nature which unites us, and that we are in pursuit of our species-

---

[21] Cf., Stephen Davies, *Empiricism and History* (New York: Palgrave, 2003).

[22] Alasdair MacIntyre, *After Virtue: A Study in Moral Theory* (Notre Dame, IN: University of Notre Dame Press, 1981). MacIntyre is actually inaccurate. Some historians of political philosophy have seriously disputed his neo-Marxian idea. See, for example, Fred D. Miller, Jr., *Nature, justice, and rights in Aristotle's Politics* (Oxford: Clarendon Press, 1995) and Brian Tierney, *The Idea of Natural Rights: Studies on Natural Rights, Natural Law, and Church Law* (Atlanta: Scholars Press, 1997).

being and are not destined to remain isolated, atomic individuals, then the rejection of community is an enormous price to pay for this abundance, one that can be paid only temporarily. And since initially Marx argued that socialism, even communism, would be more productive than capitalism, albeit in a rational way, clearly the future would be better, more progressive, than the past.[23]

Alienation at a Glance

The greatest price Marx thinks we pay for capitalism's productivity is alienation. Such is the condition of human beings when they are not living as their nature would require them to. Estrangement—being a stranger to one's true self—is what one experiences prior to the onset of communism. This is not difficult to understand.

If Marx is right and humanity is on a path of maturation, akin to what an adolescent goes through on his or her road to adulthood, one would expect that, prior to reaching maturation or emancipation, humanity would not yet be quite itself! Just as we often take it that (roughly) 15 to 22-year-olds are alienated, disoriented, in an identity crisis, so would it be reasonable to expect humanity to be such if Marx's collectivist view of human development is correct.

Alienation is one of humanity's costs for industrial capitalism's delivery of enormous productivity. It brings on longevity, wealth, abundance, diversity, technology—every advance that one can say good things about in the last 100-200 years or so, with all the science, technology, medical achievements, high-tech, and with all the explosion of research, development, and so on. But we pay the price of isolation, a lack of community, rootlessness—of alienation, which is to say, of not being in harmony with our species-being, our "human essence...the true collectivity of man." Given that we are conscious producers, our alienation, as Marx explained in the *1844 Economic and Philosophical Manuscripts*, is a relationship between the worker and the product of his labor prior

---

[23] It is this idea, mainly, that keeps many on the Left clinging to the term "progressive" in their self-depiction.

to the arrival of communism.

Most of us can gain some appreciation of this idea just by keeping abreast of our own lives and considering how we feel— or are anyway reported to be feeling by social commentators (many of whom are, of course, inspired by elements of Marxism). We are said to relate to most people around us as strangers, as if they had nothing in common with us, and as if we were in fear of most of them. And thus we get confirmation, to some extent, of Marx's point without even entering into elaborate theory. Perhaps this can even explain why so many people are always complaining. Something is always going wrong in our society, some people are always complaining, protesting, rallying for remedies, endlessly. Why, with all this incredible improvement, longevity and wealth, are so many people constantly hounding the lawyers, the legislators, and the shrinks? One may inquire, "Where is the joy that a good society is supposed to make possible?"

I am putting these points in ordinary terms, drawing on a plausible enough understanding of our everyday experiences as helped along by commentators.[24] Out of this I want to show that much of Marxism can make sense. This is one virtue we want out of a theory—that it makes at least initial sense of our numerous ordinary experiences and beliefs. The experience seems to be that millions of us in semi-capitalist societies are dissatisfied.

Here is a more personal example: At one time, as a poor refugee, I dreamed of a day I could enter a store when it began to rain and simply purchase an umbrella. Today I can buy four umbrellas if it rains. Now, however, I have other dreams. And after I reach some of those I will develop more. My desire for wealth, for commodities, for consumer goods, forever grows and I am—as are most of us—forever unsatisfied.

Marx offers a plausible explanation.

He says that at this stage of human history only the element of abundance has reached its final stage of development. But another element, the sense of belonging in a community, of feeling whole, is missing. People are estranged, alienated, even though

---

[24] See, as an apt example, Bellah, 1985.

many of them are no longer lacking in what they *need*. Alienation is, Marx points out, the immediate consequence of two factors: private property and the division of labor. Private property of course makes productivity possible. But it also isolates one from one's community and places one's relationship to most others on a basis of commodity exchange. Once again, the cash nexus!

We only have a few buddies, a few friends, a couple members of our family, perhaps. The rest of the people we come into contact with are often just means to our ends. That's all we are interested in about them. We go into Wendy's and buy a hamburger. The person who is serving us does not interest us in any other capacity than the service we need in connection with this goal. We don't say, "Hey, how's the family?," "Are you okay?," "What's going on?" but rather, "Here's my cash. Give me a hamburger." Even when we do say those things, the theory goes, we do not mean them! We don't care about these people *as human beings*!

That is the characteristic relationship, according to Marx, in a capitalistic society. He tells us that [Marx, 1977, p.185], "in modern bourgeois society, all relations are subordinated in practice to the one abstract monetary-commercial relation." And he adds [Marx, 1977, p.223], "The bourgeoisie...has left remaining no other nexus between man and man than naked self-interest, than callous 'cash payment.' " The predominant interpersonal framework is just a "cash nexus." Our relationships to people obtain not on a basis of their full humanity, but on the basis that they are instruments in our effort to obtain whatever we want, whether it be food, clothing, entertainment, etc. And, as we have seen, bourgeois economists tend to affirm this when they say that *homo economicus* fully characterizes all the ways humanity manifests itself.[25]

When I go to see a broker and we talk about how I can take a few thousand of my dollars and maybe ensure that I am not going to be poverty-stricken when I'm 75 years old, I will not treat him as a friend; not at first, at least. I'll only talk business. He probably has four kids and worries about them. Maybe his son is an abuser of recreational drugs and his daughter has run off with

---

[25] An excellent case in point is Becker, 1976.

some bum. I'm not going to talk about any of those things with him. I'm going to talk about only one thing, namely, how he can make me a little better off financially.

For Marx the question here is whether this is the way to talk to human beings? Not in the end. But for now our malaise is that in the process of humanity's development it must pass through a very productive phase, that of capitalism, which must neglect the full measure of human life that's there *potentially*. It is important to notice how often people dissatisfied with contemporary life and who go public with their complaints—e.g. in political or social movements—use slogans that express what Marx was saying in more technical terms. They say they do not want production for profit, only for satisfying needs! But "profit" is just another word for prosperity, so the issue is whether some may prosper while others are without what are regarded as the basic necessities of life. Some argue that non-owners should be treated as owners—for example, in connection with the issue of rent control, which pits tenants of residential complexes against the owners (who may be large companies or small partnerships of persons hoping to have a steady income for retirement). The reason given is that renters have become so accustomed to "their homes" that it would be unjust to alienate them from something that ought to be inalienable if they were subject to unaffordable rent rises. Others are said to be exploited—for example, when industrial plants need to be closed so as to make it possible for a firm to remain profitable. Stakeholders, not only stockholders or shareholders, are to be served; another sign of the influence of the Marxist idea that instead of prosperity what a society must aim for is human emancipation, the end of alienation. Workers who have been with a firm sometimes for decades now suddenly must find new jobs, while the owners are able to avoid losses. Adjacent businesses and other establishments must be closed when another firm can move out of the area so as to be profitable.

This is a form of alienation Marx did not spell out, but his ideas have influenced the terms in which the discussion is conducted way past the time when any explicit adherence to Marxism, as in the old Soviet Union, was the rule. Were it not for Marx, it might not be so readily accepted that the poor have a right to stop the rich from doing what the rich want with what is theirs, so long as no one's rights have been violated in the process of attaining riches. But Marx has taught us that, basically, the rich are in possession of what the poor—the workers—produced, not what they themselves have earned. Therefore, the rich are not seen as entitled—they possess what amounts to stolen surplus wealth—and the idea that they may be curtailed by government for the sake of the poor—owners of apartment houses for the sake of the renters, shareholders for the sake of stakeholders and so forth—is deemed entirely politically palatable.

Ideas do have consequences—despite what Marx argued, namely, that ideas are but the results of how the environment imprints itself on the brain. Marx's ideas have had enormous, widespread consequences in our time, although sometimes not the ones he might have wished.

Needed Function of Individualism

For example, Marx would not necessarily approve of rent control. Marx argued that every productive phase of human history, including capitalism, must play itself out fully. One cannot impose socialist or communist notions on what is still fundamentally a capitalist system. If one tries, one only thwarts productive development. Marx put it plainly [Marx, 1977, p.171]:

[T]his development of productive forces [in capitalism]...is an absolutely necessary practical premiss because without it want is merely made general, and with destitution the struggle for necessities and all the old filthy business would necessarily be reproduced; and furthermore, because only with this universal development of productive forces is a universal intercourse between men established....

Specifically, unless all the elements of capitalism are allowed to develop fully, including its fierce competition, exploitation of workers, and business cycle, then its most vital historical consequence, namely, abundance, will not emerge so as to be utilized later in the socialist and communist phases of humanity's growth. (This is why Marx might arguably have found the Soviet Union an abrogation of his historical projection—except for the possibility of Soviet expansionism, which could embrace the capitalism needed for socialist developments. But more on this later.[26])

But how might this apply to something like rent control or minimum wage legislation or stakeholder theory? Take the first issue: If one eliminates earning prospects in the housing market, via rent-control or other welfare statist measures, housing will diminish, because builders will leave the market, as will profits. Many such public policies in Western welfare states are built with reliance on Marxist concepts, yet they do not necessarily mesh with Marxism. Marx could arguably regard the programs as naive in light of his own understanding of the role of various political economic systems in the development of humanity toward its emancipation. The welfare state is, for a revolutionary Marxist, a distraction and even impediment to fostering the mindset that the workers need to mount their opposition to capitalism.

The exact implication of Marxism for contemporary political affairs is not simple to ascertain. Marxism is a dialectical and historical system and none can simply project its categories in linear fashion. Certainly it is impossible, in Marx's own terms, for communism to just supplant twentieth-century industrial quasi-capitalism.

For example, one reason why efforts to build communes (where everybody is supposed to love everybody in the way envisioned by Marx for a fully mature human society) in the midst of a capitalist system will not succeed in terms of Marx's own understanding is that the entire surroundings trap all of us into a capitalistic frame of mind. We can't just withdraw from that and suddenly create a new type of human being. That may not be possible for several generations. It might be possible to think of it but not yet possible to have it actually *be*.

---

[26] For more on this, see the Appendix, a discussion between the author and the late Sidney Hook.

Marxist Alienation

The idea of alienation looms large in contemporary culture—especially in social science education and in lamentations of the conditions of workers in industrial quasi-capitalist society. It is, therefore, proper here to explore a little further the Marxist understanding of the relationship of alienation to private property and the division of labor.

Marx states, in one of his discussions of alienation: "In general, the statement that man is alienated form his species-being means that one man is alienated from another as each of them is alienated from the human essence." [Marx, 1977. p. 83] And, as we have seen, for Marx: "The human essence is the true collectivity of man" [Marx, 1977, p. 126]. Now in a capitalist or quasi-capitalist society specialized human labor obviously is geared to efficient production. Adam Smith correctly noted that the division of labor is a means by which productivity is increased.[27] One can acquire skills that are specialized, co-ordinate them with the specialized skills of others in other areas, and thus produce very efficiently, much more so than if everyone were to do everything. The division of labor then involves specialization, including the development of single linear careers. A person who does nothing but accounting, only makes door handles, or is a dentist or insurance agent fits this model clearly.

As Marx sees it, though, one is not a whole human being when one focuses one's labors in such a narrow fashion. One thus neglects talents in other dimensions of life such as the arts, sciences or the management of productive organizations. Marx conceived of the fully developed human being more on the model of what we used to call a renaissance man, a person who is competent in a number of areas, has knowledge of a lot of things, and, if it had been fulfilling for him or her to engage in the work of these

---

[27] It's worth mentioning here that the division of labor in Plato's ideal society rests on different factors from Adam Smith's version. The former has to do with the objectively different aptitudes of individuals or classes, whereas the latter is a matter mainly off efficient productivity.

areas, it would be possible to do so. Even in our day, when we go into one of those old one-man garages, where the proprietor knows everything, we admire that. But then we go into one of the Sears auto shops and there's the guy who does horns, another seats, the next the back wheels and so forth. That's all very efficient but it's said to be not possible to experience oneself as a reasonably complete human being in such a working condition. Whereas with someone who is immerses in the craftsmanship of cars we can talk about trucks, sports cars, turbo engines, as well as family life, politics, athletics, neighborhood, and so on, and this evidences the fullness of that person's human life.

That is all true too about people who are educated in the arts, sciences, mathematics, topography, or horticulture. Some work only in some special branch of sociology, say the sociology of marriage—just in Slovakia! If men and women were fully developed and their consciousness and work were attuned to a multifaceted, fully human work process, they would find work rewarding as *human* beings instead of as clogs in a machine.[28] They would not need constant profit incentives to perform their job—it would fulfill them. This itself should suggest the immense difference between a social life that is conceivable for Marx and Marxists versus one that accommodates the capitalist, individualist alternative.

The common-sense analogs to Marx's more rigorous development of the ideal—i.e., in his terms, fully emancipated—human nature can be grasped easily enough. For Marx, a human being will be someone who fully exercises his or her multifaceted creative imagination. As a conscious producer, a human being is a social animal with a very wide, general range of possibilities in life. Marx believed that bourgeois individualism distorts this fact by making it appear that we are naturally suited to do mostly one task very well throughout our lives.[29]

---

[28] Charlie Chaplin's famous movie "Modern Times" was intended to drive this point home. Chaplin was quite sympathetic to Marxism.

[29] This Marxist ideal may be appreciated by considering the sort of individual Leonardo da Vinci had been.

But the human being is a conscious producer and conscious production can, and should, manifest itself on as many levels as human life can encompass. And although this may not be all that helpful for wealth production, communism will not necessarily have to be as economically efficient in future as capitalism had to be. Efficiency is necessary for a time when there is enormous scarcity; thus the temporary need for the division of labor and private property rights. But efficiency is no longed needed once there is no scarcity. One can slow down, relax, play a piano, criticized ideas, do science or architecture and in general be a fully developed human being.

Marx actually says that in the in the morning we can work in the fields, in the afternoon talk philosophy. There will be no hunters, doctors, educators, but only men and women who hunt, heal, teach. And they might each do a bit of everything, at their own pace.

Mature Human Beings

Marx held that since productivity—sociable, rational work— is man's basic nature, he will mature in a society where having fulfilled this idea of being human can be everyone's lot. Prior to this, people must be alienated. But that this is not yet the case has its own useful result, namely extensive production of commodity wealth.

Just how important capitalism is to Marx may be appreciated from one of the greatest ironies about Marxism, the most critical stance one can take against capitalism. For eventually it is capitalism's generation of wealth that will allow socialism and communism to give people an abundant experience of tranquility and happiness. The analogy based on the developing human individual still helps us to see the point. In adolescence we grow but experience "growing pains." In maturity we find ourselves more temperate, calm. That, at least, is a common vision of maturity, whatever the reality. Marx changes this into a vision of humanity's collective development, its harmonious future!

It is fair to say that virtually all of what Marx says about economics and political economy is ultimately derived from his conception of what human beings would be once they are fully matured, even if some of his particular or technical discussions contain independently valuable insights. Communism is, in fact, nothing else but the society of mature humanity. It is "communism" because fully mature human beings are universally communal species-beings.

All of Marx's important, theoretical judgments of capitalism and feudalism, whether in general or in particular terms, rest on his conception of human beings as members of a communist society, as species-beings. His idea of human labor and why in capitalism it is so awful, his idea of class division and why the classes are unable to resolve their *differences* without revolution and a great deal more, all derive from his firmly held conviction that humanity will some day reach its full development, its historical objective or *telos*. And it is a sign of his enormous influence that much of contemporary social science is still under the spell of these ideas and theory, from which much of contemporary social analysis and commentary derives.

Political-Economic Life and Theory

Political economy is the study of human economic affairs with normative social and legal concerns as the main focus. Examples are the proper relationship of commerce and human life, law and technological progress, economic justice, property relations, and foreign trade. In Marxist political economy the central concern is how a human community's economic affairs relate to the maturation or emancipation of human community life. In non-Marxist schools of political economy such issues as the wealth of nations and how best to achieve it, the dutiful service to God here on earth, the free flow of commerce, the protection of individual property rights, or the attainment of the general welfare may be stressed.

It is fair to claim that today what used to be called political economy is called macroeconomics, a branch of mainstream economics that deals with the way the entire society in question bears on and is affected by economic relationships. Macroeconomics concerns itself with those elements of the economic life of society that are directly and indirectly influenced by government policy—for example, Gross National Product, taxation, fluctuation of money supply, income redistribution or "transfer," balance of trade and so on.

These matters are not mainly the function of the operations of the free market, although aspects of them could be, as far as certain schools of economics have it. In mainstream political economic thinking, however, macro-economic policies have to do with legal measures enacted to shape society, through government regulation, and through other legal or public policy measures. In this as well as other matters, macro-economics and political economy have almost identical concerns. The central difference is that, while the former eschews, the latter openly indulges in value judgments—concerns with justice, equality, income distribution, minimum wage policy and the like.

Before the father of modern economics, Adam Smith, advanced his "scientific" economic analysis—which still included a great deal of concern with norms and ethics[30]—economic factors had not been thought central to the study of politics. Where Marx discusses political economy versus its study, he notes that the latter began around the sixteenth or seventeenth century. That is when writing in a broad, systematic way about the interaction of politics and economics began to proliferate in England, France and elsewhere. What Marx says is that there had always been such interaction, although few studied it. Observing that the theories about the interaction of politics and economics had arisen subsequent to the actual manifestation of that relationship, Marx denies the priority of the idea or the theory and affirms the priority of the object about which the subject matter is formed, the economic relationships themselves. He takes this to be central to his materialist approach!

---

[30] Smith was, of course, the author of a book, his own favorite, in moral theory, namely, *The Theory of Moral Sentiments* (1759) and Smith, 1939, contains ample discussions of ethical and related normative topics.

One reason one might give for maintaining that prior to the emergence of capitalism there had not been a fully developed field called political economy is that earlier there was a much slower and incremental emergence of economic factors than subsequent to the emergence of industrialization (in capitalism). So economics was not, nor was it thought to be, very significant. Most of the classical political theorists regarded economics as a sub-field of ethics or politics. Aristotle, Plato, Augustine, Aquinas and Machiavelli—all of the major political theorists—have a lot of incidental things to say about economic matters. They do not develop a field of political economy to the point where its methods become central for studying a society. Also, in earlier times the division within the various disciplines had not yet made its full appearance.[31]

Economics to them was a sub-field of ethics and/or politics, or law. Adam Smith was a professor of moral philosophy, not (or not called) an economist. Nobody was called an economist at the time. Smith's *Wealth of Nations* is perhaps the first major (and of course prominent) tract that addressed more or less technically and systematically the wealth of a society. Earlier major tracts had been concerned with honor, justice, virtue and the goals of a good human community. Or they were concerned with the "economic" question of the just price and whether usury is appropriate or morally objectionable. Here is how the issues of commerce arose back then: could thrift and frugality be realized in those forms of activity where economics has considerable significance? That is when people began to talk about economic matters because of course this is where those virtues, if they were virtues, would have their application. Household management, exchange of goods and services in a marketplace, are spheres in which people are tempted by the sins of greed or callousness. They may fail to practice prudence, which is the first of the four cardinal virtues. Anyway, writers looked at economic matters under the

---

[31] See, for more on this, op cit., Davies, *Empiricism and History*.

rubric of moral and political norms.[32]

In Marxism and, in a roundabout way, even in the study of economics itself, there is a general interest not only in political economy but also in political theory, political philosophy, and the possible impact of economic matters on, for example, the stability, justice, and power of the state. Most political theorists have prized stability and order. "Law and order" is a popular political phrase. A society that enjoys a kind of steadiness, an absence of deep uncertainty and the presence of some measure of dependability is regarded as a better society, everything else being equal, than one that lacks such ingredients.

Now, one of the macro-economic phenomena that has puzzled students of political economy is that of business cycles—upheavals, downturns—in the general marketplace: the destruction of the value of money, credit-crunches, soaring interest rates, unemployment, relocation, bankruptcy, slumps, followed by their polar opposites. (Consider the scare that the October 1987 New York Stock Market dip of 22.6% produced for most investors!)

Furthermore, one of the current, as well as classical economic concepts, apparently divorced from politics and philosophy, is that of equilibrium. What does the word "equilibrium" mean? It means that various forces have evened themselves out and are in a steady state. The concept of equilibrium, although it is definable in all sorts of formalistic ways, ultimately means no more than economic stability or order in a society. Thus, if most people in society suffer massive psychological depression while employment is high and supply fully meets demand, from the economist's point of view this society enjoys a state of equilibrium.

One problem with markets that most economic theorists acknowledge is periodic booms and busts. Most economists have argued that by its inherent characteristics the marketplace, unhampered by either major cataclysmic natural interference or more government interference, would rebound from cycles, even itself

---

[32] The newer approach was the result, also, of the emergence of the so called scientific study of society, encouraged especially by the reductive materialist philosophy of Thomas Hobbes.

out, that a full balance between production and consumption would eventually emerge. Nobody claims, of course, that in any particular industry or line of production there could not be a temporary imbalance between supply and demand.

Because of the problem of time-lapse and absence of perfect information about demand and scarcity one would not be able to read the marketplace precisely enough to learn how much one should produce of any particular item. This observation does not even take into account the effects of such normal human factors as oversight, laziness, frustration, absent-mindedness, preoccupation and the like, matters that tended to be avoided in the budding *scientistic* atmosphere of scholarship. There is too much information lag and uncertainty, so, even if managers of firms are very careful and watch the market meticulously, there will simply emerge situations in which they have to plan far ahead and will either underestimate or overestimate future demand. The problem of over-employment or underemployment will occur: there may be too few people to do the work that needs to be done or too many people to do the work. There are also the recurring problems caused by dislocations and distortions engendered by non-market influences.

But bourgeois political economic theory has always proposed that while these gyrations occur within various industries, the total market, if left to itself, would always even itself out much better than if government steps in. Once a firm manufactures so many shoes, there might be a drop in the expected purchase of shoes. But that drop will be made up by a simultaneous rise in the purchase of gloves, for example, or hats or, say, baby carriages. And while a certain amount of instability is admitted to during the period that a realignment of the employment situation occurs and people for example leave the shoe-manufacturing industry and move gradually to the glove-manufacturing industry, once that adjustment has occurred, things are supposed to even out and the market will once again approximate equilibrium or optimal productivity.

But, Marx observes, it never happens exactly like that. Capitalism has always involved booms and busts. Things look very good for a while and then start to look very, very bad at other times. We have ourselves experienced some of this in our own time. High inflation, high unemployment, market panics—or Alan Greenspan's "irrational exuberance"—imbalance of trade, excessive dislocation, high budget deficits, rise in interest rates—make for temporary inefficiencies. Adjustments to these inefficiencies are being made when people speak of tightening belts; or when people talk about conservation and growth reduction, going to a "zero growth policy." At such times people]=are considering public policies thought to facilitate stability and prevent major jarring disruptions of the economy.

Most bourgeois—especially the "Austrian"—economists hold that business cycles are a result of various forms of government intervention. They hold that a central government bureaucracy, in contrast to the millions of market agents acting on their own judgment based largely on local knowledge, cannot predict what needs to be produced, where consumption is going to occur, what inventories are shrinking, how circumstances of scarcity or demand or technology change, and so forth. Bourgeois economists say government will inevitably mismanage supply and demand in whatever area it enters because of the epistemological problem.[33] There clearly seem to be few solvent government businesses. Think of the even the partially privatized Post Office, think of Amtrak, let alone any state's DMV. Think of the New York City subway system.

In almost any government enterprise one can think of, whether in production or consumption of goods or services, there seems to be a misalignment—some kind of a failure, an underestimation of how much things will cost, an understatement of the budget. So-called free market economists tend, accordingly, to attribute the business cycle to periodic, more or less severe government in-

---

[33] Ludwig von Mises is perhaps best known for advancing this thesis, along with his numerous more or less loyal students. See his *Epistemological Problems of Economics*, trans. George Reisman (Princeton, NJ: Van Nostrand, 1960). See also F. A Hayek, "The Use of Knowledge in Society," *The American Economic Review*, Vol. XXXV, No. 4 (September 1945), pp. 519-30.

tervention in the economy. If anything appears to substantiate these ideas that is fully evident to any ordinary educated person, the demise of the Soviet Union and its satellite countries would be good cases in point. The failure of those centrally planned economies appears to have been established as a matter of empirical history. Of course, Marxists would not agree with this because of the peculiar version of socialist economics of the USSR, one that engendered what Marx himself characterized generally as the "socialization of poverty." He thought that would be the fate of societies that hadn't passed through a capitalist phase of production. That, for example, Czechoslovakia clearly had passed through such a stage suggests that Marx's analysis was flawed even here.

Now the bourgeois idea has been that the way to establish and maintain economic progress and stability is to disengage the government from as much of the economy as is possible, without jeopardizing the security of a country. Marx thought this was another example of naive bourgeois economic thinking, of "insipid illusions."

For example, Marx observed that it is a myth to think that one could have a bourgeois capitalist economic system in which the government could ever stay out of lending a helping hand to some interests in that system. It is a hopeless naiveté to think that, for example, the economically powerful classes would not employ the government to bail them out whenever they face some trouble. In late 20th century America this was shown most notably in the case of the Chrysler Corporation. Chrysler's Lee Iacocca changed the tune from free enterprise to federal bailouts when it was his own firm that was on the brink of bankruptcy. It was no longer, "Let market forces rule, do not regulate the auto industry, do not interfere with us, we want to face the competition and win based on open, unencumbered competition." "Forget it," he said, "we're suffering. Please, Uncle Sam, help us out." Later, when Chrysler bought American Motors and then had to shut down the plant in Kenosha, Wisconsin, many protested—most notably then Democratic presidential aspirant, Jesse Jackson—that, if the government could bail the firm out, it ought also to prevent it from closing the plant and leaving 5,500 workers out of jobs.

In any case, those commercial interests possess enough economic and political power, a Marxist analysis would maintain, to ensure that whenever they are threatened they will successfully implore the government to help them. So keeping the government out of the economy and letting the market forces determine all on their own what will happen—this is a silly myth.

Marx then plainly did not accept the very possibility of an ongoing, lasting, truly free market. He could not imagine that in capitalist systems firms would refuse to run to the state for help or that states would be able to resist such calls. The idea of a constitutional separation of church and state might have made sense to him, since he did not think churches have much economic power (for a gruesome picture of the unprincipled behavior of many who run the major corporations of the world, see [32]), but the idea of separating of economy and state, the ideal of free market capitalism, was for Marx an impossibility. For example, he explicitly rejected the analysis of the American economist, Henry Carey, that explained distortions in the economy by reference to what Marx called "malicious perversions on the part of governments" [Marx, 1971,p.19].

Instead, the link between (monopoly) capital and state is unavoidable. It follows from the class conflict, based on economic determinism, whereby the ruling class controls society's culture and institutions—law, morality, religion. The idea that production could carry on merrily and in harmony, with no trade cycles, if government only let things be—*laissez-faire, laissez passer*—is to Marx totally naive. Governments at this stage of history are unavoidably the agents of capitalists, not impartial adjudicators!

Social Revolution and Economics

But there are other problems aside from class conflict and the ever-growing number of unemployed created through the monopolization of capital. (In later Marxian terms it may not be literally unemployed but "immiserated," impoverished workers who fill the bill here.) The latter involves the process of competing firms whereby the weaker competitors are gradually eliminated.

Here Marx effectively models economic competition on the sports tournament in which eventually just one victor remains. For instance, new technology will take the place of the employed. Thus the labor force is going to be unemployed or relegated to primarily unskilled, inexpensive labor. This further contributes to the antagonism set up between the proletariat and the capitalists, since all profits—surplus (stolen) value in capitalism—go to the latter.

There is also the problem of degeneration of credit, investment and ultimately production, which is often overextended in the process of monopolistic competition. In other words, capitalists borrow a lot of money, which for a while makes possible capitalization, investment, building, expansion, etc. That takes money out of the consuming portion of the economy. In turn what is built and produced is not going to be readily purchased. It will take quite a time before new consumer money is generated to replace money that was lent out—new consumer money to enable the consumers to purchase all the things that were built with the money that was borrowed. And that also means that the purchasing power of the consuming public will take some time to be regenerated, if at all. In the meantime unemployment or diminished (or cheap) employment continues. This produces repeated, ongoing dislocations and dissatisfaction among the workers. And once this has gone on for a while, the dissatisfaction grows to the level that is necessary to create the condition for a fundamental (though not necessarily violent) revolution, the abolition (in certain places such as England and North America, [Marx, 1977, p. 594] via the electoral process) of the basic institutions of capitalism itself.

Marx does not deny that in any particular industry readjustments can be made in the wake of such upheavals. But the crux of his argument is that after a while, with little bits of booms and busts going on, there emerges a total antagonism for the marketplace in capitalism.

In ordinary common-sense terms this should not be terribly surprising. If someone loses his job four or five times in four or five years, he will be frustrated with the uncertainty that this creates in his life. Can one plan on anything, buy anything, invest anywhere, keep one's family intact, hold on to one's friends? A social antagonism, not just an economic antagonism, develops toward capitalism. There is disenchantment with its capacity to meet human needs of a more general kind. The problem isn't about money, tape recorders, hair-dos, shoes, cars and food, but about the desire for stability.

This attitude is well illustrated vis-à-vis globalization, especially outsourcing. Sure, free market ideologues hold that in the long run jobs will reappear after they have disappeared, since the money saved via outsourcing is going to be invested and spent on alternative goods and services. But Marx would respond that this doesn't make up for the loss of stability and community. That, in turn, feeds the revolutionary sentiment in society. Combine all this with alienation, the rise in unemployment rate, monopoly capital, and later on (when one adds to this some neo-Marxist considerations bearing on international relations) imperialism, and all these provide the necessary and sufficient conditions for the ultimate demise of the capitalist system.

It doesn't have to come overnight, obviously. None of this is supposed to be a rapid occurrence, but instead a process that can draw itself out for many, many generations. (Never mind now that Marx himself, in his private behavior, sometimes acted as if it would come in a couple of months. He behaved both as a theorist and as one of history's movers.)

Marxism and Reform

Many Marxists and, as we have seen, Marx as well, regarded it as quite un-Marxist to advocate stalling measures—such as unemployment compensation and antitrust laws—which would give capitalism longevity, albeit in an impure rendition. They saw the welfare state itself as ultimately counterproductive.

Around the turn of the nineteenth century very heated debates arose between the members of the Communist and the Social Democratic Parties of Europe. Social Democrats—now democratic socialists, even so called "market" socialists—believed in liberal democracy and in trying to change their countries gradually, to establish social policies, combine bourgeois features of a society with socialist ones, build something like the welfare state or, in the post-Soviet era, "the third way." But hard-core Marxists do not understand democracy in a liberal mode. They use the term to mean total socialization of the means of production—the society run *for* the people, not necessarily *by* the people. So the two sides would often clash on particular public policy measures and legislation.

Communists opposed reform because it pushed back the revolution beyond their reach. Even more recently, when someone like Tom Hayden, a "soft" late-60s-type Marxist, eventually a member of the California state government, spoke someplace, a little band of revolutionary communists would surround and boo him—a miniature manifestation of this long-drawn-out debate between the revolutionary communists and the democratic socialists who want socialism but want to do it in a nice, humane fashion. (Hayden's Campaign for Economic Democracy had been basically soft-socialism and was opposed by the Marxists of this revolutionary communist type, who were much more interested in a drastic, radical transformation of the society with no mercy for or compromise with the bourgeoisie.) Marx himself allows conflicting interpretations concerning this matter. It is possible to read into Marx a very serious commitment to democracy, if by this concept is meant "government for the people." (See, again, the Appendix for more on this issue.)

As far as leaving the choice of government and its administrator to the people, that is another matter. Marx was too concerned even about the false consciousness of the proletariat [Marx, 1977, p. 594], not to mention reactionary elements in post-revolutionary societies, to regard the full and unregimented political participation of the people as acceptable. He clearly wonders whether the proletariat are ever going to vote democratically for socialism, a strain of his thinking picked up later in full measure by Lenin. What if they are mistakenly but quite sincerely satisfied with what capitalism does for them? Wouldn't that mean that something has to be done to eliminate the sluggishness of the democratic process, a process that might on its own not even go in the direction of socialism? Those who still consider socialism to be the right system could think that a leadership must be established to usher it in—exactly what Lenin and Josef Stalin proclaimed about the matter and why in Soviet-type Marxism liberal democracy had been demeaned, disdained, and dismissed.

There is yet another reason why full-scale liberal political democracy and Marxist socialism are incompatible. The latter involves the total abolition of private property rights in capital goods, the means of production. All that would remain is some manner of personal property, that is, the ownership of intimate articles (which could, of course, involve a home, a vacation spot, horses, cars, etc.).[34] Yet one of the preconditions of a functioning liberal democracy is that citizens can remain relatively independent of government provisions. Without this independence one is not able to exercise one's own independent—un-impeded or intimidated—judgment in political matters. Democracy, in fact, is inherently individualistic because in such a system *at the outset* every citizen may stand apart from the rest. Everyone is supposed to figure out what side of an issue to support and everyone is, in principle, free to reject the dominant political authority and, even after ending up on the losing side, retire to his or her own dominion or sphere of personal jurisdiction. That is exactly the function of the right to private property in a *bona fide*, functioning democratic polity—individuals need not be beholden to the state and have the right to stand apart from it.[35]

Yet under socialism it is just this individual independence that is ruled out. Could it be argued that this is fine and that it is

---

[34] For more on this see Thomas Keyes, "The Marxian Concept of Property: Individual/ Social," in Tibor R. Machan, ed., *The Main Debate: Communism versus Capitalism* (New York: Random House, 1987).

[35] This is a crucial flaw in the kind of democracy envisioned by Richard Rorty and Jürgen Habermas, one that makes no room for a basic *right* to private property.

enough if the state acts on behalf of the best interests of the people, regardless of whether the people find this acceptable? I doubt it, because there are losses to autonomy that are hard to stomach on this scheme. As J. Roger Lee has argued, the loss of freedom is itself a kind of harm.[36] There can be arguments for this—Marx would advance the idea that, when for centuries members of the proletariat have had their minds focused on nothing more complicated than how to carve out a meager subsistence, one could not expect them to have a clear view of what is best for them, not, at least, until their consciousness had been fully raised. But whether or not this is correct, the point here is that from the Marxist perspective the kind of democracy that is acceptable does not involve the full political participation of independent citizens.

In fact, Marx would frown on this idea as a convenient myth that ignores the real history of the population in so-called democratic capitalist societies. This real history simply conditions workers to accommodate the ruling class and gives them only the appearance of political independence. What the workers actually experience is dependence on the capitalists, and they vote accordingly—at least until they become utterly exasperated and incensed, so they will vote in socialism. What remains after that, however, is not the type of democracy that liberalism envisages but a collective dictatorship presumably aimed toward the objective improvement of the lot of the working class.

An example from the United States might make the point in less abstract fashion. In the late 1970s in a California referendum political activist Bill Press conducted a campaign to tax the oil companies quite heavily (it was called Proposition 11—with TV ads supporting it asking why don't we move in on the "pigs" and get them to pay up). It was roundly defeated. Thereupon, led by Bill Press, California's economic democrats flatly rejected the result and denied that it amounted to a proper democratic outcome. They maintained that the population voting against the measure was "paid off," duped. It was paid off not directly, but

---

[36] J. Roger Lee, "Choice and Harms," in Tibor R. Machan and M. Bruce Johnson, eds., *Rights and Regulation* (Boston: Ballinger, 1983).

through the media, manipulation, advertising, and other more subtle means the oil companies used to dupe the public. Here is the contemporary though somewhat watered down manifestation of the concept of false consciousness in an attempt to discredit the very democratic process initially taken to be the solution.

Since Marx postulated both democracy *and* false consciousness, advocacy of two kinds of political process can emerge out of Marxism, one of which is committed at least for a time to liberal political democracy. When applied currently this allows for the slow, gradual transformation of society toward socialism. The other advocacy disregards democracy and suggests instead the need for a temporary dictatorial type of organizational effort, often sanctioning violence, purges, liquidation and terrorism in order to overcome the impediments created through the false consciousness of the proletariat. That's what was attempted first in the Soviet Union and later also in its dominated states. Thus Marxism-Leninism-Stalinism flowered into brutal national terrorist domestic policy, most clearly in the hands of Stalin, who met with widespread resistance, not only from much of the population but from his very own allies in the Communist Party, but also already from Lenin. Stalin proceeded to execute his sometimes imaginary opponents, because he saw himself as one of the very few people without false consciousness.

In Marxist terms Stalinism could be accounted for along such lines. Stalin, like many other Soviet leaders, was a peasant-intellectual who saw it as his task to give ideological guidance in the revolutionary struggle of the proletariat. Stalin may certainly not have been in full accord with the spirit and letter of Marxism. Yet he was not exactly out of line with it either.

Of course, Marx does consistently endorse a planned economy for a mature society. He does not say, however, that the plan has to be implemented and devised by four or five old Russians. Marx could be interpreted as having advocated both a democratic, participatory socialism, along lines proposed by the late Sidney Hook, and, as others saw him, a centrally planned socialist system.

Socialist Planning versus Capitalist "Anarchy"

At this point it will be helpful to provide some of the differences between a market and a socialized economy (or mercantilist one, the two being structurally very similar[37]). Perhaps the central difference is that in principle in socialized or mercantilist systems there is collective ownership of the means of production, whereas in capitalist systems every individual human being's right to ownership of resources (or "the means of production") is acknowledged and protected. (This includes human labor power.[38]) It is vital to note that "collective ownership" or "public ownership" means that while legal title is held by "the people," or "the citizenry," it is the government of such a society that has effective ownership, given that it is the government that makes decisions concerning the use and disposal of public property. And that, in turn, means that certain individuals in public office are making these decisions. In a monarchy, for example, public ownership means the king or queen or royal family owns everything and it is these agents who decide the use and disposal of the resources involved. In a socialist system it is those who represent the people of the country—a party or some individuals—who occupy this role. They may, however, delegate some of these decisions to individuals or groups (at times corporations or other economic agents)—that would be the case in a market socialist system. This was also so in the British monarchy of the 19 century—as in the case of The East India Company.

In a capitalist society the constitutional right to private property, resting as it does conceptually on a natural right, entitles everyone to elect to seek to obtain and hold resources or to pool resources held privately with other private owners and establish corporate bodies with officers authorized to make the decisions about the use and disposal or these resources for various pur-

---

[37] Spanish mercantilist kings gave land grants, and the British kings and queens licensed privateers too, yet they retained the legal authority to revoke their grants, so they didn't acknowledge the existence of a right to private property.

[38] For a discussion of this by a neo-Marxist economists, see Robert L. Heilbroner, *Marxism: For and Against* (New York: Norton, 1980). Given Marx's labor theory of value, it follows that a socialist system involves public ownership of human labor.

poses. In both cases some human beings make decisions—in the socialist or mercantilist society they do this in the name or for the benefit of all the people, in the capitalist society they make them in the name or for the benefit of various individuals or voluntary groups.

When speaking of a socialized economy, it is crucial to keep in mind that whatever it is that socialization involves is not brought about with the consent of individual members of the citizenry. Socialized economic systems we are considering are supposed to be socialized as a matter of the natural condition of human life, not through a voluntary arrangement made by numerous individuals to pool their various resources. Socialism in the political context is supposed to be the state individuals would naturally fit into, not enter into as a matter of choice.

Even this needs some clarification. One might argue that even if a socialist system does naturally fit human beings, yet they must still choose it; just as in human life generally even what is natural to human beings ought to be a matter of choice. But the Marxist conception of socialism contrasts significantly with, say, the socialism of Henri Saint-Simon, Charles Fourier or Robert Owen (the so-called utopian socialists), as well as of Auguste Comte, all of whom wanted to bring socialism about by way of moral persuasion and thus assumed that human beings ought to choose the system.

Marx saw socialism coming about as a matter of natural evolution (or revolution), not as a matter of the free choices of individual human beings, some of whom might choose—perhaps wrongly—some other system to live under. Socialism of this sort sees society, in Marx's own words, as "an organic body" or "organic whole" [Marx, 1977, p.351]. Individuals are parts of the larger social *organism*. Thus when Marxist socialists speak of planning, they see society as a whole doing the planning *of its life*, just as sometimes individuals plan their lives.

This aspect of socialism is a problem for most of those who sympathize with it but also cling to certain classical liberal notions and ideals about personal autonomy, choice, freedom and the like in certain areas such as religion, journalism, the expression of ideas, scientific independence and democracy. Even those who favor the milder versions of socialism, such as communitarianism and market socialism, have a difficulty with the idea that in Marx all members of society are related rather like ants in their colonies or bees in their hives, rather than by their own free choices as are individual human beings in an association, club or corporation. Some of the odd public policy notions among those who prefer the hybrid of socialism and liberalism may be accounted for because of the bad fit between these two political traditions at a certain basic level—thus liberal minded socialists reject private property rights but not, notably, in body parts or even labor (unlike, say, Soviet Socialists, who held firmly to the idea that everyone's labor belongs to the collective). Also, wealth redistribution is often favored by such liberal minded socialists but excludes the wealth one may have in one's special physical condition or beauty (thus precluding any public policy of people having to share one of their two healthy kidneys or eyes with another who needs one). Marx is a far more consistent, coherent socialist than most of those who sympathize with him "up to a point."

The capitalist market, in turn, is conceived of as a gathering place where individuals or their groups (firms, companies, partnerships, clubs, teams, corporations, etc.) come together to do business. The market is the commercial forum of a society in which these individuals are supposed to be sovereign citizens. They are deemed to be the kind of beings who can choose to enter the market, the playing fields, church, the academy, or the scientific laboratory and interact with other individuals if these others will choose to do so on agreeable terms.

Capitalism is the kind of political economy in which markets—which is to say their freely acting participants—are supposed to be unimpeded by law in their peaceful conduct, in which men and women are deemed to have the natural, basic right to private property—just as in such a political system they would have the basic right to privacy in sex, thought, religious worship, sport, etc. They are supposed to be making their choices in all these realms within the constraints of their circumstances but not by taking jurisdiction from others. They have the right of free choice *vis-à-vis* their lives, not those of other people. But this realm may be *different* in scope or size—for a person with limited skills, holdings, or ambition, there will not be much to trade; but for one with extensive skills, holdings, or ambition there may be a great deal to trade. Socialism sees at least holdings but often also skills and labor as collective property. Capitalism sees all of it as private, not because of some artificial "atomistic" individualist idea of human nature but because capitalists assume a conception of the mature, grown-up human individual as having the capacity (though not always the willingness) to think and act on his or her own considered judgment.[39]

While there is planning in the market, it is at the level of individuals or their voluntary cooperative/social establishments. The market assumes the recognition of private property. So, when market agents plan, they usually do so with their own resources or with resources they have been given. They are not permitted, legally, to just take the resources of others without the owner's consent. When in such a system government wants some land, it must gain the owner's permission or must meet his terms. Governments do of course invoke eminent domain laws in most so-called capitalist countries, but in a purely capitalist version of such countries this would only rarely be possible, strictly for public use. So the market is inherently decentralized, even when there are quite a few firms that have managed to serve very large groups of people all on their own. The economy is "anarchic" (except for rules that direct the line of ownership through a lineage of voluntary exchange of legitimately owned property). This also suggests that political power cannot be retained without considerable satisfaction by the citizenry. Without such satisfaction, the citizens will withdraw their support. And although this is not utopia, it does appear to make extensive political and even cultural diversity possible.

---

[39] For a fuller discussion, see Machan, 1998, especially chapter 14, "Individualism versus Its Critics." See also Norton, 1976.

In socialist systems, where government is the "head" of the people as a whole, one's plans will be forced to square with what the government regards as the plan that best serves the interest of society. There may not be great diversity but we can at least imagine that such a system can lead to the well being of the people. And so far this could mean a type of democratic socialist system in which decisions about society's concerns might be aimed at what is "for the people."

But when we add to this the Marxist idea of false consciousness, whereby many who are actually members of the working class still are not quite aware of their own best interest, planning for at least a certain period of time must be carried out by central authorities who represent everyone. And if Marx is wrong about what the workers really will develop into, then all this will require extensive coercive force in order to be put into effect. ("Coercive" here is a loaded term. If one sees such force as involving the violation of the rights of individuals, then it is coercive. But if such force is appropriate, indeed required, for the society to flourish and individual rights are seen as mere reactionary myths, then it is thought not to be coercive at all.)

Here is where Leninism-Stalinism can come in as a very natural adjunct to something Marx conceived of but need not have linked with such force. This is what lent Marx's support to many of the official repressive, tyrannical, anti-liberal activities of a Stalinist-type Marxist government.

Marx may not have intended—nor would he have regarded it a natural development—that socialism should arise in this dictatorial form. Nevertheless, certain crucial Marxist ideas had a hand in paving the way for Soviet (Leninist-Stalinist) credibility. In short, the centrist socialist system can be validated by reference to Marx's belief that false consciousness impedes the working class's determination to lead the revolution. And even after that revolution there must be a period of adjustment during which there may be much room for sometimes pretty brutal force.

Now even if Marxism were understood without the concept of false consciousness, the kind of political democracy that is prized within the liberal tradition would not be compatible with it. As we have seen, such democracy requires the principles of private property rights at its base, so that dissident citizens could at least have a reasonable chance to withstand attempted state pressures exerted on the minority—sometimes of one! But, at least during the undermining of capitalism, political democracy could be part of the process of ushering in socialism. Marxism with false consciousness would not make the emergence of socialism depend on political democracy. Marx himself suggested both possibilities.

All the time one must keep in mind that Marx makes a serious projection of a new human nature for the future. As Marx saw it, human beings in his time were characterized by avaricious behavior and an avaricious state of mind, so that it is unthinkable that socialism, let alone communism, could at present work. For that it is necessary that human nature undergo its dialectical development. Thereafter, in socialism—and of course in communism—no incentive programs would be necessary to encourage production. People would behave roughly as musicians do at jam sessions. They would work spontaneously for the love of work itself. All labor would be a labor of love, not hardship or chore.

Marx: Socialist or Communist?

Is Marx a socialist or a communist? He is a communist, but he sees that the advancement of communism on a scientific basis must admit of a stage between capitalism and communism. Between adolescence and adulthood, we have young adulthood. That stage, namely socialism, is not a goal of history at all. Marx believed that the state is only necessary to maintain the ruling class against competing classes. The only competing class in socialism is the dying-out, reactionary capitalist class. The moment that class dies out, the state—an extremely forceful government—has no function. The state is not productive; it only protects the interests of the ruling class. In socialism the state still protects the ruling classes, namely, the interests of the workers, but only until the workers learn how to do this themselves.

When one asks what Marx thought communism would look like, one can expect only very rough hints. That is because communism ushers in humanity's adulthood. Presumably adults are free and able to determine creatively and quite unexpectedly various ways in which to lead their lives. Children go through definite stages. Human adults are precisely those creatures who are free and self-creating. This doesn't mean people who are stunted or arrested adults. We are talking about the mature adult, one who is really looking creatively at a life to be led and not one who is still living down childhood traits. That is the image or model one has to use to understand Marxism. (When talking about ideal circles, one doesn't talk about the sloppy ones drawn on blackboards.)

Marx says that we cannot have a blueprint of communism. We cannot now know exactly what will happen because communist society will be populated by an emancipated human race that has overcome the necessities of scarcity, of class-consciousness, of class-conflict, of alienation and of exploitation. In consequence of all this, such a society has the capacity to develop freely and creatively. Making detailed predictions about it is impossible; we are not there yet.

Now one could ask the question, of course, why shouldn't the free and mature people in communist society re-institute numerous aspects of capitalism? There is nothing in Marx's thinking that would preclude such a prospect. After all, Marx was the first to call attention to the fact that communism would have at least its abundance in common with capitalism. Moreover, communism will finish what liberal bourgeois society has started to do, namely, diminish government's role in human life. It will let the state wither away and become unnecessary.

Some Marxists have even argued that certain aspects of communism will call to mind what capitalists think of as the free marketplace but what never really occurred under capitalism, namely, truly free exchange of goods and services, but with the appropriate respect for the true value of these. Does this seem a bit crazy? Well, doesn't a commune in some respects resemble the marketplace? People interact on a voluntary basis, just as they would do under capitalism. Only they don't require police supervision of their interaction but do it spontaneously, freely, of their own choice. And supposedly they are guided by their sense of proper respect for the contributions of all the members.

At any rate, communism is supposed to be the mature stage of human life and can contain elements of preceding stages, just as a mature individual today may exhibit traits that are reminiscent of his or her childhood and adolescence. After the business cycle has precipitated the revolution—violent or peaceful (i.e. forced or carried out via democratic politics)—a stage of social management, socialism, must come into effect. Thereafter communism, the spontaneous manifestation of the wisdom of that management, will finally emerge.

And no one can deny that this is a very plausible scenario in our own time. What with economic uncertainty and upheavals making everyone in capitalist societies extremely dissatisfied and nervous, the communist alternative—with its unalienated humanity, unexploited labor, whole or fully integrated individuals, and cooperatively managed continued economic abundance—would certainly appear to be a breath of fresh air. It can seem that way, clearly.

Chapter 4. People,
Capitalism, and Exploitation

Homo Economicus

Earlier, I discussed the difference between the Marxist concept that man has a nature (albeit to be fully realized only in communism) versus the Hobbesian view that human nature is basically something that we assign or impose "nominally," in name only. We were talking about the contrast between someone who believes that there is a human nature versus someone who believes there is no human nature. Now we come to the difference in content between Marx's conception of human nature and Hobbes's nominalist idea.

The Hobbesian materialism presupposed in economic science goes roughly as follows: nature is composed of matter-in-motion. What this means in concrete terms may be gleaned by imagining a hustling-bustling reality populated by little atoms that are always moving and swirling. That is not so unrealistic—a good many modern physicists envisage that in the last analysis there really is nothing but swirling matter-in-motion, e.g. bits of subatomic particles dashing about. Hobbes and other materialists of the sixteenth, seventeenth and eighteenth centuries imagined that nature was composed of matter-in-motion, which Newton described in a comprehensive and universal physical system. This mechanistic physics is, to a large extent, still the world view of intellectuals and scientific people of the last three centuries—although not of the general population or priests. I am referring to those who were beginning to think of physical nature as the basis for understanding everything else. (Hobbes himself followed his friend Galileo's lead here and extrapolated mechanical laws to everything in nature. Newtonian physics, which defines the principles of the motion of [material objects], presumably gives us the most fundamental laws of nature.) The Hobbesian understanding of human behavior, accordingly, turned out to be mostly what most economists assume people to be, at least for purposes of analyzing market events.

Economists think that every person is a utility maximizer—that is, all people pursue their desired goals. Underlying the most advanced (neo-classical) economic point of view is a conception of human beings as entities seeking out things to acquire or enjoy. As one Marxist scholar, C. B. Macpherson, characterizes the ideology underlying classical and neo-classical economics, human beings in this ideology are conceived of as possessive individuals, and therefore they mainly engage in deals, buying and selling and so forth. Marx, too, saw bourgeois society as reduced to a "cash nexus." This is the picture that according to Marx (and many anti-Marxists) underlies capitalism. Capitalism is supposed to rest on a model of the acquisitive, possessive, utility-maximizing person.

What would life be like for such a human being? To put it roughly, here we have the perpetual wheeler and dealer. And modern economic theory confirms this image of people. The core of that theory aims at explaining only market behavior, but very often economists extend this beyond behavior in markets. (See Machan, 1990, for a full discussion of this economic approach to human life.)

There are economists who study marriage, crime and religious conduct on the model of market behavior. In other words, although core economic theory requires that this model explain only market behavior, in fact it is actually applied across the board to the nature of human behavior as such, not just the nature of human behavior as it manifests itself in the market.

Marx, too, believed that in the capitalist phase of humanity's development this is exactly the case. What could we expect of people when they go grocery shopping? Well, once we know that they are going grocery shopping, we can tell, also, that they want to make a good deal. This is only sensible on their part, and the bulk of them probably carry on in this sensible way. They want to turn in their coupons, get bargains on the best peas, orange juice, TV set, rent-a-car, blue-chip stock and everything else they desire. This is what shopping is all about.

But not all those in the grocery store are shopping; some are just milling around; some husbands are reading magazines; some people are escaping the rain outside. But they are the exceptions. The bulk of the activity going on in the grocery store, and in markets in general, has to do with buying and selling. And the motivation that explains this best is to obtain desired goods and services at the least cost. That is the model for economics: people want the most for the least. Observe anyone who goes shopping. No one says, "Oh, the sugar costs five dollars; here is an extra ten, just as a bonus." Not unless the merchant is a friend or member of the family. Even the least commercial among us behave mostly as market agents when we are out shopping—poets, musicians, philosophers or whatever. So what the economist uses is a perfectly adequate model for such human behavior.

Economic Imperialism

But economists sometimes want to explain more than just plain, straightforward market behavior. They want to become social theorists. They wish to offer an economic explanation of all of human behavior. Becker, already mentioned [Becker, 1976], takes the model we agree makes perfectly good sense of going shopping (or market behavior) and expands it to cover going to church, making love, bird watching, playing sports, holding up banks, and everything (for a good critique, see McKenzie's *Limits of Economic Science* [McKenzie, 1971]).

Indeed, the seventeenth-century field of political economy also used the model of selfish behavior (pursuing one's self-interest) to explain what happens in all of society. For example, Hobbes's explanation of government went roughly as follows: if everyone seeks his or her self-interest—tries to avoid death and tries to reach as much satisfaction as possible (the two ingredients of seeking one's self-interest)—eventually, in one another's vicinity, there will be a "war of all against all." Because this would happen, and because we are rational, we reach a solution by introducing government. It will restrain us in the pursuit of our self-interest by the introduction of laws and regulations strictly enforced by administrator(s).

The entire explanation of the nature of government emerges out of conceiving of human beings on the model of self-interested rational actors or, even more basically, as pieces of matter seeking to keep in motion. (The social contract of Hobbes and many contemporary Hobbesians, such as Jan Narveson, David Gauthier, Bernard Gert, James Buchanan and Robert Frank, rests on this idea. But, of course, since the Hobbesian idea of human nature is fully deterministic, there is not much that can be done even if a given contractual outcome were to have binding moral force. We will just continue to do what we must, regardless!)

Anyway, what would a selfish person want to do or what would motivate him? He wouldn't want to die and he would want to get as much wealth as he could. Wealth is simply whatever the actor desires to have, whether leisure, lots of bananas, lots of money, lots of heroin, or whatever: it makes no difference. According to this conception of human beings, we are constantly in motion, seeking to survive and "enhance" ourselves. This is actually the application of the principles of motion (governing all the particles that move in the world) to social life. It is an extrapolation, a lifting of a principle from one sphere of interest and then extending it to another.

This model has for some time guided much of the understanding of political economy in most bourgeois—near-capitalist or fully capitalist—societies, including when Marx was examining these issues. In classical economics the major principle of Adam Smith, for example, is that, through pursuing their private or self-interests (understood mainly in terms of gaining worldly prosperity), people will achieve the public interest (again understood economically). They will be motivated selfishly, not "from benevolence." Yet their self-serving motivation, to increase their own wealth, will, if not squashed by government interference such as taxes and levies and criminal acts such as theft and robbery, also increase the public wealth.

Adam Smith's *The Wealth of Nations* is concerned, mainly, with the wealth of nations. But in the analysis he also proposes that, by leaving individuals unimpeded in their efforts to pursue their own economic ends, they will be ingenious and will bargain and produce and wheel and deal. This will ultimately make the whole pie—the wealth of the entire community—bigger than it would otherwise be. This is the basic viewpoint of mainstream, neo-classical, including supply-side, economics—all are, at heart, but an update of Smith's economic views: if the regulations and restrictions are removed from the marketplace, there will be a freer, more vigorous flow of commerce, because the built-in proclivity that motivates us all will be unleashed. That is the central theme of classical liberalism.

And all this liberated economic energy will increase the government's wealth, since although taxes may be low (for high taxes are a disincentive to production) the total tax bill may turn out to be much higher in the long run. Even those who care not a jot about governments getting richer may endorse this theme of supply-side economics. All they need to wish for is a wealthier community and, only in consequence, government that would appear to be impossible under the more restrictive systems of socialism or the welfare state.

Economists versus Socialists

Now, it is this ahistorical or even anti-historical economistic conception of human life and behavior in society that was one of Marx's major targets. He denied the soundness of the idea that throughout human history the principles of one kind of political economy could remain stable. Humanity, like the individual person, undergoes a process of maturation. When the classical and even neo-classical (contemporary) economists held that, as far as our economic life is concerned, the principles which govern it have been firmly placed already, Marx thought they had to be wrong and indeed bad scientists! They prejudicially extrapolated limited historical principles into trans-historical ones. In particular, these economists have believed that human beings have ever been, are and will be self-interested, self-aggrandizing, self-promoting conscious beings. They failed thus to see that this state of humanity, contrary to being in their essential nature, is merely a passing, albeit necessary, stage of development toward a far more emancipated, improved end.

Briefly we should note that it is one thing to claim that the classical and neo-classical economists get it wrong about human nature. (Actually as Marx sees it they were right enough for a certain period of human history, just the way adolescent psychology tells it right, when it does, about the adolescent personality, but not about human personality as such.) It is another thing to say that *their very method of seeking to answer questions* had been (and is) erroneous. Moreover, the suggested error is something directly contrary to what any scientist and thinker would wish to claim, namely, that he is objective, unbiased, faithful to what the facts dictate rather than to what personal or some other subjective interest may desire. Marx accused the classical economist not just of being wrong but of being helplessly biased—indeed, it is a central thesis of Marxism that these economists cannot help but be mouthpieces of the bourgeoisie. They have no choice about the matter—it is indeed their historic role to spout their ideas and serve as rationalizers of the temporary rule of the class whose interest they represent.

As a result of this analysis by Marx, his accusation is ambiguous. Marx was never clear about whether human beings have personal moral responsibility, at least prior to the onset of communism. Thus whatever faulty methodology economists might practice, there isn't anything else they could have done. So perhaps the indictment should be taken to be more of a hyperbole or tactic. (Indeed, when we consider the nature of revolution as Marx saw it, we will understand better how Marx may well have construed the function of his own moralizing invectives against others, namely, as inducements to social change performed by him in his role in the dialectic of human history.)

It seems that Marx, a historical determinist, had to find some deterministic way to explain why the classical economists said the (wrong) things they did say. It could not simply be that they made mistakes. Something *must* have caused them to do misunderstand things, something historically vital. And indeed they— Adam Smith and David Ricardo—were said by Marx to be suffering from "insipid illusions" [Marx, 1971, p. 16] for a historical purpose: to help rationalize the necessary but temporary phase of capitalism, to help give it historical staying power.[40]

We should also note that most economists, then and now, do not actually talk about human nature but rather about human behavior, at least when they wax philosophical. They tend to simply hold that what we call human beings *behave* in certain ways which to the economists seem crucial. In the framework that yields this social scientific idea about human behavior, namely, Hobbes's mechanistic materialism, this really means that all behavior may be reduced to that of matter-in-motion, *a la* Isaac Newton.[41] So, of course, human behavior, too, must come to no more nor less than trying to keep in motion and resisting being stopped—self-preservation and fear of death. And for them, everything in the past, everything in the present and the future that human beings do, especially socially, could be explained according to this view.

But all this is as good as having an idea of human nature, even if the epistemological status we might require would be weakened, even down to the level of nominalism. Let's just say the modern economist tends to deal with human beings as if they had the nature they presuppose in how they view human behavior, namely, as naturally, instinctively seeking to prosper, commercially prudential agents. Marx might have said only that this view is wrong. Yet he also wanted to say that holding it had its

---

[40] Marx sees the error of his opponents' thinking arising "from the ideological point of view...since the belief in the eternity of these ideas...is, of course, in every way confirmed, nourished and inculcated by the ruling classes." [Marx, 1971. p. 73]. "This abstraction or idea [of "money relationships, in the developed exchange system" of modern capitalist economies] is merely the theoretical expression of the material relationships that dominate individuals" [Ibid].

[41] Of course Newton's materialism was combined with a theological perspective, what can be construed as deism.

natural causes, namely, the vested interests of those who espouse it, or of those in whose employ the theorists are—the ruling classes. "Just as the economists are the scientific representatives of the bourgeois class, so the Socialists and the Communists are the theoreticians of the proletarian class" [Marx, 1977, p. 212].

By Marx's account, the well to do, of course, welcomed their status at the time. For them treating the situation as if it were the manifestation of the laws of nature—scientific laws of economics—was clearly unobjectionable. Marx held that, sometimes intentionally—"subjectively"—but mostly as a matter of wearing theoretical blinkers, the founders of classical economics (as well as their contemporary descendants, the neo-classical economists who dominate college and university departments of economics in our time) occupy the role of sophisticated propagandists.[42]

Imagine someone who got so enamored with adolescence that he focused on nothing else in the lives of individuals than this period. He would proclaim that what adolescents do is indeed *the* mature way to act. Surely this would be a welcome message to the bulk of adolescents! Their immature lives would appear to be vindicated. And how could this turn into propaganda? Suppose that after a while someone demonstrates that adolescence is in fact just a phase in the process toward maturity. But now those who welcomed the mistaken theory would gladly see to it that the earlier mistake continues to be published as truth!

Marx and his followers argue that the ruling (capitalist) class supports an army of—sometimes unwitting—propagandists (or apologists) spreading convenient falsehoods. Marx and Marxists refer to these individuals as ideologues and to their so-called scientific economics as ideology, that is, the rationalization of capitalism. Like some contemporary Marxists both East and West, Marx did not even respect these "reactionary ideologues" enough to treat them as genuine participants in a social scientific dispute. Marx himself often lashed out at the nasty economists with venom.

---

[42] This is just how they are often viewed by their fellow academics, who regard members of faculty in schools of business or department of economics as a rather odd bunch, more apologists for the bourgeoisie than as scholars.

Yet there are many passages where he took them quite seriously, of course. He agreed that these founders of economics understood capitalism quite well! What he denied is that the principles of capitalist, market economics are *the* principles of human economic affairs. That idea then made room for the presentation of his alternative, historicist vision.

Historical Political Economy

In contrast to what he took to be the narrow and therefore reactionary neo-classical idea of human nature, Marx advanced an emerging, growing, dynamic model. In it he proposes that human nature changes from epoch to epoch, depending on which stage of the dialectic of history humanity has reached. True, in the capitalist era the bulk of the population is engaged in a hustle for material wealth—the proletariat, because it is exploited and needs every bit it can get just to keep at a level of subsistence; the propertied class, because it is constantly being threatened by fierce competition. So at the stage of capitalist development Marx would agree that the mainstream economists' model of human behavior applies: greed or avarice motivates us all or, to use the technical term, we are all utility maximizers (or at least most of us are).[43]

In contrast Marx presents the idea that human nature, when fully realized, will flourish in a communist, co-operative society and human behavior will be noncompetitive, generous, kind, loving, caring and devoted to work for the love of it, not for the external rewards it offers [Marx, 1977, p. 82]:

> ...it is in the working over of the objective world that man first really affirms himself as species-being. This production is his active species-life. Through it nature appears as his work and his reality. The object of work is therefore the objectification of the species-life of man; for he duplicates himself not only intellectually, in his mind, but also actively in reality and thus can look at his image in a world he has created.

---

[43] "The individual may by chance get rid" of these tendencies, "but not the masses that are ruled by them...." [Marx, 1971, p. 72]

One way to appreciate the Marxist image of work is to think of the jam sessions of certain musicians. These extremely demanding yet wholly fulfilling work sessions are not done for purposes other than what they themselves contain. Most of us work to earn a living. In jam sessions musicians are doing their living, not earning it. Marx notes [Marx, 1977, p. 368]:

> Really free labor, the composition of music for example, is at the same time damned serious and demands the greatest effort. The labor concerned with material production can only have this character if (1) it is of a social nature, (2) it has a scientific character and at the same time is general work, i.e. if it ceases to be human effort as definite, trained natural force, gives up its purely natural, primitive aspects and becomes the activity of a subject controlling all the forces of nature in the production process.

But of course this kind of labor, and the human nature which is presupposed by it, can only be the result of extensive development. It requires that humanity as an "organic body" grow out of its adolescent stage and into maturity. People in capitalism are not in fact fully human yet, any more than an 18-year-old is a grown person as we now see things. Rather humanity will be mature eventually, after it has passed through its process of growth. Capitalism does not represent human maturity but merely a stage toward it. So economists who identify the science of economics with the principles of capitalism are elevating temporary conditions into general ones.

The process of exploitation is natural to capitalism, just as the process of dependence is natural to adolescence. The worker is exploited by the capitalist, not individually and not in any sort of blameworthy fashion. As we saw once before, Marx noted that for him "individuals are dealt with only in so far as they are the personifications of economic categories, embodiments of particular class relations and class interests. My standpoint views human life as natural history" [Marx, 1977, p. 417].

Natural historians view humanity as botanists view any given plant or biologists view any living animal, growing from infancy to maturity through several stages. That in a certain stage some being is vulnerable to mishaps—e.g. infants are prone to falls, teenagers susceptible to hero-worship, adolescents likely to be wild and reckless—does not prove individual fault or personal failing, any more than a sapling's inability to withstand high winds is its own fault, for which it should be held personally responsible.

Now Marx did not always speak as if he absolved individuals of such responsibility. He often uses phrases that suggest an underlying belief in people's ability to do better, a belief in freedom of choice. But this can be appreciated too. Such language can have the force of reform. A parent might very well both expect his teenage son to get into mishaps and also scold him for it. Yet, judging by how often parents resent it if someone else condemns their children, they do not really regard the misbehavior as something over which the child had much control. Rather the scolding, rebuke, chiding and so forth serve as a kind of spur to betterment, an inducement to maturation.

Similarly, Marx's moralizing language could be understood as part of his revolutionary activism. He lambasted capitalists, aiming to point out thereby the immature character of the kind of society in which capitalists flourished. When capitalists are said to exploit the workers, then, this is not so much a moral indictment—that is, chastisement of something they ought not to do—as a report about the dynamics of capitalist production, somewhat akin to saying that fungi live off certain other living beings. The fungi are not guilty of anything, nor are the capitalists. Nevertheless, both victimize something else. The victims of the capitalists—or, perhaps, the casualties of their mode of existence—are the workers whose well-being is made impossible by the way capitalists flourish. Exploitation, then, is a necessary and untoward condition of the capitalist phase of human existence. It is only characterized as a form of stealing or unjust deprivation for rhetorical purposes—perhaps in the spirit of urging on the revolutionary process of change.

In its details exploitation involves the fact that, even though workers produce items or services that fetch a certain return in exchange on the market, they receive only as much of what these items and services fetch as enables them to come back to work to continue their productive activity. In short, the working class receives a subsistence wage, the market-value but not use-value of their product—a wage required for them to reproduce their labor but a wage less than what the capitalist will fetch from what the laborer produced. The capitalist keeps the rest of the value of the workers' product and contributes nothing to the production process; nothing, at least, as a capitalist (owner). All of what capitalists own is ultimately explained, by Marx, by the contributions of the workers—labor, labor power, skill, time, etc. Capitalists cannot make any contribution to the products they sell and often profit from; for they do not labor.

By most accounts, this would mean the capitalists are thieves, unjustly depriving workers of what workers own. But by Marx's account they are doing what they must, as a matter of the laws of economic motion. There is no room for morality or immorality in all this, no room for personal, individual responsibility. Indeed, one reason Marx may not recognize any contribution from the owners to the production in his view of human nature or of the profit-making process is that there is no room for desert— deserved rewards for taking risks, making good judgments as to forgoing consumption now so as to gain more returns later.

In fairness, however, there is not much room for such an idea in the economist's picture either. However, the economist regards profit as an incentive for the capitalist to exploit workers in a socially useful way (for the time being). The worker, we may assume, could not embark on any such grandiose scheme and thus could not become the engine of production all on his own. He is without capital goods, mainly because, historically (according to Marx and his followers), he emerged from the serf class of feudal times, while the capitalist emerged from—although also in opposition to—the landed nobility. And it is plausible enough, even for classical liberals, to see the relationship between the landowners and the serfs as one of exploitation! Never mind that the actual history of the situation is far more complicated than Marxists would have it. (For example, most of the workers who provided the labor of early industrial capitalism simply would not have been alive without the benefits of industrialization, mass production, and technology [see Hayek, 1960; Heller, 1972, and Acton, 1971], and thus they were not serfs.)

Scientific Communism

Marx was adamant about the moral neutrality of his outlook when he stressed, as we noted earlier, that "Communists do not preach morality...." He explained: "They do not put to people the moral demand: love one another, do not be egoists, etc.; on the contrary, they are very well aware that egoism, just as much as self-sacrifice, is in definite circumstances a necessary form of the self-assertion of individuals" [Marx, 1977, p. 183]. This is the substance of historical determinism—human beings must necessarily—that is to say, by natural necessity—act in certain ways during different periods of human history. He made clear that from his historical approach it makes no sense to try "to do away with the 'private individual' for the sake of the 'general,' self-sacrificing man...." So instead of conceiving of capitalism and its untoward elements, such as alienation and exploitation, as if these were morally evil and the fault of some human beings who just ought to act differently, Marx, at least in some of his reflections, saw the matter as a neutral scientist might see the development of some living organism. At the early stages of its development a given living entity will compare unfavorably with its fully mature stage.

But those initial stages are still absolutely necessary, and without them the ensuing maturation becomes impossible. For example, Marx notes that in order to have a revolution "the great mass of humanity [must become] 'propertyless'...." And for socialism to emerge [Marx, 1977, p. 170] the "development of productive forces...is an absolutely necessary premise because without it want is merely made general, and with destitution the struggle for necessities and all the old filthy business would necessarily be reproduced...." The historical process must necessarily go through the stages Marx identified because without this there would not really be any development but general regression.

One reason that many Western Marxists deny that the Soviet Union had been following Marxism is that Russia never experienced a capitalist stage of development. Marx himself warned the Russians "If the Russian Revolution becomes the signal for a proletarian revolution in the West, so that both complement each other, the present Russian common ownership of land may serve as the starting-point for a communist development" [Marx, 1977, p. 584]. But, without this internationalization—a type of globalization—of the communist revolution, the Soviet Union could not develop toward communism from its semi-feudal socialist stage.

It could be argued, in fact, that all of the so-called communist societies—the USSR and its satellite countries, now reduced to Cuba and North Korea—had been and continue to be feeble, wrong-headed attempts at following the Marxist framework, since none has experienced the full development of capitalism. The full development of laissez faire (not state or even crony) capitalism is necessary for a viable socialism. Such a system requires abundance so as to eliminate the objective need for the kind of egoistic, competitive productive process that characterizes capitalism. Marx stressed this fact repeatedly.

Yet it could also be argued that, since the whole development of humanity transcends national boundaries, the main issue is not whether some particular country has gone through the capitalist phase of development, but whether humanity itself has done this—somewhere, anywhere. In this light Marx's remark, as well as others he makes when discussing the prospects of Russia's being transformed into socialism without going through capitalism, makes sense in Marx's own terms. It suggests that communism might have been properly advanced by the start of a socialist revolution in Russia, despite that country's backwardness, provided the revolution had been successfully internationalized.

Capitalism may alienate the workers and exploit them, but it is first and foremost the most efficient productive engine of humanity—so it is contended in Marxism. Marx declares, in the famous *Communist Manifesto* [Marx, 1977, p. 225], that:

> The bourgeoisie, during its rule of scarcely one hundred years, has created more massive and more colossal productive forces than have all preceding generations together. Subjecting Nature's forces to man, machinery, application of chemistry to industry and agriculture, steam-navigation, railways, electric telegraphs, clearing of whole continents for cultivation, *canalization* of rivers, whole populations conjured out of the ground—what earlier century had even a presentiment that such productive forces slumbered in the lap of social labor?

Nevertheless, the capitalist class has done all this at great sacrifice—or, at least, inescapable cost. It has done it without making it possible for the most active members of the productive process, the workers, to benefit decisively from capitalism itself. At least this is how Marx saw things.

We can now see a clear connection in Marx's position between his conception of what it is to be a person or a mature human being, the socio-economic system of capitalism, and the processes of alienation and exploitation. Human nature is developing in accordance with the dialectical movement of society. It will reach its fulfillment in communism. Capitalism is the stage just prior to socialism, which is itself virtually the fulfillment of human development, except that a socialist society must still involve some government. Communism allows a completely self-regulated society, somewhat in the order of a successful commune. Capitalism is the adolescence of human social development.

Alienation is inevitable because none of us is yet fully human, so just like an adolescent, we are all merely on the way to our full maturity. Exploitation, in turn, is the driving force of capitalism, the vehicle by which it does what it is best noted for, namely, produce wealth. Capitalists must exploit workers and then use the exploited wealth to produce even more wealth, on and on, until finally the system collapses under its own weight. We will talk more about that collapse later, but it is crucial to note that exploitation is a necessary ingredient of human development, not some disease humanity is suffering from. Without capitalists exploiting laborers there would be no wealth to administer rationally in a socialist economic system, one in which the objective is not the most efficient way to produce goods and services but the most rational way to administer resources, to make sure that the principle "from each according to his ability, to each according to his needs" will be implemented through and through.

Despite all of the moralizing language Marx himself and many of his followers engage in, Marxism finds nothing morally blameworthy in one class exploiting another class, nothing that it might regard as unjust. Ideas of morality do not apply at all in the context of Marxism. The only function such moralizing language can have is performative—to prompt revolutionary conduct, to bring to awareness the conditions that are to be realized next in human development. For Marx the development of humanity is a process of natural history, a process of a kind of biological growth, in which every kind of human activity has a function, including moral exhortation, blame and praise. And that function is to drive humanity on toward its emancipation.

As suggested before, moralizing itself seems to have a function in human life, not however as blame or praise, with any basis in the supposed free choice and personal moral responsibility everyone possesses. Rather moralizing is a kind of consciousness-raising process—calling to the minds of people what the future has to offer. Protesting against exploitation, imperialism, injustice, alienation from a faithful Marxist viewpoint anything but implies that things could be different for the time being. But it can be a means by which to prepare for the future. And even if the moralizing appears extremely odd, contradictory to the determinism of Marxism, so much the better. It has to feel real and believable in order for it to have the proper impact of making people aware of a better future alternative.

Chapter 5. Socialism as
Reactionary Conservatism[*]

Capitalism as Reaction

A central tenet of Marx is that capitalism is only a phase of humanity's development, characterized by ferocious competition, which is the muscle building that readies the social organism for full maturity or emancipation. He made clear his disdain for capitalism—i.e. standard classical economics—as a generally valid theory [Marx, 1971, pp. 21, 11 & 39]:

> [T]he so-called general conditions of all production are nothing but abstract conceptions which do not go to make up any real stage in the history of production...even the most abstract categories, in spite of their applicability to all epochs—just because of their abstract character—are by the very definiteness of the abstraction a product of historical conditions as well, and are fully applicable only to and under those conditions.

True to his Hegelian teachings, Marx held economic principles to be relative to the means and forms of production: "Capital, for example, does not mean anything without wage-labor, value, money, price, etc." [Marx, 1977, p. 351].

Marx, moreover, took it that there must be a definite development from one social stage to the next, so that the economic truths of the past not only may not but also cannot apply today, while those true for now cannot apply tomorrow. Yet Marx and his followers blatantly contradict themselves when at the same time

---

[*] A version of this chapter appeared (as "Socialism as Reactionism") in Kurt Leube and Albert Ziabinger (Eds.), *The Political Economy of Freedom: Essays in Honor of F.A. Hayek*, Munchen: Philosophia Verlag, 1984, pp. 47-60.

they attribute some determinate function to those who disagree with them. With historical necessity so much a part of their viewpoint, why are they so eager to smear those who reject their faith?

Of course, if we allow that Marxists are involved in a strategic task to obtain power, then this all makes better sense. They would not be the first group of people who committed themselves to some ideal vision and then devised various means, including faking adherence to various "scientific" doctrines, so as to facilitate the realization of these ideas. The crusade to wrest power for the laboring class—never mind the plain fact that not all members of that class may be deserving of the advantage that will come with that power, nor are all those who now hold that power undeserving of their present advantage—could well make use of the tactic of moral condemnation, scientific proclamation, prophecy, name calling, denunciation, etc. All these can be useful, even if none are intellectually tenable!

Marxists viciously attack those who find the Marxist economic story so much utopianism that could only lead to social catastrophe if taken seriously. Herbert Finer, back in 1949, accused F .A. Hayek (author of *The Road to Serfdom,* a scathing critique of the welfare state and the prospects of its degeneration into socialism) of being a reactionary. He was thus imputing to Hayek a power that by the Marxist account no one can have, namely, the power to turn back the clock. Similarly, when American "democratic" socialist Michael Harrington charged Milton Friedman, on the latter's TV series, "Free to Choose," with holding on to reactionary economics, he was alleging that Friedman was rationalizing the "injustices of capitalism." He was also assuming, in a highly un-Marxist fashion, that Friedman could have some impact and may even delay progress.

Yet, if these are to be treated as meaningful charges, the entire picture painted by Marx must be given up and all this notion of humanity's inevitable progress recognized as nothing but fraudulent "revolutionary" claptrap. Indeed, wherever Marxists have gained political power for a while, be it in Russia, Hungary, or Nicaragua, the first order of business had to be the silencing of their opponents, lest their reactionary thought undermine this breezy progress of humanity's history. And in the end the Marxist confidence in history came to no more than a confidence in the power of the gun, the power of the gulags, the power of terror.[44]

This may seem harsh, given how much sense there appears to be in Marx, at least from a certain perspective. Yet virtually all the vicious acts of human beings can be painted in a tolerable mode. One may be sure that most of the criminals sitting in jails went about their crime by first accepting it as something necessary, unavoidable, even noble for them to embark upon.

One must appreciate equally the Marxist historicist idea. There is initial plausibility to it. When free market economists allege the generality of their own economic theories, they do appear to be stretching things a bit. After all, the most crucial preconditions for markets were absent in most historical periods, including mainly the legal protection of the private ownership of property. Where a market is to be found, traders are necessary. But if only a small fraction of the human community can ascend to the status of a merchant, then market conditions are effectively lacking for the rest and are highly distorted where they do make their appearance.

Marx explains the absence of market conditions by ascribing to human life a determinate development. Only when a certain stage has been reached will there be markets. This is like saying that only at a certain stage of the development of individuals will adolescence emerge, neither earlier nor later. To this the mainstream economic scientist has little to say except to ignore it. But Marxists know they have something of a case here and it is important to respond to them cogently.

Some Revisions of Capitalist Economic "Science"

The principles of the free market are not purely positive nor descriptive, contrary to what many economists maintain. One

---

[44] This, of course, assumes Marxism is wrong, so in order to attempt implementing the revolutionary progress of history, it is ultimately futile to wait for natural, especially democratic developments to that end. Instead history will require "little helpers." And when that doesn't quite pan out, the resort to violence and brutality is extremely tempting. In the end, though, the effort will fail, as history has shown.

ought to see them for what they are, namely, hypothetical, instrumental or *conditional* political economic propositions. *If* the circumstances of the market are instituted, maintained, and preserved, *then* certain consequences will ensue—e.g. productivity will increase, wealth will be fostered, satisfaction of desires will be more widespread than otherwise. If governments do not meddle with production and consumption, then various individually satisfactory consequences will obtain. Also, if these circumstances are not instituted, then certain consequences will also obtain in view of their disregard—for example, a country will begin to travel "the road to serfdom."[45]

In defending the market system, economists may be saying merely what follows their analytic and empirical investigations. Most often, however, they also advise that the circumstances that facilitate free market measures be made possible by public policy. That comes very close to endorsing them. Neo-classical economists will freely claim that rent control is undesirable from the economic point of view, or that minimum wage laws are economically destructive for unskilled workers. And in saying such things, these scholars have tacitly put themselves on the side of economic health, of widespread prosperity, as a major objective in social life.

But is economic health such a noble objective? This they have not shown. There is nothing in the value-free social science of economics to establish the *value* of prosperity. Yet policy advisers from the ranks of these scientists do lend their prestige to this social goal. When probed, they will report that they are simply showing how to do what everyone, after all, wants. But when one notes that not everyone wants prosperity—commonly taken to be some measure of exchangeable wealth—as a high priority, they deny this. They claim that there is a misunderstanding there. And the way to demonstrate that there is a misunderstanding is sim-

---

[45] Some supporters of free market capitalism make too dire predictions for societies that abandon free market principles. People do not always follow the logic of initial decisions. So public policies that would, if consistently followed, lead to ruin are often rescinded or modified once their disastrous implications begin to be appreciated.

ple: everyone wants something, whatever if may be—all people seek ends, seek to obtain goals. Therefore, everyone wants prosperity. Prosperity simply is whatever people want.

Yet, of course, this turns out to be a vacuous thesis. Some people may want quietude, reflection, peace of mind, a satisfactory line of work, bondage with others, and everlasting salvation—e.g. the life of those in a kibbutz, convent or monastery. They do not seek wealth and prosperity, at least not as a priority. Well, such objectives are not obtained primarily in the marketplace even if market processes do assist in their pursuit. To conjoin those places with a marketplace, simply because in both people do what they want, is to obliterate significant differences. Some of these *differences* pertain indeed to values, to what is a better kind of life for people. And the economist ignores them in favor of the kind of life he or she studies!

The economist's assumptions about the merits of economic prosperity, as commonly understood, are not descriptive, positive notions. Clearly, *one needs to defend the belief that it is good to satisfy individuals, that prosperity is a value that individuals ought to strive to attain* [see Machan, 1975; Machan, 1989, and Machan, 1998]. This will then help establish the conclusion that a system that makes all that possible rather than one that does not is better for human beings to institute—even if there are some exceptions. If it can also be shown that such a system can make room for the exceptions (convents, communes, kibitzes, monasteries) then this system will be shown to be truly better for people. And yet when the principles of the operation of such a system are considered, researched, analyzed and tested, that inquiry will still qualify as bona fide science.

But to believe that economics offers us pure, value-free principles—in the sense that no value assumption is embedded in them—is plainly wrong. Consider that the market system requires the possibility of exchange. That in turn requires that there be values that individuals be authorized, in law, to put up for sale. But for the law to secure this authorization, it has to be established, first, that individuals ought to have a sphere of private jurisdiction, in short, private property rights.

The myth of wholly value-free economics requires the sort of cumbersome economic analysis produced by desperate economic reductionists. Economists such as Professor Gary Becker attempt to argue that every sort of human behavior is best understood as a form of utility maximization—desire satisfaction—but this simply misses the point that the economic approach is only going to help us understand a limited aspect of what people do and why they do these things.

For example, it is true enough that religion, marriage, friendship, patriotism, and science all have economic aspects—it takes prudent allocation of resources to build a church, run a household, hone friends, devote oneself to political action and search for truth. But surely all by itself the fact that people want to allocate resources prudently does not explain why they choose to do so for one purpose rather than another. Why do secular humanists spend so much time organizing meetings at which they criticize religion, and why do believers spend so much time making their own costly efforts attacking secular humanists? Why do some people devote so much energy to cultivating friends, others little or none at all? And why are there people who choose to invest in the commission of crimes rather than productivity, while others are never tempted by that "entrepreneurial" opportunity?

The plain fact is that for a reasonably comprehensive understanding of human affairs the economic approach is insufficient. And it undermines itself by making the attempt to come up with such an understanding [Machan, 1989].

If I explain legitimate productive endeavors like baking and selling bread or selling computers, as well as criminal conduct like rape and stealing company secrets, by reference to people's desire to satisfy themselves, I become theoretically impoverished; for I have not really found the variable that shows me the difference between the two sorts of behavior. I fail to understand, actually, what makes one behavior what it is and the other what it is. An explanation needs to help in showing me the difference between the two kinds of conduct and, if it fails at this, it does not work as an explanation at all.

Furthermore, the economic reductionists or imperialists wish to explain society fully even when nothing conducive to market transactions is present—e.g. where half the population is enslaved by the other half, or when bureaucrats command production, invention and consumption at whim. There are, of course, discernible consequences one can count on when markets are shut down. But it is doubtful, judging by the hopeless vacuity of economic reductionism, that economic analysis is sufficient to predict these. No, what is required is the admission that economic science establishes only "if-then" propositions and that, if the antecedents are absent, all bets are off. In other words, if there is a framework for market behavior—if the law respects private property rights and the right of a person to trade what belongs to him or her with others also willing to trade—then a good deal of what happens in the market can be explained by reference to the fact that people are motivated to make deals, to gain more than they would give up in an exchange. But this makes good sense mostly of distinctly market behavior—of the behavior of those professionals who work to increase wealth for themselves or their clients.

Once we mix the market with other spheres of human concern—science, religion, politics, art and so forth—the economic approach to human behavior will provide only partial understanding. For example, if an economist works hard to reach some understanding of economic principles, the fact that she wants to earn a good return on her invested effort is not sufficient to understand her behavior. Why is she doing this as an economist rather than as a housewife or trapeze artist? Why is she not willing to sacrifice her honest insights for political power? What would it take to get her to change her profession now? All these are issues not fully explained by reference to principles of market behavior—mainly because there are other principles at work, some of them normative or moral ones.

Instead of attempting to out-science the supreme scientists, the answer to Marxists is that we *should* establish and preserve market conditions, however often they have been absent in the past and however unlikely it is they may be permanently preserved. We need to admit that there was something wrong with societies through much of human history, as there is today, and much of this can be described, just as Marx himself suggests, as the "malicious perversion on the part of government" [Marx, 1971, p. 19]. The perversion involves corrupting the institution from what it ought to have been, namely, a protector or securer of the peace, of civilized life—of individual rights—to one that oppresses citizens and indeed perpetrates violence on them quite routinely (in the fashion of rogue cops, we might say).

Unfortunately, most mainstream economists do not admit to the underlying normative element in their analysis. They will not insist on what must be stressed, that the undermining of free markets is morally pernicious. They just content themselves with the naive view that, if only everyone knew about the efficiency of the capitalist system, they would rally to its support. In short, they believe that not supporting capitalism is merely an information problem.

Marx, too, rejects the ethical or moral approach but does wish to admit that there is a value element in political economics. Thus he revises science to fit his value-laden progressivist outlook. According to him, the metaphysical machinery of the Hegelian *dialectic*—turned upside-down by Marx—drives humanity toward its perfection and human nature itself will change as a matter of natural law. This absurd idea has lately been abandoned even by some of Marx's most faithful followers. The Hungarian Marxist Agnes Heller [Heller, 1972, p. 76] puts what may well be Marx's point thus:

As Marxists, who have made our decision for communism, who have recognized the *possibility of* communism within *existing* societies, who struggle for the realization of this alternative, this *dynamis—we believe in the invincibility of the human substance.*

Expressed in this way, we can see that Marxism is one of the more intricate normative—though not necessarily moral or ethical—systems aiming to capture our hearts and minds. It proclaims a confidence or faith in human collective emancipation, the full realization of *the human substance* as an *organic whole.*

Marxism's central problem is that it ignores that the human substance is individual and that there is no transcendent [collective] human substance. So if you and I and the rest of us do not fully realize ourselves by the time we die, then that is it, and it remains for the next generation of individual human beings to make this attempt. The question of political economy is what kind of general system secures the best conditions for the constantly renewed possibilities for individuals to of this. There is, in short, no one-time accomplishment after which we can all rest forever.

Capitalism is a radically different conception of how human beings *should* live in one another's company. It is not merely a stage of humanity's inevitable progress toward some myth of collective self-realization. Its basic principles are not just temporarily descriptive but are universally normative—they prescribe how we should live with each other, what our institutions should be, etc. It prescribes adoption of the theory of individual natural human rights and the development of institutions which protect them.

It is true enough that the concrete shape capitalism can take in the twentieth century is not identical to some possible capitalist order of the past. Had there been a society of sovereign individuals some time in the past with their moral space clearly specified and protected, the capitalist system of that era would have looked quite different from a capitalist system of our time. But its principles would have been similar. Had slavery been abolished in ancient Greece or Egypt and had all people been treated as worthy of their own lives—not at the disposal of others—this may not have given rise to exactly the kind of legal order that we now associate with that ideal. Nor would such a system have been the sort most societies had in fact lived under.

But, one might ask from a Marxist viewpoint, could one even conceive of such a society? Would that not have been premature?

Would humanity itself have developed far enough for that kind of life? Of course, from Marx's viewpoint, that idea would be nonsense. Marx is a complete historicist—following, with certain serious modifications, in the footsteps of Hegel.

The principles of a proper social order at one time in human history cannot be those appropriate to another time. But is there reason to agree with Marx? That is the issue. It will not do simply to say that the bourgeoisie cannot accept the possibility of its own short-lived fate, its temporary status in humanity's history. It requires proof. And Marx offers no proof. He offers a plausible scheme but not any actual historical research to show that what occurred under the regime of ancient Egypt is what had to occur then; nor that capitalism had to develop from feudalism.

Indeed, we see in our era that many feudal systems prevail, even in the midst of modern technological advancement. Even Stalinist Soviet Union and Maoist People's Republic of China could be viewed quite fruitfully as versions of feudal states. In turn, there is evidence from anthropology that the supposed homogeneous tribal -life of early humans never happened. Instead there were quite different forms of early human life. The native American Indians are a good case in point. Their different communities exhibited a great variety of forms of life, even within roughly similar stages of technological development.

Here Marx seems to succumb to what he himself was astute enough to criticize in others, namely, reductionism. To make everything fit into his dialectical scheme, he read into history what suited him and left out what didn't suit him.

It is perfectly plausible to view things differently. Marx held the view that one cannot become truly free until one escapes the bounds of nature, the necessity of focusing all effort on satisfying basic needs. Of course, even in communism the basic needs have to be met, it's just that they are met efficiently. This made sense because he envisaged humanity extricating itself from that condition and becoming free in communism, when true general abundance would arrive. But, if one rejects this unfounded projection and judges the prospects of humanity's future in the light of the more realistic, factually supported alternative human beings face, one can come to very different conclusions.

Indeed, which political economic alternative is to be accepted is a matter of the choices of actual people. Communism promises to deliver human beings from their struggles for self-improvement, from the condition of constant exertion and need to make intelligent choices. It rejects the persistent condition of differences among human beings and the apparent permanent presence of many human problems. It looks for a utopia, despite Marx's protestation that communism is not for him "an ideal" but a real movement.

A sensible statement of capitalism promises neither utopia nor the everlasting, automatic social bliss that Marx forecasts for humanity. It is not a mere bourgeois ideology, serving to protect some vested interest with rationalizations aiming to cover up the fact that it is really just a ploy by which to expropriate wealth from those who truly deserve it. Rather it is a system that most accurately reflects the human condition, for good and bad, but which demands of those in society to respect the one equality in all men, namely, the moral equality that means that we are all equally responsible to strive to make the best of our lives.

True, among contemporary neo-classical economists and even some members of the Austrian School, the idea that free market economics will solve all human problems can now and then be heard. It is curious to find this coming from the ranks of those who regard economics as a pure, value-free social science. It is still argued that such a system is unrelated to any ethical or political ideals. But this is a mistake not of the economists *per se*, but of the prevailing ideas about science among such scientists. Ultimately, responsibility for that lies not with economists but with philosophers. It was they who argued that ethics is impossible. Economists just followed suit.[46]

---

[46] An element of Marxism that is still extremely appealing is his historicism, the idea that the proper way to look at ethics, politics and political economy is historically relative and that those who seek for stable, lasting principles are taking a wholly defunct ahistorical approach, reading back into history ideas that are sound now but were not back then. (Some call this the Whig theory of history.) This is a vast topic but essentially the right response is that while some features of human life, personal, social, even international, are

Philosophers argued that given what it takes to know something—namely, direct sensory evidence—we could never really know that something is right or wrong for human beings to do. This famous "is/ought" gap put on record by David Hume (whereby no true statements of fact could establish, deductively, the truth of statements made about what people ought or ought not to do) served not only to discourage the idealism of some rationalists and theologians (what Hume evidently aimed for) but also fostered distrust of any sensible role for argument in ethics (e.g., that espoused by Aristotle). It is arguable that from professional philosophers little that is of help has caught on prominently since the time of Hume. Kant's efforts to ground morality resulted in a view of a fundamentally divided reality—the scientific and the moral. This, naturally, could not be acceptable to most people who have their feet firmly planted on earth—with scientists or those who respect science.

Perhaps it is understandable that at its heart Marxism is rarely challenged head on. In fact Marx is a traditionalist. His dislike of private property, his altruism, his so-called compassion, his hatred of the bourgeoisie, and his disdain for privacy and distinctiveness among human beings, echo the similar themes we find in many of the world's most prominent religions. His refusal to try to conceive of a good society that also recognizes that evil is always going to be possible to human beings—though perhaps sometimes it is quite unjustly spread—follows the dreamy visions of utopians. The difference is that he dressed it all up in scientistic garb, one more suited to his times than to the cultures addressed by his forerunners.

With a few exceptions, even in our time most philosophers now defend the welfare state and socialism, a watered-down ver-

---

lasting and stable—principles of justice, medical ethics, what have you—while others change—applied medical or childrearing practices, for instance. Nutrition is a field the findings of which gradually change the prescriptions for healthy eating because of improved understanding. But this doesn't fit, say, its basic organic chemical *principles*, or those of economics. It is certainly so, too, with biology or astronomy and probably applies only with great care to sociology, psychology and other disciplines. Op. cit., Machan, *Libertarianism Defended*.

sions of the hard-line doctrine Marx advocated. That is why scholarly critiques of Marxism and of the language it has unleashed on the community of political controversy are largely lacking today. That is why the social scientists and political economists of a free society must suffer the *ad hominem* attacks endured by F. A. Hayek and by Milton Friedman throughout their careers, being routinely labeled "ideologues" and such. This may also be why some who favor the pure laissez-faire system yet also aim to be respectable within mainstream circles eschew any kind of *principled* adherence to it.[47]

But the times may be changing now. Marxism is no longer such a mystery, and its philosophical substance is beginning to be seen for what it is, a rather flawed totalist secular religion.

Socialism as Modern Feudalism/Mercantilism

Without its progressivist metaphysical camouflage, Marxist socialism is a dream, a vision, and not a pretty one at that. Ultimately it is the last gasp of privileged rule, resting on the language of compassion for the poor. There is no secret about Marx's own personal admiration of various feudal social traits. He admired feudalism's respect for close-knit community life—except perhaps the specifics between the lord and the serf—and he held in high esteem the sort of economic interaction prevalent in feudal and tribal societies. He valued producing for use, not for profit. What he disliked about feudalism was that it failed to produce abundance for the masses. For this, he admitted, capitalism was required. And what he wanted was not so much to make a world that is safe for the proletariat but to make one that will transform the proletariat into a new aristocracy—with every worker a theoretical scientist, with ample leisure, while all the gadgets created by the mad productivity of capitalism handle the dirty work.

It is true that when capitalism was first unleashed, adjustment

---

[47] See, e.g., Jeffrey Friedman, "What's Wrong with Libertarianism," *Critical Review* 11, no. 3 (1997). See Bruce Ramsay's essay at http://www.vonmises.org/fullstory.aspx?Id=1626.

to it came with some difficulty. There were too many whose feudal privileges were left intact and too many whose unjust treatment in the past was never remedied. But that had little to do with capitalism and a lot to do with the inadequate efforts to bring all of its principles to bear on the new societies in which it had been introduced in a half-hearted, hurried, undeveloped fashion. Yet that is not what Marx held against capitalism. He found its recognition of the principle of private wealth acquisition abhorrent in itself. The right to private property at first did perpetuate injustices and it might have been taken as an obstacle to compassion and humanity among people. Yet Marx himself realized that, with the kind of poverty most people suffered in precapitalist societies, it was impossible to be kind to all. He held capitalism responsible, but in fact capitalism should have been credited with making possible the beginning of the end of unjust holdings.

For Marx capitalism lacked the kind of humanism he perceived in tribal and feudal systems. Capitalism is decidedly not collectivist. Under capitalism the masses could produce but would live alienated from their allegedly true nature, namely, as essentially social beings who are through and through interwoven with all other parts of the organic whole of society.

In the last analysis, however, socialism means merely tribalism and its more modern rendition, feudalism. Every single instance of a contemporary socialist economic system demonstrates this. Given that Marx's dialectical/historical materialist ideas are seriously flawed and baseless—even for Hegel their base was extremely suspect—it is no wonder that what Marx regarded as progress was exactly the opposite, especially from a moral and economic point of view.

A Meager Competitor

But where can one find something to stand up against Marx's vision? Where is there a comparably robust, promising, yet also realistic and comprehensive alternative? The welfare state certainly doesn't qualify. Nor does its kin, market socialism.

Contemporary economic analysis ultimately becomes an off-shoot of classical economics. Between F. A. Hayek and Milton Friedman there is not much difference from a fundamental philosophical standpoint. But its philosophical base is too limited. Something is necessary other than the arid stuff of value-free economic analysis to demonstrate that promise lies not with the idealistic utopianism of the alleged scientific Marx but with the moderately optimistic vision of the free society and free market.

Neo-classical economics is basically the elaboration of the principles of human interaction in a society in which individual rights, including (and most pertinently for this purpose) property rights and the right to enter into contractual relationships, are legally defended. That kind of a social system is, in turn, sound not because it is some pinnacle of humanity's maturation process but because it is in political accord with the moral viewpoint that each individual's responsibility in life is *to choose to excel as a human individual*. And each person may well also fail at this or come not nearly close enough to complete success.

It is Marx who is the reactionary. Capitalism is the radical realistic idea, coming as a viable alternative—combined, of course, with all of the non-economic adjuncts of its culture—after many centuries of muddling through with varieties of statism, what as we saw Marx derisively called "malicious perversions on the part of governments" [Marx, 1971, p.19]. As a determinist and historicist, Marx could not abide by the possibility that all through history some institutions had been *allowed* to *pervert* human community life—such as slavery, subjugation, taxation, serfdom. No, for him these all were necessary, unavoidable matters, as is capitalism itself.

There is, admittedly, no guarantee of resisting a reactionary route, contrary to what Marx assumed (namely, that history is necessarily progressive). Certainly there are neo-Marxist groups—we have already seen Agnes Heller's revisionism along such lines—that try to avoid the Marxist line about history. The Frankfurt School—led by Jürgen Habermas—has watered down Marx to the point where all that's left of it is a kind of liberalized Hegelian progress of Idea or Spirit through the intellectual "democratic" discourse of humanity. (Yet, with all that open-ended criticism Habermas champions, one wonders how it is already known that socialism provides the best setting for it? Moreover, why proclaim this open-endedness when in fact criticism, the hallmark of this neo-Marxism, necessarily presupposes some kind of criteria that must be invoked?) In this neo-Marxist framework material history is no longer driving toward its own completion. Rather a kind of epiphenomenon, human language, is evolving in a quasi-random fashion, through the criticism and self-criticism engaged in by the disciples of Marx, something that presumably will guide society to progress.

Frankly, it would be far more honest and straightforward to be faced with the historical determinist Karl Marx, instead of with all these revisionists who wish to make Marx palatable without those very elements of his thinking that rendered his position conceptual integrated and coherent.[48] But, unfortunately, as much as Marx himself protested at being considered a Marxist, he must ultimately shoulder part of the responsibility for giving rise to all the confusion.

Marx labored to construct a quasi-mechanistic system to spur the masses into following his reactionary dream to modernize tribal collectivism. Yet he also wanted to pay homage to the unavoidable moral element in human life: the element that marks human nature off from the rest of the living world.

However, doing justice to the moral nature of human beings is impossible without rejecting the collectivism and determinism so dear to Marx. Only if individuals are in some crucial respect independent, free agents, not mere "species-beings," can it be said truly that what a person does is something for which he must take personal responsibility. Marx himself could not avoid holding this perspective on human life when he dealt with his own friends and intellectual adversaries. But his dialectical mechanistic system required that he take it all back and explain their wrong

---

[48] A case in point is James P. Sterba's use of the concept of "surplus" wealth. See, op. cit., Sterba, *Justice.*

thinking as just one of the many ways in which history, not the theorist himself, behaves.

In our time Marxists still want it both ways. Neo-classical scholars and other champions of market economics are to be blamed for thwarting history's glorious progress. (My own second book [Machan, 1975] was also attacked in the old hard-line Marxist *Pravda* as an apology for militaristic warmongering imperialism on 10 December 1976. While Marx cannot be blamed for this, his idea that his opponents simply entertain "insipid illusions" has something to do with the ease with which criticism of this alleged science can be dismissed by the "Marxist" faithful.) Yet at the same time, supposedly they really cannot help what they are doing, being as they are products of historical forces.

It is odd, is it not, that this progress that defenders of the free market allegedly try to thwart is inevitable and foreordained, somehow despite all this "reactionary" thinking? One may wonder then what is the point of worrying about the reactionaries.

The reality of the situation is that eating one's cake and having it too has come to be the true substance of reactionary thinking. Such confusions are what undermine, more than most other factors, the only kind of non-technological progress that is possible to human beings. This is the progress of living in societies that secure the greatest possible degree of individual human liberty for their members, a progress, however, that is all too fragile.[49]

In a free—capitalist or libertarian—society, all people have the best chance of making the most of the arduous but quite possibly—yet never certainly—rewarding task of choosing their way of life without thwarting (and very often assisting, *voluntarily*) the lives of their fellows. That is what progress must amount to for human social life, namely, enabling the moral nature of human life to flower at the hands of the individuals who may or may not

---

[49] For an example of a classical liberal admitting to this, see Milton Friedman, "Is a Free Society Stable?" in T. R. Machan, ed., *The Libertarian Alternative* (Chicago: Nelson-Hall, 1974), pp. 408-418.

fully realize that nature.[50]

In reactionary socialist systems all that is held out for human beings is the remote luck that they will end up as part of a small cadre of rulers—members of politburos, central committees, military gangs, Mullahs or secret police functionaries. For anyone to suggest that the prevention of this kind of development in human societies amounts to engaging in reactionary thinking is to perpetrate yet another of the frauds we have come to expect from too many Marxists, paralleling their doctrines of "true freedom is slavery," "individualism is collectivism," and "morality is terrorism," ideas that have made it possible to overlook the brutality of Stalin and other Soviet leaders and to condemn the late Sidney Hook for his skepticism about the merits of the Soviet system even after the documented revelations of the nature of that system.[51]

---

[50] This contrasts sharply with the sort of coercive enabling promoted by welfare state supporters, including, unfortunately, Amartya Sen, in his otherwise excellent *Rationality and Freedom* (Cambridge: Harvard University Press, 2002).

[51] For a revealing discussion of this by parties to all sides, see Matthew J. Cotter, ed., *Sidney Hook Reconsidered* (Buffalo, NY: Prometheus Books, 2004).

Chapter 6. Liberty versus
Marxist Liberation

Ideas of Freedom

Everyone who reads even local newspapers should have heard of the idea of liberation over the last decades of the 20th century. Women are seeking liberation. There are national liberation movements. The Soviet Union claimed to have liberated Czechoslovakia and Hungary in the Second World War, while the U.S. made the same claim about France (and Iraq).

A good deal of talk about liberation is linked to Marxism. A while back the late Pontiff, John Paul II, warned Roman Catholic priests in Latin American countries about espousing Marxist-oriented "liberation" theology. And of course still now quite a few groups in the Middle East and Africa regarded as aiming for the liberation of the people are guided by at least the spirit of Marxism.

Yet liberation is also an important ideal for Americans who have no affinity with Marxism. To liberate a country has been a pre-eminently professed American objective in several of the wars the country has fought. To liberate black slaves during the Civil War was also closely linked to the American political tradition.

It is no secret that these two sources of thought about liberation are not always identical in their basic meaning. We know that both Marxists and anti-Marxists subscribe to the ideal of liberty or freedom, yet just because of this they do not aim for the same thing. The best way to appreciate this is to consider two important but distinct senses of the term "freedom": "negative" and "positive." Those who embrace the one will often declare that theirs represents the true sense of "freedom," and we'll get to that. For now let's see what these two senses of freedom mean.

Negative Freedom

When we ask what is the characteristically American sense of the term freedom we can satisfy our curiosity by considering that the American ideal has usually meant "Don't tread on me" or "Hands off." More precisely, negative freedom means being left to one's own judgments, decisions, choices, actions and so forth by other people. That is the crux of it—others leaving one be makes one free.[52]

Negative freedom is a type of political liberty, espoused mainly within the classical liberal tradition of politics, that aims to free men and women from the intrusiveness of others, including governments. Whenever it is understood that every individual must be left to make his or her own decisions in life and must be left to act on these without the intrusion of other people, we are considering political liberty, such as the absence of censorship, the prohibition of murder, assault, theft, or variations of these. One may not be prevented from associating with other willing parties, from joining churches or clubs, from reading the books one wants to read, from enjoying one's own selected entertainment, etc. Free trade, too, is a part of negative liberty: none may prevent others from engaging in trade—domestically or internationally.

Thus far I have explained negative freedom somewhat casually. But when we wish to get a clear understanding of it, we need to do a bit more elaborate thinking. For one, although most of us have a clear enough idea about what it is to leave one free, in more complicated situations we need principles or standards by which we can tell. Copyright laws, for instance, spell out the standards for telling the difference between intruding and not intruding in the lives of others by means of, for example, plagiarism. Trespassing laws spell out what it is to let people be free to enjoy their property. And so forth.

The capitalist tradition of thought embraces political liberty as

---

[52] This accords with the analysis of Isaiah Berlin, *Four Essays on Liberty* (New York: Oxford University Press, 1969).

something government is established to defend. There can be many other values for people in such a system, but government is concerned with securing just this value, political freedom or non-intervention by others in one's life.

In the American political tradition the standards of such liberty are identified in the Declaration of Independence and for their legal protection specified in the US Constitution, particularly in the Bill of Rights. In the political theory that undergirds this tradition, a theory of natural individual human rights spells out the principles which, if adhered to, will preserve negative political liberty.[53]

Positive Freedom

When one complains about not being free from a headache or from financial worries or to pursue a career, one might be complaining not about other people's intrusions but about one's own limitations, imposed by nature or social circumstances. That is where we come near to the idea of positive freedom. One without eyes is not free to see. One without wealth is not free to spend on health. One who is ignorant is not free to know. And one who is evil is not free to reach for human excellence. So for this Hegelian conception of freedom [Pelczynski, 1971, p. 9]:

> The highest type of freedom—freedom in the ethical sphere—is the guidance of one's actions by the living, actual principles of one's community, clearly understood and deliberately accepted, and in secure confidence that other community members will act in the same way.

This is the statement by a conservative advocate of positive freedom. The socialist statement of the doctrine is not very different [Campbell, 1983, p. 213, my emphasis].

---

[53] For a full discussion, see Ronald Hamowy, "The Declaration of Independence, " in Tibor R. Machan, ed., *Individual Rights Reconsidered: Are the Truths of the U.S. Declaration of Independence Lasting?* (Stanford, CA : Hoover Institution Press, 2001).

Socialist rights are more positive, less dependent on the activation of the right-holder, more directed towards the protection and furtherance of those concerns which express the needs of active and creatively productive social beings than is the case with capitalist rights. Socialist rights are more organizational than political in that they inform the cooperative social effort rather than represent demands to be disputed and traded off against each other. *They are devices to secure the benefits which can be derived from harmonious communal living, not protections for the individual against the predations of others. Socialist rights are highly dependent on others fulfilling their correlative obligations, but are not conditional on the right-holders fulfilling their own obligations,* although in practice socialist rights and socialist duties tend to coalesce, as in the case of the right and duty to work.

In short, positive liberty means to have the ability to do what will be best for one. And just as negative liberty is generally associated with the doctrine of negative individual rights, so positive liberty is associated with a doctrine of positive rights.

Such considerations, expressed here by a socialist thinker, give clear indications of the main difference between the ways Marxists and capitalists are likely to use the concepts "freedom" or "liberty" and "rights." As an example, the Marxist former president of Nicaragua, Daniel Ortega, gave a clear indication of this when he explained what he understands by "freedom" [quoted in Davis, 1986]:

I always think of freedom in the plural. Freedom is for the people here, not for the individual. Freedom has an integral character linking the individual to the group. It is not simply what the individual feels, it is the action of the individual within society which organizes the rights of each to the benefit of all. Society limits, of course, those aspects of individual freedom that go against the common effort in all phases of life.

This is almost identical to Marx's own characterization of socialist freedom, and not surprisingly, when we consider that Ortega is an explicit Marxist.

In general, doctrines of positive freedom or liberty conform somewhat to our non-political usage of these terms, e.g. one can easily think of being free of a headache, of having a sense of liberation once a worry has been removed. I will return to this topic shortly, but first a word about the related idea of rights.

Some even deny that there is anything such thing as the right to liberty in the negative sense because, they argue, no negative liberty can exist without government's protection of it, which would then depend on a positive right to such protection.[54]

This line of reasoning reaffirms a venerable contention, namely, that rights are all conventional, invented and granted by governments, so that no natural rights, prior to government, can exist at all. Yet that idea undercuts a vital element of the theory of consent, since the basis of the claim that consent is a requirement for just government rests on the idea that everyone has the right to give or withhold consent—go along with the establishment of government, for example. This notion that all rights are post-political also grants those who govern carte blanche since their rule isn't checked by standards of justice.

Rights

So, then, positive rights do not exist—the idea is an empty abstraction that some people entertain in the complete absence of firm conceptual support. Rights are just the sort of moral principles that concern the establishment of limits and liberties in the relationships among human beings. At the basic level, rights come to be liberties, signals to others to ask for permission before they come in, before they enter one's sphere of jurisdiction—one's "moral space," as the late Robert Nozick called the sphere of sovereignty that each individual moral agent requires in society. Rights

---

[54] For this line of argument see Henry Shue, *Basic Rights* (Princeton, NJ: Princeton University Press, 1980), Stephen Holmes and Cass Sunstein, *The Cost of Rights, Why Liberty Depends on Taxes* (New York: W. W. Norton, 1999).

emerged in political theory because it became evident that as moral agents, with responsibilities to choose to act the right way and the possibility of failing to honor such responsibilities, human beings required sovereignty, a sphere of personal authority to govern their lives.[55] My right to my life imposes an obligation on others but only negatively: they may not take it. But this makes sense only if others are capable of respecting such an obligation.

In socialist rights doctrines, however, one is supposed to have all sorts of rights even though others may not at all be able to respect them. The right to education, employment, health care, affordable housing, education, pregnancy leave, a job, etc.—to use some popular examples—would lead one to believe that one is owed numerous goods and extensive services of all sort—which is to say, *involuntary servitude*—from others. And so if goods and services, including labor time, are in short supply, this would mean one has a right to something no one can provide. Certainly if someone does not *choose* to do the work "I have a right to," it must still be provided, which is to say, they may be coerced to do the work or to pay for others to do it. That is the reason Nozick called taxation "on par with forced labor."[56] This is the very opposite of the idea of liberty that is so closely linked with natural human individual rights!

The negative rights theory on which free market, *laissez-faire* capitalism rests is plain enough: if one has a right to freedom from aggression—from murder, assault, theft, etc.—others can always respect it, even though at times only by exercising great self-discipline (as when they restrain themselves and do not steal though they are very eager for support). *Not* to murder, assault, or steal from people is something one always has the option to do—it requires one to *abstain* from performing actions, not to *do* them.[57] On the rare occasions when the restraint required from

---

[55] Op. cit., Tierney, *The Idea of Natural Rights*.

[56] Robert Nozick, *Anarchy, State, and Utopia* (New York: Basic Books, 1974), p. 169.

[57] James P. Sterba claims that since it is unreasonable to require a starving person to abstain from raiding the "surplus" wealth of those who have it, such persons have a welfare right to such wealth. It is here that the liberal with sympathies for socialism runs into the trouble of having to defend both basic rights to life and liberty—no one may deprive one of an

others in their respect of rights would mean forgoing essential benefits, there is still the option, especially in a substantially free society, of making requests for help or offering one's services for trade.[58]

Of course, in emergency cases, when it is impossible any longer to maintain peace in a human community because of catastrophic circumstances, talk of rights becomes nonsense, and persons will have to muddle through with the kind of emergency moral law that afflicts those who are now and then caught unprepared on the high seas. But we are not discussing a social reality that is constantly under siege from nature. We are talking about the principles of a human community that enjoys relative normality, where production is generally possible, and where indigence is a rarity, often brought on by human failing, not by natural disaster.

Indeed, the entire tradition of capitalist rights has to do with freedom of action, not with freedom from trouble or hardship. Underlying that tradition is the belief that if others just co-operate in upholding peace—do not initiate forcible intrusion on any-one's life—securing "freedom from trouble or hardship" is something that men and women enjoying peace can always accomplish, indeed better than if they were forced by others to try.

So the doctrine of positive rights is ultimately nonsense, a point with which Marx, incidentally, agrees. He denied that there are any universal human rights at all, negative or positive! He thought such rights were fictions: "...the right of man to freedom is not based on the union of man with man, but on the separation of man from man. It is the right to this separation, the rights of the limited individual who is limited to himself" [Marx, 1977, p. 531. Marx understood, of course, that "The practical application of the rights of man to freedom is the right of man to private

---

extra kidney or eye, no matter how desperate the need—and the "right" of the very poor may deprive one of resources one may well have earned by working hard (prior to becoming wealthy). See for one of his presentations of his case, James P. Sterba, *Justice: Alternative Perspectives* (Belmont, CA: Wadsworth Publ. Co., 1991). Cf., Tibor R. Machan, "The Nonexistence of Basic Welfare Rights," in James Sterba, ed., *Justice: Alternative Political Perspectives* (Belmont, CA: Wadsworth Publishing Co., 1992) and "Does Libertarianism Imply a Welfare State," *Res Publica* Vol. III, No. 2 (Autumn 1997) .

[58] For more on this see Machan, 1975.

property" [Marx, 1977, p. 53]. He did not ultimately approve of private property rights, because the principle protects those engaged in recklessness—such as misuse of resources—but he saw its usefulness for a certain period in human history, because it created enormous productivity in a society. But Marx did not ultimately subscribe to any doctrine of human rights, least of all individual rights.

On the issue of positive freedom Marx was firm: he was for it. He called it "real freedom" [Marx, 1971, pp. 124 et seq.]. He debunked free competition by arguing that "it is not individuals but capital that establishes itself freely in free competition...the movement of individuals within the pure conditions of capital will seem to be free" [Marx, 1971, p. 129]. He continues, as we have already seen [Marx, 1971, p. 131]:

> This kind of individual liberty is thus at the same time the most complete suppression of all individual liberty and total subjugation of individuality to social conditions which take the form of material forces—and even of all powerful objects that are independent of the individual relating to them.

Now the reason Marx demeaned the negative liberty, which goes by the name "the right to individual liberty" in capitalist political systems, is that he thought most individuals are powerless to take advantage of it.[59] Marx, as we saw before, thinks of people as belonging to classes. And these classes are formed in response to the productive circumstances of a society. Thus members of these classes are largely passive respondents to their situations. This is what it means to say that one cannot "make the individual re-

---

[59] As Anatole France, the French novelist and poet, later put it, "The law, in its majestic equality, forbids the rich as well as the poor to sleep under bridges, to beg in the streets and steal bread." This slam at bourgeois liberty has been repeated over and over again by critics of capitalism, yet it is only by respect for and protection of such liberty that the poor have a chance to extricate themselves from dire straits. The critics claim without first being provided for, the poor are helpless. The bourgeois replies that without first being free from the shackles of others, one cannot produce even minimal sustenance, so that liberty must be is first. See my discussion at http://www-hoover.stanford.edu/publications/he/he20.html.

sponsible for relations whose creature he socially remains, however much he may subjectively raise himself above them." In other words, although here and there one might see some workers taking good advantage of economic freedom, the bulk cannot do this because they are struggling to survive. That is a law of capitalist economics.

So for Marx, liberty must involve something more than the liberty we usually have in mind when we talk about economic freedom, civil liberty, the freedom of the press, freedom from slavery or subjugation. We tend to mean by all this being free from the initiation of forcible intrusion by other people. We tend to believe, on the whole, that even if there is some difficulty, once we have that kind of freedom we can pretty much take care of other needs except in catastrophic situations or emergencies.

The ideal of freedom or liberty associated with America is thus very different from the Marxist ideal of real human freedom. This freedom is a kind of total mental and physical well-being. It is the freedom from trouble, hardship, limitations, poverty, disease and so forth. One of my students, from China, made an apt remark about this topic: "The Chinese Cultural Revolution was a laboratory proving the fallacy of the doctrine of positive rights."

National Liberation

Accordingly, when Marxists and related leftists speak about freedom, liberation and the like, they mean providing everyone with what it takes to achieve freedom from trouble, hardship, poverty, disease and so forth. Consider when we hear of Marxist liberation movements in Africa, Central and Latin America, and elsewhere. The liberation involved here has to do with changing society through and through. It does not simply mean removing the oppression imposed by some people on others, although sometimes that is also implied. But this last type of liberation is akin to what Americans did when they liberated France from German occupation. When the Soviet Union used to engage in liberation, something very different was meant. That involved total revolution, the changing of the entire society.

There are many reasons why societies might deserve changing. Some have oppressive governments. Some have a tyrant. Some have corrupt administrations. Some have legal institutions that do not conform to ideals of justice. Sometimes, however, it is held that even though the people wish to bring about certain kinds of changes—e.g. establish democratic political rule—they are not wise enough for that and must be liberated from their own ignorance.

The Marxists who for a time ruled Nicaragua's government have argued this way. They did not believe that an ignorant population is qualified to elect political representatives. Accordingly, the people first needed to be liberated. This would have required many things, including indoctrination into revolutionary ideology, which was called the abolition of illiteracy in Nicaragua's case. The point is that when imposed on a population by the liberating forces, it is incompatible with the idea of negative liberty or political sovereignty—for reasons Marxism explains.

Although no Marxist leadership ever fully follows Marx, the philosophical source of this kind of liberation of the people is the Marxist notion of freedom or liberty, one that despite the major failures of Marxist type regimes is still promulgated by various political advocates and parties in parts of South America. The people are helpless, indeed, quite gullible—beset with "false consciousness" that will lead them in the wrong direction unless they are provided with firm guidance. Some of the motives underlying such power grabbing can be quite noble, as can be the motivation underlying other kinds of brutal discipline imposed on people. But this does not change the fact that such "liberation" ultimately regards human beings as vulnerable, passive entities who must be firmly guided.

Marxism is committed to the idea that, until we reach communism, we are not really ready for the kind of individual political freedom that has been associated with the American political tradition. And once we reach that kind of social situation, we will have no use for it! Strictly speaking—and here is where many New Leftists and other socialists depart from Marx—the individual liberty we associate with America has an important function, according to Marx. It allows the free flow and development of capital. And that is a very good, though not sufficiently good, thing indeed. It produces abundance, wealth, and riches. It does so recklessly—through the production of such bizarre things as pet rocks and 14 types of underarm deodorant. But that, like the muscle-building recklessness of adolescence, is ultimately to the good of humankind.

Women's Liberation: Two Versions

We may finally illustrate the difference between Marxist and capitalist ideals of freedom by reference to the current women's movement. There are two versions of what it means for women to become liberated. The same point applies when we talk about women's rights.

On the one hand, the ideal of women's liberation means that no initiation of force should be permitted against women. No institutions that express such initiation of force should be sanctioned. Thus, for instance, women may not be kept from serving on juries, enlisting in the military, acquiring property, deciding whom they will marry, or seeking a job. The same point may be made in reference to how we may understand the claim that women have rights, just as anyone else does. They have the right to their lives, liberties and property. Which means that they need ask no one's permission to live, to act and to produce, acquire, hold or dispose of valued things. In other words, other people must not interfere with women doing these sorts of things. In practical terms this would simply mean that all women may trade freely, ask no official permission for working or pursuing a career, and so forth. The best expression of following through with the ideal of women's rights understood in this capitalist fashion is the extension of the vote to women.

On the other hand, women are often said to be liberated only when they have had their consciousness raised, when they have matured, when they have escaped from old-fashioned roles and taken up new ones. This view maintains that there is a right way for women to live and, until they have come to live in this right way, they are not free. Women's liberation, within this framework, means that women must be led to become liberated, they must be guided toward the right way for them to live. And women's rights would mean providing women with what they need for the full attainment of the right way of life for them. In practical terms, this latter view would involve government programs that provide women with child-care facilities, re-education opportunities, centers for psychological treatment, and so forth.

Underlying the two views we find again a fundamental difference about what human beings are. The former view says that if only left to their own resources, ingenuity, inventiveness, creativity, productivity and so forth, they will flourish. Of course, different women may require different degrees of effort to reach certain levels of achievement, but that is true even without any prior oppression against them. People are not equal in their capacities and interests, so it is irrational to expect equality of results. What may be expected is that none shall be kept down by anyone else.

In the Marxist vision human nature is basically passive and so it isn't sufficient to free people of the oppression of others [Marx, 1971, p. 497]:

> Freedom in this field [production] can only consist in *socialized* man, the associated producers, rationally regulating their interchange with Nature, bringing it under their common control, instead of being ruled by it as by the blind forces of Nature; and achieving this with the least expenditure of energy and under conditions most favourable to, and worthy of, their human nature. But it none the less still remains a realm of necessity. Beyond it begins that development of human energy which is an end in itself, the true realm of freedom, which, however, can blossom forth only with this realm of necessity as its basis.

For Marx, freedom means escaping the realm of necessity. This requires giving people special treatment. Affirmative action programs reflect this view very well. Businesses must be forced to hire women; it isn't enough to wipe from the books all the laws that made it hard to hire them in the past. Freedom will come eventually but only to mankind as a whole, never to individuals!

Chapter 7. Socialism:
Democratic or Dictatorial?

Marx on Democracy

It will be useful to return here for a little while to the question of whether Marxism is democratic. Some Western intellectuals, e.g. those who supported the Cuban and Nicaraguan revolutions, insist that Marxism offers true democracy. Other Westerners are often puzzled when Marxists call themselves supporters of democracy. They were even appalled and outraged when Soviet bloc countries were officially called democracies—e.g. the former German Democratic Republic for socialist East Germany. But, before they yielded merely to their emotional revulsion, Westerners would have done well to understand that there are arguments behind the Marxist claim that it is only socialism that can be truly democratic.

As far as capitalist democracy is concerned, Marx held that "the struggle between democracy, aristocracy, and monarchy, the struggle for the franchise etc., etc., are merely the illusory form in which the real struggles of the different classes are fought out among one another" [Marx, 1977, p. 169]. So Marx repudiates the belief that capitalist democracy—what now goes by the term bourgeois or democratic capitalism—is fundamentally different from, say, feudalism. He make clear that "the old democratic litany familiar to all: universal suffrage, direct legislation, popular rights, a people's militia, etc." represents "demands which in so far as they are not exaggerated in fantastic presentation, have already been realized" [Marx, 1977, p. 565]. In short, he admits that some measure of political democracy had been achieved in bourgeois societies but that was not a fundamental enough change in human living. (How fundamental one can get in changing human life is, of course, a very interesting question that one can appreciate only by considering the basic elements of Marxism—e.g., dialectical change in humanity's history.)

But ultimately Marx rejects this bourgeois conception of democracy—which concentrates on the rights of all citizens to participate in the political process, but in a context in which the political process pertains to limited matters of concern to people (e.g. the administration of justice, the securing of rights, and the protection of the country from aggression). Instead he embraces a kind of totalitarian, democracy, the "dictatorship of the working class [or proletariat]" [Marx, 1977, p. 291]. This comes through in the previously quoted notes Marx made on Bakunin's *Statism and Anarchy.*

To bring all this together, let us recall that Marx thinks that human beings a what he calls *species-beings:* "Man is a species-being not only in that practically and theoretically he makes both his own and other species into his objects, but also...he relates to himself as to a universal and therefore free being" [Marx, 1977, p. 8]. By this Marx has in mind what we have in mind when we regard humankind as one being and each individual as part of this organic whole. Moreover, Marx also suggests that we, as humankind, are really the rulers of nature. (Some people dismiss this as Marx's early, pre-scientific thinking, taken from the philosopher Ludwig Feuerbach. But in fact it is reflected in his discussions of alienation and the role of the working class throughout all his writings.)

Essentially, Marxist democracy is shaped by his idea of human nature. Indeed, Marx's conception of human nature pretty much guides all of his thinking. As man is a communal being—when fully developed—he can only be fully realized when he fully participates in the government of himself or engages in self-government. But this does not mean governing his individual life. Rather it means being party to collective social organization. Socialism is the socio-economic system in which privacy is fully abolished. Everyone owns all valued things collectively, although *personal* property is sanctioned.[60] Democratic socialism is the system in which everyone also fully participates in the management of everything of value.

There are people who read Marx as advocating such a democratic socialist society, while others claim he advocated one which is democratic only in intent but in practice amounts to a party dictatorship. In the Soviet Union, for example, there was clearly no democratic socialist government, but those who claimed that the Soviet Union was democratic would have argued that, since the Central Committee of the Communist Party governs for all the people and expresses the will of all of the people, the country is properly a democracy. This may seem double-talk to most of us, and ultimately may very well be, but there is enough palatability to it that it needs to be understood precisely before one considers it critically. In a way many Americans think that democracy should mean that we govern ourselves collectively. In many clubs, unions, even classrooms, there are efforts to give everyone a fair stake in what is important. Well, political democracy does not satisfy this. Simply because we can all vote, it does not follow that we will all have for ourselves what is of value in our country. So many Westerners tend to agree that democracy needs to be extended. We should bring corporate governance under democratic control because corporations deal with so much wealth. Or there should be democratic control of the public airways, since they are so influential.

All in all, however, Americans embrace the capitalist idea of democracy. They resent having their personal lives and values, including their property, subjected to collective governance. Such institutions as municipal architectural boards, building departments, Coastal Commissions and the like are received well by those who want major public reform but resented by many who are being governed through them. In short, we are more individualist than collectivist in this culture, even if we cannot fully

---

[60] For more on this, see Thomas Keyes, "The Marxian Concept of Property: Individual/Social," in Tibor R. Machan, *The Main Debate, Communism versus Capitalism* (New York: Random House, 1987), pp. 311-330.

defend it and intellectually feel a bit guilty about it.

The socialist democratic picture that emerges from reading Marx in certain ways collectivizes all values and purposes so that society becomes a huge commune. All decisions are to be made in common. It is rather like a world-wide town hall meeting. The idea is that, from the debate that will precede the final decision, the best results will emerge, and everyone will welcome the results so long as everyone has had a fair chance of participating. It seems very benign, all things considered. But is it really? We will get back to that shortly.

"Democratic" Centrism

But there is another side to the Marxist picture. Most Western defenders of Karl Marx try to hang this on Lenin and claim that Marx really was a democratic socialist. But Marx may also be read as a democratic centrist. By this I mean someone who regards all human concerns as subject to social democratic decision making but does not yet regard the public as emancipated enough actually to make its own decisions. Rather, some representative group must do this. In the Soviet Union this [was to have been] the Central Committee of the Communist Party [(Bolshevik)] and the even smaller group, the Politburo.

As I noted above, some believe that Marx and Engels were genuine democrats. Alfred G. Meyer claims [Meyer, 1967, p. 6]:

> Marxism is based on the belief that the working class is rational. A consequence of this belief is a general faith in democratic processes; and for this reason Marxist politicians have generally been in favor of constitutional government, widening of the franchise, civil liberties, and the like....

The Russian communists, however, could not follow Marx and Engels all the way in these thoughts. For in Russia, where the proletariat was still in the minority, the democratic republic would not give a spell to proletarian rule [24, p. 33]. Thinkers like Meyer, then, attribute the one-party dictatorial rule of so-called communist societies to the distortions of Marxism at the hands of the likes of Plekhanov, Lenin and Bukharin, all central-planning socialists.

But we must ask, where did Lenin *et al.*, devoted students of Marx, obtain their ideas about what needs to be done in Russia? The following lines from *The Communist Manifesto* itself should answer that question [Marx, 1977, p. 231]:

> The communists, therefore, are on the one hand, practically, the most advanced and resolute section of the working-class parties of every country, that section which pushes forward all others; on the other hand, theoretically, they have over the great mass of the proletariat the advantage of clearly understanding the line of march, the conditions, and the ultimate general results of the proletarian movement.... The immediate aim of the Communists is the same as that of all the other proletarian parties: formation of the proletariat into a class, overthrow of the bourgeois supremacy, conquest of political power by the proletariat.

While the *Manifesto* is a political statement—embodying some compromises and ambiguities—it clearly offers in this passage an opening for introducing the idea of a revolutionary cadre. In addition, Marx argued that in certain places the working class in capitalist societies "did not know how to wield their power and use their liberties, both of which they possess legally" [Marx, 1977, p. 594].

But with regard to the communist movement in Russia, Marx's sanction of nondemocratic, centrist socialism is even more easily justified. This is because he believed, as we have already seen, that any phase of human history, including and especially capitalism, must rest on a previous phase that makes it possible. In other words, since Russia had not experienced capitalist productive development, it really had no basis for a genuine democratic socialist revolution unless led by a group that fully understands what must be done to foster revolutionary change.

So any Marxist could infer from Marx's works—read the way Lenin and other Russians read him—that in Russia and everywhere else, where capitalism had not played itself out fully, the socialists could only rule by firm—some might say "brute"—force. That is not merely something that Marxism implies unintentionally. It is arguably part of Marxist theory, something Marx had to be aware of, given his own words and his encouragement of Russian revolutionaries in the face of Russia's essentially peasant-feudal society. If we add to this that Marxism is very possibly wrong, then the use of force in implementing its vision is clearly needed, since the theory about the self-consciousness of the proletariat turns out to be wishful thinking. It will beg to be supplemented by "firm" leadership on various occasions in the building toward communism!

Let me bring back my analogy of the growing individual. Marx sees humanity as a growing, developing individual, and he applauds its maturation, indeed would probably like to see it come about rapidly. He had predicted proletarian revolutions for several countries, as well as the onset of socialism and communism, even though theoretically he did not have to. At any rate, Marx could accept that some parts of the organic body, humanity, might mature faster than others; but not without a price to pay. And that is like the case of individuals.

Some of us grow up *too* fast, but this can mean that certain critical developments do not take place. If Russia moves from *feudalism* to socialism, it will still be poor and will lack a working class large enough to wage a democratic transformation of society. So Russia will have to employ drastic means—liquidation, purges, police state practices, etc. When Marx says that "without it want is merely made general, etc.," he is referring to the point, which flows from his theory, that without capitalism there would be shortages. Indeed, the experience of the Soviet Union and its satellite nations, all of them prematurely socialist in Marx's own terms, testifies to this for any faithful Marxist. Never mind for now that there may be another explanation for this, quite apart from Marxism. All that is crucial here is that trying to skip the capitalist stage of production is costly even from a Marxist standpoint. But Marx consciously, with full awareness, was willing to subject societies to these severe costs. The experience of Lenin and Stalin and of the recent police state in these nations flows directly from going on with a plan Marx himself sanctioned.

When developments do not come forth peacefully, spontaneously, discipline must be instituted. This is true in individuals. Marx simply extrapolates from them. When we try to take short cuts—e.g., if someone tries to learn a sport or a musical instrument in later life, the self-control, the severity of self-discipline, will have to be greater. So, for someone who views humanity as an individual, it should come as no surprise that humanity will have to be put through some horrors before things can get better.

That is what underlies the Stalinist experiences of Russia from a Marxist point of view—not that Lenin or Stalin distorted Marx, as so many people wish to believe. Some may still argue that if Russia was not ready for democratic socialism, it was not ready for socialism at all. Yet Marx himself answers this when in the preface to the Russian edition of the *Manifesto* he makes clear that under certain circumstances, namely, when a country has annexed regions that had gone through capitalism, the socialist movement may be started in a country like Russia.

Revolution the Non-violent Way

In contrast, Marx did not even believe in the need of a violent revolution for democratic capitalist societies [Marx, 1977, p. 594]:

> We are aware of the importance that must be accorded to the institutions, customs, and traditions of different countries; and we do not deny that there are countries like America, England (and, if I know your institutions better, I would add Holland), where the workers can achieve their aims by peaceful means.

What is clear from this is that the common belief that Marxist revolutions must be violent is false.

Revolutions do require the fundamental reformation of society. Marxists have always had disdain for mere reformers because such people do not see what the Marxists see, namely, that the only way to upgrade society is to abolish its basic constitution. But despite the fact that revolutions aim to overturn the fundamentals of a social system, they can still be peaceful. They must be violent only where capitalist democracy has not been achieved and no other avenues for progress exist. From a Marxist point of view, this includes many countries that do a lot of business with major capitalist societies, such as those in Central and Latin America, the Middle East, and so forth. The reason is that although these countries share some capitalist features, they are politically almost feudal. They fall into the capitalist group because of their close trade links with the United States, Great Britain and other industrial nations of the West, which are more capitalist in all respects than the rest. So any workers' revolt in Central or Latin America is a kind of socialist revolution, but not aimed at their own government but against these Western societies, indirectly. Since the workers cannot vote to influence the governments of the United States and other Western countries, from the Marxist point of view they can only resort to violent revolution.

In the United States, for example, there is no need for that kind of rough stuff, not as far as Marxism is concerned. Bit by bit, step by step, at municipal, county, state and the federal levels of government, socialism can be instituted by democratic process.[61]

One can easily make out a case for this already. As Marx made clear, "the theory of the Communists may be summed up in the single sentence: Abolition of private [though not all *personal*] property" [Marx, 1977, p. 232]. Where in Western societies is there any evidence of full respect for private property rights? Nowhere. Everywhere this principle is being eroded. Regulators, inspectors, supervisors and the rest, at municipal, county, state and federal levels, are now in charge of property. One needs permits to add a small room to one's private home, not just to annex to one's factory or warehouse. One must go through several layers

---

[61] For a revealing chronicling of this trend, see Steven Greenhut, *Abuse of Power, How the Government Misuses Eminent Domain* (Santa Ana: Seven Locks Press, 2004).

of bureaucracies to begin a small business venture, never mind a major industrial development. And, since all these interventions with the right to private property are the result of more or less democratic processes, we could argue that Marxist theory is nearly being realized in practice. Of course, all this could be explained differently, but we will come to that later.

For now we need realize simply that Marx speaks with a forked tongue. Democratic socialism is the spoken ideal—the historical promise—but when it does not come about, well, centrist, dictatorial "democracy" will do nicely too.

There are clear indications of this in our day-to-day politics. Recall the example of Californian New Leftist Bill Press. Apparently the people were "too stupid" to discern the truth, so their full legal participation in the referendum process did not really manage to be democratic. Which is precisely the point Marx made about the English workers. And it is just the sort of reasoning that ushers in elite communist cadres who prove to be necessary in the face of mass ignorance, including the proletariat. This kind of thinking is now part and parcel of Marxism. Many Marxists have developed it further. We hear from them all about the way capitalism manipulates the workers, numbs their revolutionary consciousness, and bombards them with consumer goods they are incapable of resisting, just so that they become captive to capitalism itself.

Some would exempt Marx from any responsibility for this kind of reasoning, laying all the blame on Lenin and other neo-Marxists. But, as we have seen, Marx laid the groundwork on which Lenin, Stalin and Marcuse could build to their heart's content.

Chapter 8. Communism:
Humanity Matured?

Communism Is No Ideal

Marx never bothered to say a whole lot about communism. But he said enough for us to get a fairly clear idea about what it might amount to.

First of all, we should keep in mind that for Marx communism is not some vision, some ideal, or some desirable state of affairs that people should work to implement. He was clear about this [Marx, 1977, p. 171]:

> Communism is for us not a state of affairs which is to be established, an ideal to which reality will have to adjust itself. We call communism the real movement which abolishes the present state of things. The conditions of this movement result from the premises now in existence.

Just as a caterpillar becomes a butterfly, an adolescent a young adult, so humanity will become communist.

We tend to look at socialism, communism, or any other type of society differently. We tend to regard it as in our power—at least in the long run—to change a society from one kind to another. If enough of us will it so, then such a transformation is possible, so long as the idea of that society makes some semblance of sense. That is how we view the history of the American republic. It had at one time been part of the feudal state but, because enough people wanted to change it, it became a constitutional republic. It was a matter of deciding to change things, essentially.

But Marxism does not allow for that kind of thinking. For Marx that amounted to utopianism. He thought that those who tried to change things were naive visionaries [Marx, 1977, p. 183]:

> The communists do not preach morality at all.... They do not
> put to people the moral demand: love one another, do not be
> egoists, etc.; on the contrary, they are very well aware that
> egoism, just as much as self-sacrifice, is in definite circum-
> stances a necessary form of the self-assertion of individuals.
> Hence the communists by no means want...to do away with
> the "private individual" for the sake of the "general," self-
> sacrificing man....

The reason is not difficult to identify in Marx. For him, as we
have already noted early on in this work, ideals of the sort which
we often believe motivate people are really just products created
in the human mind by economic circumstances—"ideals" are
phantoms. Yet there is much to be said for the view that Jacques
Maritain advanced and that is related to us in these terms by John
C. O'Brien [O'Brien, 1987, p. 61]:

> Although when he became a communist, Marx excluded from
> his arguments all moral and juridical arguments, allowing
> henceforth only economic and social considerations, Maritain
> points out that Marx was unequivocally committed to the bet-
> terment of the oppressed and the exploited, to "laborers who
> must sell themselves piecemeal" to the alienated. Moreover,
> says Maritain, although Marx may have substituted the phrase
> *social claim* for such moral expressions as *justice* and *right*,
> what is the fighting value, the persuasive force of a claim if it
> is not just? Thus, justice, adds Maritain, cannot efface the mark
> of its Judaeo-Christian origins.

Nevertheless, for the mature dialectical materialist, Marx's communism is not some good social system which people *ought to*
produce. Rather it is the mature form humanity *will* finally take!
(As we have already noted, the role of moralizing in Marx may be
seen as a type of revolutionary action rather than any kind of pre-

scription or expression of what the personal responsibility of someone might be. We can, after all, rail at dumb brutes, with the expectation that they will reform and behave better next time as a result of just such scolding.)

Furthermore, does the Judeo-Christian morality—e.g. its conceptions of "justice" and "right"—exhaust the possible renditions of ethical terms? A far older tradition exists in which such terms make their appearance, namely, Socratic-Platonic-Aristotelian moral philosophy. And while some of this tradition does accord with the Judeo-Christian (and Marxist) ideals of collectivist humanism, some of it clearly does not.

It is arguable—and I do argue this [Machan, 1975 and Machan, 1989]—that a version of the kind of morality Marx and many Christians reject, namely, one stressing the prime responsibility of the individual to excel as a human being primarily *for his very own good*, can be linked to Aristotle's eudemonism. One need not be a hedonistic, narrow-mindedly self-interested individualist to reject the ideal of collectivist humanism (religious or secular). One can see the superiority of the ethics of self-actualization, self-enhancement, and flourishing or rational self-interest as these notions emerge from within the Aristotelian eudemonistic ethical tradition [Norton, 1976].

Communism: Each Living the Life of Renaissance Man

Let us now ask, but what will communism be like? What will this haven for humankind amount to? How will it realize the ethical and moral ideals Marx at least subsumes in his scientific analysis? Marx gives only hints. He tells us, for example, that in communist society human beings will engage in really free labor, one which will not consist of any professional specializations [Marx, 1939, pp. 22-3]:

For as soon as labor is distributed, each man has a particular exclusive sphere of activity, which is forced upon him and from which he cannot escape. He is a hunter, a fisherman, a shepherd, or a critical critic, and must remain so if he does not want to lose his means of livelihood; while in communist society, where nobody has one exclusive sphere of activity but each can become accomplished in any branch he wishes, society regulates the general production and thus makes it possible for me to do one thing today and another tomorrow, to hunt in the morning, fish in the afternoon, rear cattle in the evening, criticize after dinner, just as I have a mind, without ever becoming hunter, fisherman, shepherd or critic.

And "In a communist society there are no painters but, at most, people who engage in painting among other activities" [Marx, 1977, p. 190].

One should be very careful not just to dismiss this vision. Marx starts with the belief that material labor—work of any kind, for him—is what essentially characterizes human life. Since material labor for him is necessarily a social activity, one can only be fully mature as a material laborer if one is in a communal, socialized economic system where one is a full participant in the organization of work.

In Marx's view, however, being essentially a material laborer also means being essentially non-specialized. To restrict someone to one kind of work is, then, for Marx, to truncate that person, to alienate him from what he really would be if fully healthy. There is some of this in our ordinary thinking, as well, when we openly or secretly admire the "renaissance man," the "Jack of all trades," the well-rounded individual, the whole man and the like.

In less ambitious ways, we give evidence of sharing some of Marx's notions, quite without being anything akin to a Marxist, when we admire the musician who plays numerous instruments—and is a racing driver on top of that! More systematically, many people are dissatisfied with having to do the same kind of thing all their adult lives. At first they may have found satisfaction in their work but later it becomes stale. This tends to produce that famous modern malaise, the mid-life crisis. Some people uproot themselves completely, renounce all normal responsibilities, and take off to the hinterlands or the wide-open seas. (Many return after a while, having learned that it's tough going out there.)

Marx argues that when humanity reaches full maturity—once we are emancipated, not politically (as by his account we nearly are) but as human beings—it will be a place of serious joy, complete self-fulfillment (as a material, laboring social being), for all. We get another clue from what he says about work in such a mature social setting [Marx, 1977, p. 368]:

> Really free labor, the composing of music for example, is at the same time damned serious and demands the greatest effort. The labor concerned with material production can only have this character if (1) it is of a social nature, (2) it has a scientific character and at the same time is general work, i.e. if it ceases to be human effort as a definite, trained natural force, gives up its purely natural, primitive aspects and becomes the activity of a subject controlling all the forces of nature in the productive process.

If one has trouble envisaging what this could mean, I suggest recalling a jam session with a group of musicians. There is no doubt that such a session involves hard work. It is, however, not done for the sake of some external reward, or for payment. (They are not playing a gig!) It is spontaneous. But it is a limited case.

We should remember that Marx fully anticipates that in capitalism there would be no room yet for general labor, for work that is not subject to the division of labor. Here and there some people might escape the general principles that govern capitalist production. Marx was never one who believed in any kind of iron law, some geometrical principle, which governs human development. Rather he thinks of his scientific perspective more along biological lines. The principles involving class relations and the like are more statistical than anything else. "It is very 'possible' that particular individuals are not always influenced in their attitude by the class to which they belong, but this has as little effect upon the class struggle as the secession of a few nobles to the *tiers état* had on the French Revolution" [Marx, 1977, p. 216].

What emerges then about communism is that we would all work for the love of the work itself, certainly not for any remuneration. The entire notion that underlies, for example, supply-side economics, namely, that people need incentive in order to produce diligently, would be superseded. Humanity would have transcended that phase of its existence when the main objective, from its historical perspective, had been the creation of abundance.

And this is crucial. It does not upset a Marxist if one suggests that socialism is less productive than capitalism. Productive of what? It certainly will not serve the sort of desires capitalism is so apt at serving—whims, fads, tastes and the like, with total disregard for what the productive effort satisfying these could do elsewhere. Rather, communism would usher in a peace of mind for working men and women. They would do things they wanted to do, and all such things would be productive because what they are would be decided by the entire society, collectively. "From everybody according to his ability, to everybody according to his need."

Evidence of Communist "Progress"

We have plenty of evidence of this kind of thinking already in our midst. When people complain that people work for profit but not for use, that developers of apartment houses concentrate too much on earning high returns on their investment and not enough on suiting those who need dwellings, that kind of thought clearly gives expression to the conception of the good society which guided Marx's thinking, namely something on the order of a kibbutz or commune based on intimate relations, uniform and common purpose. Indeed, that conception is not unfamiliar to Western civilization. Sharing had been an ideal in many religions and aiming to profit, not to mention usury, had been for many centuries sinful. Aristotle, the great Greek philosopher who forged many of our ideas, condemned profit making and so did most of the great religious leaders throughout human history.

What should by now be evident is that apart from the peculiar format of Marxism—its dialectical materialist base—there is not much revolutionary about it. The vision of humanity as a great family is familiar to us from sources that are in other respects quite alien to Marxism. And all this is easy enough to explain.

As we have already noted, one of the men Marx admired was Ludwig Feuerbach, the German philosopher, whose main claim to fame inventing materialist humanism. The explicit objective of this invention was to make religion less otherworldly and to transform man's love for a mystical God into his love of Man or humankind. In a way, we can claim that Feuerbach, and later Marx, tried take the value system of the Western religious tradition and naturalize it, bring it down to earth, give humankind a promise of heaven—not after life but in the actual, reachable future.

We can ask, of course, whether that itself was a good idea. Perhaps the major religions did not convey to us an accurate idea of what the human good really comes to. Perhaps we have been misled about the picture of human emancipation, not just with respect to its occurrence in a supernatural dimension but even so far as its character is concerned. In short, are we to accept that the only difference between Marxism and the truth is that Marx promised a truth for this world that can only be achieved in another?

Chapter 9. Marxism versus Free Capitalism

The Main Debate

As Jean-Paul Sartre, the major twentieth-century representative of Existentialism noted, Marxism had been *the* going idea in most of the 20th century.[62] It had been the central topic for debate—all other controversies were rather negligible in comparison. And some of this hasn't changed, even after the demise of the society most closely identified with Marxian aspirations.

Almost every attack on capitalism, or even Western liberalism (as a somewhat ambiguous contemporary stance), still draws on the vocabulary of Marxism. Even defenses of the *welfare* state require Marxist notions about exploitation, property, human nature, alienation, exchange, participatory democracy, planning, labor and so forth. When capitalism is charged with being wasteful, cruel, reactionary, unjust, dehumanizing, or crass—the charges reek of Marxist underpinnings.

So the main debate in our time is between the political economy of capitalism and the historicist view of humanity's development put before us by Karl Marx. If capitalism means to be a significant intellectual-political alternative in our time, it must confront the Marxist system head-on. Yet among capitalist thinkers very few today are concerned with Marx. In the past it was somewhat different. Some members of the Austrian School of economics—notably Böhm-Bawerk and von Mises—have addressed Marx's economics. Hayek, too, has dealt with certain central aspirations of socialists. In a roundabout way, but focused mainly on economic matters, Marxism had to be contended with by those who found capitalism a promising socio-economic system. Yet,

---

[62] Jean Paul Sartre, *Search for a Method*, translated and with an introduction by Hazel E. Barnes (New York: Knopf, 1963).

apart from Thomas Sowell's [Sowell, 1985] and Roberts and Stephenson's [Roberts and Stephenson, 1979], few capitalist criticisms of Marxism exist. (I have already mentioned that David Conway's *A Farewell to Marx* is a welcome addition, as is N. Scott Arnold's *Marx's Radical Critique of Capitalist Society* (London: Oxford University Press, 1990).

We have seen Marxism in reasonable detail and now, after some hints as to what individualism comes to, we can turn to a discussion of which is the better system and why. Of course, I have, in the above discussions, already alluded to some of what I take to be the advantages of the individualist approach. I have also suggested where it needs to be revised, given that most people conceive of it in *homo economicus* terms.

I will simply contrast the two systems and explain why it is that Marxism is a failure. The essence of the contrast is that Marxism does not see value in the life of an individual human being, whereas individualism considers the crux of value to be nothing other than the life of an individual human being.

Individualism: True and False

In recent years there have been renewed attacks on individualism, the ideology that is closely associated with the political traditions and history of the United States. Most notably, Professor Robert Bellah, Amitai Etzioni, and Charles Taylor have been engaged in lambasting America's (allegedly "atomistic") individualism. Earlier this century the same kind of anti-individualist crusade was conducted by the likes of the philosopher John Dewey, but the latter had at least a more constructive tone to it. Even Alexis de Tocqueville took issue with it (while, however, offering a useful alternative that is still individualist in its essence).

Bellah, as we have already noticed, argues that it is a mistake to link individualism to the ideal of a free society, quite the contrary. Individualism is in fact a threat to human liberty, argues Bellah, citing, somewhat misleadingly, Alexis de Tocqueville as the authority in support of his thesis.

But does Bellah tell us what he means by American individualism? Actually the conception of the individual person he has in mind has little to do with the American political tradition. His target cannot be associated with the philosophy of the Founding Fathers or the framers of the Constitution, all of whom were concerned to a considerable degree with the political sovereignty of every person and with the protection of individual rights. What Bellah has in mind is a very different kind of individualism, namely, one that appears in the works of theoretical economists, about the individual who is exclusively concerned with advancing on the economic front, who wants only to acquire more goods and services. This caricature of individualism is the very same idea that Karl Marx took to task and slanderously associated with liberal capitalism.

Now there is little doubt that many people in America and throughout the world partly fit this characterization. Of course, in the rest of the world the chances are remote that people can indulge in extensive acquisition—they are rarely permitted to do so and their institutions pose extensive obstacles for them if they try. But in America one is largely free to pursue economic well being, true enough. And the fact that many people have spent much time on this objective is also understandable—they recall the not-so-distant periods of history when only a very small and privileged proportion of a country's population had been allowed to gain wealth. The rest were usually held in servitude and lived by the grace of these few. So the concern for wealth is surely understandable—especially in a country where people are largely the offspring of destitute immigrants.

But, even in such a country, is it really true that most people are obsessed with wealth acquisition as such, as depicted by the caricature of individualism Bellah would have us endorse? Or are they rather concerned with obtaining some of the benefits attainable in human life which had been denied to their ancestors—home, transportation, entertainment, arts, medical care, and education for the kids? Moreover, is it not true that what individualism remains in the United States—for in fact there is little of it left on the political front where the *welfare* state has pretty much wiped out the idea of individual responsibility—often generates considerable commitment? Is there indeed not extensive commitment in America to numerous artistic, spiritual, scientific, intellectual, literary, philanthropic and related community projects?

Though they often have higher hopes for it, most economists use their model of acquisitive human nature for purposes of understanding the way the market works, the place where we do our buying and selling. No wonder then that they do not concentrate on other elements of individualism. But sociologists would seem to have the responsibility to take seriously different aspects of individualism when they consider its implications.

Let us note that American individualism means mainly that people must make decisions about their lives. No one may take over that role for them. Whatever associations people enter, they are responsible for what they have done and cannot defer to God, tradition or family as the agents who should take the credit or blame for this action. American individualism means, ultimately, *moral* independence—the responsibility of every person to make the choice between good and evil, right and wrong, and not abdicate his role as an active agent in his life.

American individualism is not some arid, callous and silly idea that we ought to live as hermits and renounce the company of our fellow human beings. Nor does it cut us off from freely chosen responsibilities to our fellows, to our country, to our culture. But it does deny that we are all really just one thing, some totalitarian *Einheit* or "oneness" that swallows up individuals and makes them the subjects of the larger organism, the state. Instead, American individualism is far more akin to what Ayn Rand describes when she notes that "Man is not a lone wolf and he is not a social animal. He is a *contractual* animal. He has to plan his life long-range, make his own choices, and deal with other men by voluntary agreement (and he has to be able to rely on their observance of the agreement they entered)."[63]

Statism appears to be the preferred alternative suggested by the distorted attack on American individualism that Bellah & Co.

---

[63] Ayn Rand, "A Nation's Unity," *Ayn Rand Letter*, Vol. II, 2, p. 3.

are undertaking. Such attacks suggest nostalgia for an age when individuals had no say about their lives, when communities (i.e., chiefs, Caesars, tyrants, tsars, despots, kings) ran our lives and no one asked the great majority of individuals what they wanted out of life.

I am afraid that attacks on individualism are in fact mostly attacks on the sovereignty of people as far as making decisions about their lives is at issue. Those doing the attacking help, willingly or not, those who would have us surrender to them our freedom to decide how we will live and spend our labors.

Of course, every viewpoint has its ridiculous version, including individualism. The real question is which basic social philosophy is more suited to human nature, one that stresses individual responsibility and choice or one that treats people as parts of some larger, superior whole. There are clearly those who favor the latter view. And the kind of attacks carried out by Professor Bellah on American individualism seem to me to serve their purposes rather than to help avoid the occasional excesses of individualism that is at heart the social philosophy most respectful to human beings that has ever been proposed.

The Paradox of Limitations

There is one interesting explanation for the lack of adequate concern with Marxism. This is that capitalist theorists have a narrow focus. Capitalists are committed to allowing only a minimal portion of life to be tied to politics. They want to stress only one political point, namely, "Don't tread on me!" or "My life is off limits unless I say otherwise." Expressed a bit curtly, that is the central capitalist ideal. But this leaves capitalists philosophically united on very little, which is their strength and weakness. Capitalists know that *vis-à-vis* strangers the only thing one must always keep in mind is a negative duty or a prohibition. They need only remember and respect the rights of others—one may not commit murder, assault and theft, and all the variations of these in their complex legal renditions associated with a rapidly developing technological era. And so long as others do the same, capitalists will be theoretically satisfied.

Yet life involves far more than politics. There is family, the arts, sciences, entertainment, sports, hobbies, friendship and all the variations of these, plus a lot more we think up as we carry on with living. There are problems, challenges, puzzles, mysteries, connected with all of these realms. And there are millions of different ways to tackle them, depending on who faces them and under what circumstances.

None of this falls within the purview of the politics of capitalism, which is wonderful as well as scary. It is wonderful because capitalists can refuse to be pretentious. They can remain modest, just as their political outlook requires of them, and they can remain true to their political ideals when they keep all this clearly in mind. It is scary, also, because as capitalists they will probably confront Marxism and other systems of thought in a wide variety of ways, thus making themselves vulnerable to the charge of being confused and divided on crucial issues.

Marxism: Totalitarian in Spirit

Marxism, by contrast, knows it all. One can see this even if one is just watching from the sidelines. Marxists know it all about women's problems, workers' problems, education, drugs, divorce, poverty, technology, psychology, racial conflict, history and all. Marxism strives to be a total system of thought and action. It is also totalitarian, politicizing everything from the nurturing of one's psyche to the building of one's dwellings, all the way to how to plan an economic community.

Marxism is not just geopolitically expansionist, something even some capitalists wish to deny. But as Shirley Christian wrote: "Internationalism—the assistance of fellow revolutionaries—is a key element of the faith to Marxist-Leninists, and telling them not to practice it is like telling priests not to pray" [Christian, 1983, p. 20]. Some may protest: "But that is Marxist-Leninism, not Marxism!" Yet Marx himself, as we noted earlier, said pretty much the same thing. It's okay to start socialism in Russia but it is vital that the revolution be exported! Since Marx also noted that each productive phase of humanity must be fully realized, so it would be impossible to move to communism from socialism without incorporating the attainments of capitalism, even if only by colonizing (near-)capitalist societies.

My concern is not just with the geopolitical expansionism we witnessed at the hands of the Soviets. I am interested in the propensity of Marxists and neo-Marxists to take hold of every issue, ignore completely the idea of specialization and make every subject their full possession, however artificial their treatment of it ultimately proves to be.

Yes, this is all quite natural within Marxism. Marx thought of humanity as an "organic whole" or, to use another translation of the same phrase, "organic body." And just as holistic medicine does not permit the separate treatment of various portions of an individual's body, so Marxism does not permit treating sociology or economics or history or psychology or political science as if these could be mastered independently of mastering all the others.

The mastery tends, ultimately, to be prejudicial. It is based on some key formula—in this case the dialectic principle—some notion which has very little to do with the facts at hand. Yet it does appear to be a formidable approach, one that can impress many of those eager to grasp things intellectually. The philosopher's stone has been the hope of the ambitious intellectuals who want to skip dealing with reality's multi-faceted nature and the consequent irreducibility of the principles that govern its various domains.

Reassessing the Red Balloon

In the end there really is a good deal of hot air in the Marxist dirigible. But it is difficult to tell. And there is just enough substance there that serves some vital intellectual needs that, unless one's attack on the system is well-grounded, one can easily be gobbled up by it.

For one thing, it isn't enough to retort to Marxism that it is economically naive. Marxism does not pretend to be an economic theory. At the least Marxism proposes a political economy, with emphasis on the "political." Then, also, Marxism has solid rebuttals to those who believe that economics can be a pure, value-free science. Marxists can note that economics studies trade or exchange. And trade or exchange presupposes that some things are owned. But ownership is not a value-free concept, since it means: "None but X (or Y or Z) may decide what is to be done with the owned item." If this were not presupposed in market analysis, why would it be assumed that, without mutually satisfactory terms, no exchange will ensue? If the valued item is not really *owned*, why worry about failure to come to terms? It could simply be acquired without mutually satisfactory terms.

And in other areas, too, Marx can shake things up with impressive ideas. Economic individualism assumes that people pursue self-interest. But it has a rather barren idea of what the self amounts to, and Marx has nailed it for that good and hard (in his "On the Jewish Question" [Marx, 1977, pp. 53 et seq.]. And the list could go on.

What I am trying to get across is that, however inadequate it ultimately is, Marxism provides interesting and impressive ammunition against the classical liberal conception of capitalism. And since capitalists agree on very little besides their ideal of negative liberty (which itself appears on first inspection to be a bit shallow, failing to provide a clear standard for distinguishing liberty from its infringement, unless one also buys into a system of natural individual rights or some other doctrine), many of them find themselves barred from answering Marx fully.

Going on the Offensive

But there is a way to take the bull by the horns. It is to realize that one isn't just a citizen or political animal but a complete human being. And that means one needs a way of thinking about life that will supply us with something to obstruct the path of the Marxist Pac-Man.

Now I myself think that we need a philosophic system to do this. And I think there is such a system available to us whose tenets will successfully rebuff Marxism. I'll apply this philosophical framework to crucial Marxist ideas.

(1) Marx thinks the world develops dialectically, in a three-fold process, toward its perfection in the end. That is why Marx prophesies communism as the last stage of humanity's predictable development—the natural maturation of the organism, as it were. But even if the dialectic method could be found here and there, it is quite evidently not all-pervasive. In other words, there is not only one principle of growth or development in nature, even in that part of it which is humanity.

(2) Marx accepts the collectivist idea that humanity is the being one should think of as the individual that may be harmed or benefited; "The human essence is the true collectivity of man." He added that "isolation from this essence is out of all proportion more universal, insupportable, terrifying, and full of contradictions than isolation from the political collectivity..." [Marx, 1977, p. 126]. This means that the most advanced form of human society not only gathers individuals into a political unity—e.g. by way of equal principles of justice or rights—but gathers them into a cohesive cultural body, a "true collectivity." In short, one is happiest when one is but a cell within the organic body of humanity.

Now this seems absurd. If everyone were really a member of one family unit, we would be emotionally crippled all the time. All the deaths, births, anniversaries, illnesses, weddings, joys and sorrows of all persons would have to be as meaningful to each of us as are these matters now when involving our intimates. But intimacy is based on individuality and special relations. Collectivity would demand of us that we die emotionally so as to survive all of what happens to everyone in the world. If we really tried to live as if humanity were a large family, we could not do it. Yet that is exactly what Marx demands of the communist—he must regard everyone in humankind as an intimate!

Marx takes this notion quite seriously. All its problems seem not to concern him. Aside from the above, for example, the human essence involves, first and foremost, people having goals, *determining* purposes, making decisions, choosing values and so forth. These are just what individuals only, not groups of people, can do—even biologically to think otherwise is absurd.

There is more. Marx carries to the ridiculous a dreamy conception we find in much of philosophy, East and West, namely, the view that humankind is all one, that we form not just a large species with much to benefit from interaction but that there really are no selves and what humankind is comes to one gigantic being. (Another version of this view is that the universe is just one large being of which we are a part, perhaps the conscious part!) We can put it differently. Marx, following such other thinkers as Plato, accepts the idea that the term "human being" is a name for one entity, that the universal concept by which we mean each separate one of us really means just one transcendent being.

The universal concept became a real, concrete *entity* for Marx. It is as if one would argue that the concept "chair" really stands not for millions of individual chairs but for one large chair comprising the rest. For Plato this idea may have served as a kind of myth. It was to remind us of the fact that members of the same species really are members of a species, not disparate, totally separate, isolated entities. As we saw, Marx, too, was reacting to a different extremism which had maintained that we are all independent, isolated atoms. Marx went to the opposite extreme and relegated our individuality to total insignificance. He looked on humankind as a materially real entity of its own, undergoing an individual development.

All the collectivist talk about species-being, liberation, human (but not individual) emancipation and the like attests plainly enough to Marx's view that all people are really part of this large person who is growing up. But, it turns out, this large person has no brain, no eyes, no memory, no imagination, no regrets, sorrows, joys or delights. Humanity has no consciousness. So what Marx took to be the most important aspect of humankind is really not human at all but some imaginary blob of being, even by his own account of it. If I may venture a suggestion, for Marx, humanity will have grown up when it has reached the dumb state of an ant colony or beehive—carrying on without purpose or thought, just automatically. Marx quite explicitly denied that we are human beings. He revered a state of untroubled bliss.

(3) From the above, basically metaphysical, problems there flow numerous other flaws. If humanity cannot really be the depository of human nature, what is? Well, it is our human individuality. This is a bit different from what we get in the individualism of classical liberalism, but some elements of that courageous tradition remain. What the classical liberals got wrong is the view that each of us is only individual in that we each count for one being among many others—somewhat as a chair in an auditorium is an individual chair among many others. Rather we are that and more, namely beings who create much of what is crucial about ourselves quite on our own. We are separate not just physically and materially, but morally. We possess individual responsibility for becoming what we will be. That is a major addition to the individualist tradition, one advanced by Ayn Rand and also by David L. Norton, resting on a neo-Aristotelian conception of the objective knowability of human nature and the basically individualist implications of the resulting knowledge.[64]

What this comes to is crucial. Individuals are vitally important to humanity, indeed the most important aspect of humanity. Actually, humanity is no more than individuals—no abstract universal being "humanity" exists, there is, contrary to Marx, no "organic body" that is humanity. Just as the classes I teach at my college aren't anything other than the students taking those classes with some common objectives shared among them, so humanity isn't something apart from the billions of individuals who comprise it. Since the individuality of these members of humanity is highly diverse and varied, both because of circumstance and because of personal variation in effort and capacity (e.g. talent), a society's constitution—its laws and public policies—must honor individuality first and foremost, in order to be humanly appropriate, good, fit, just or excellent.

(4) For Marx the exchange economy is a temporary phase of

---

[64] Many dispute that it is important to have a well grounded moral outlook—they think simply embracing various moral notions is sufficient for guiding one's life properly. See, for example, Niclas Berggren, "Does Belief in Ethical Subjectivism Pose a Challenge to Classical Liberalism," *Reason Papers*, No. 27, pp. 69-86. However, without a solid support, a moral outlook is easily challenged by another that can plausibly claim to be well founded.

humanity's growth—a kind of adolescence of humanity. It is wild, crude, reckless, but it helps build the organism into a powerful machine. Capitalism, Marx held, was the most productive system of human organization. It is also indispensable—that is why the Soviet Union must conquer us and must have an internationalist expansionist foreign policy; because, without capitalism at home and abroad it has no capacity for survival, let alone for flourishing, in Marx's own theory. It is as if a person skipped adolescence and failed to gain all the muscles. He or she would have to remedy matters by taking these from elsewhere or by becoming dependent on those who possess them.

But now, with the individual person back in the center of the important things in human life, what about capitalism? It turns out to be the best system because it can best—though not *always,* and certainly *not necessarily*—accommodate any individual's highest rational aspirations. The fact that capitalism has only in recent centuries been identified by political economists for the integrated, coherent economic order that it is does not mean that its principles have only now come into existence. Many facts of science have come to light only recently yet have in fact been those facts all along, ever since the entities to which they pertain have existed, way before human beings have managed to identify this. That same thing is true about the principles by which human community life ought to be governed, even though this may not have been realized or adhered to in some periods of history. Not everything about human life has such permanence and stability, of course—fashion, technology, the system of travel, and such are far less universal and stable than these very basic principles (because the latter rest on our human nature, which is stable and lasting enough in nature).[65]

(5) There is a lot more. Marx's conception of social science

---

[65] Does this square with the principles of evolutionary biology? There is no reason to think that in the course of evolution, as it plays out in all living species, periods of considerable stability and permanence are excluded. This is a matter of discovery; it depends on what the facts are and what the evidence shows us, it is not something that's theory-driven. By all accounts, the human species has been what it is for approximately 100,000 years. See, Vitaly Shevoroshkin, "The Mother Tongue," *The Sciences*, May/June 1990, pp. 20-27.

and his attempt to forge a theory of value that conforms to it; his class analysis; his conception of human being as for the time being passive, etc. All this must be given up once it is understood that individuals, not collectives, are the essence of humanity. And in the wake of this realization, the capitalist market is vindicated. The vindication is, moreover, a moral and scientific one.

The central failing of Marxism is its faulty ontology where human nature is concerned. What we can tell about human existence plainly contradicts it. The main contention that Marx has advanced, namely, that each person is first and foremost a collective or species-being, does not fit the facts as disclosed by our experiences with human beings, including, ironically, with Marx himself. Individuality is a central characteristic of every human being, no less important than our natural affinity to community life.[66] It is not just that each person counts indeed for one instance of a kind of thing, but that each person is centrally, essentially a self-made being, in need of the constant initiation of his or her life processes.

Summary of Marx's Problems

When I say that Marx's collectivism is wrong I am not saying that the idea of the human individual is not a relatively recent one in human history. As Collin Morris observes [Morris, 1972, p. 2], "Western individualism is...far from expressing the common experience of humanity. Taking a world view, one might almost regard it as an eccentricity among cultures." Marx himself made much of the fact that [Marx, 1971, p. 17]:

[t]he further back we go into history, the more the individual, and, therefore, the producing individual seems to depend on

---

[66] As Ayn Rand points out, "Man gains enormous values from dealing with other men: living in a human society is his proper way of life—but only on certain conditions. Man is not a lone wolf and he is not a social animal. He is a *contractual* animal. He has to plan his life long-range, make his own choices, and deal with other men by voluntary agreement (and he has to be able to rely on their observance of the agreement they entered)." ["A Nation's Unity," *Ayn Rand Letter*, Vol. II, 2, p. 3.]

and belong to a larger whole: at first it is, quite naturally, the family and the clan, which is but an enlarged family; later on, it is the community growing up in its different forms out of the clash and the amalgamation of clans. It is only in the eighteenth century, in "civil society," that the different forms of social union confront the individual as a mere means to his private ends, as an external necessity.

Yet there is nothing terribly odd about the recognition that individuality has been suppressed in many epochs throughout human history. There is no clearly evident advantage to those who oppress others in fostering laws and public policies that encourage and promote the idea of individuality, and to let it gain prominence.[67] Moreover, many ideas come to light antecedent to the facts that are meant by them—as Morris puts it in his title, the individual had been *discovered*, not invented! (This, incidentally, is denied by such prominent thinkers as Alasdair MacIntyre [MacIntyre, 1984] who argues, following Marx, that the individual was indeed "invented" in the modern era. But see also J. D. P. Bolton [Bolton, 1973] for a demonstration of the lingering presence of the idea of individualism from Homer to Christianity.)

The issue of whether human beings are essentially individuals is not itself a historical but a factual question, a very basic ontological one. It seems evident, based on the kind of activity that is most central to human life, namely, volitional rational consciousness as a guide to behavior, that it is impossible to understand the human situation without granting the essential individuality of every human being. In a sense it is odd that modern philosophy admits of the existence of the human individual, since this philosophy is largely in the grip of mechanistic materialism and can make room only for what David Norton calls "quantitative individuality." After all, self-determination in a framework of efficient causal relationships is inconceivable. Kant could make

---

[67] This is evident in our time when there so much evidence of hostility both abroad and at many American universities of hostility toward individualism—relinquishing power to individuals themselves doesn't sit well with those elites who possess it.

room for the autonomous self only by inventing the noumenal reality, a kind of supernatural realm that transcends mechanistic science. Only after a naturalistic pluralism could be philosophically identified, philosophy having been freed of its positivist/empiricist biases, could we find true individuality!

The human essence, then, is more sensibly thought of as the true individuality of every person. The recognition of the bourgeois person constitutes the first time in human history that men and women have not been thought of and treated as first of all members of a tribe or a clan or even a family, but as possessing what is most essentially human, namely, their self-responsibility. Bourgeois men and women belong to no one, they are sovereign, they are capable of using this sovereignty for good or for ill, and they require a political community that pays relentless, sustained attention to this fact.

There is a central reason why Marxism must end in totalitarianism. This, of course, goes contrary to what so many of Marx's admirers and he himself in his more democratically sounding passages maintain. It is that without brutal regimentation, the collectivist idea of human nature cannot be made to fit human community life. This collectivist view is the fundamental flaw of Marxism. It infects the entire system, even where it makes some eminently valuable points—e.g. about the importance of meaningful work!

Failure to acknowledge that each person is by nature a choosing agent, not a limb or part or segment of some larger entity such as humanity or society, is the source of the central failure of Marxism. And it seems that, gradually, in those societies where an attempt has been made to make practical use of the system, it is slowly dawning on many people that Marxism is not the solution to the problems of human life.

Marxism has offered some very valuable criticisms about certain versions of liberalism, namely, the ones that derive from the reductive materialism of Thomas Hobbes and the subsequent individualist, *homo economicus* approaches to political economy. But Marxism advanced a far more flawed system, one with much more serious problems. As I have said in another context, "The choice, then, may be between market exchange, which can involve some 'exploitation,' meaning the opportunity of some to take advantage of the circumstances of others, and totalitarian rule, which *guarantees* that exploitation will occur, as a permanent and unalterable feature of the system."

As with many attempts to address the problems of human beings, Marxism produced its share of valid insights but also managed to create havoc because of its flaws. We can hope not to be similarly plagued with our own efforts.

Communism isn't, as Marx imagined, the best society for human beings. The legal framework that makes capitalism possible, however, is that society. That is because such a society gives the most faithful recognition to the diversity and individuality of members of its human population. And capitalism serves this population best in the capacity of satisfying many of its legitimate, even ultimately honorable objectives, needs, desires and wants. This is why central planning does not work—because in the end it fails to do justice to the individuality of the men and women who comprise a human community, lacking the requisite knowledge of what enables these individuals to thrive.

Appendix: A Dialogue* on Marxism
by Sidney Hook and Tibor Machan

Marx and Marxism

Machan: Marxism is probably most popular—not only among intellectuals but also among ordinary people of the world in Central America, Asia and Africa—why is that so?

Hook: Well, I think that's evidence that Marx's ideas still have relevance to what's going on in the world today, and to the possibilities open to human beings, both as to what he said and as to what people think he said. It seems to me quite clear that, unless one has some understanding of what Marx taught and how people are interpreting his teachings, they couldn't understand the world in which they live; it is as if you were trying to understand the Middle Ages without any knowledge of Christianity.

Machan: Why is someone who wrote 100 years ago, and in very complicated prose, about matters such as revolution, the dialectic and alienation—how can such a person attract the hearts and spirits of poor folk everywhere?

Hook: Because of the way in which he's being expounded by those who call themselves his followers, and because the central appeal that Marx has made to human beings. Not so much because of these...doctrines which appeal to intellectuals but rather the kind of promise of transforming the world close to human desires.

Machan: There's been some suggestion that in Marxism you find a kind of secularized version of certain elements of Christianity. Do you agree with that?

---

* This exchange occurred on October 31, 1986, New York City. The slightly edited transcript is used with the generous permission of the Palmer R. Chitester Fund, Erie, Pennsylvania.

Hook: Well, if the emphasis is on the secularized version, yes; but one should recall that Marx himself was militantly atheistic. Indeed he thought that the critique of religion was the beginning of the critique of all institutions in society. At the same time his vision of history promised a society in which all human desires could be easily gratified so that...in one sense what he was offering was a secular equivalent for heaven on earth. But I think it would be an exaggeration to account for his influence in terms of the literal expectation of that. Yet there is a passion behind Marxism which is a quest for social justice but which, interestingly enough, he himself was not concerned with because he maintained that he wasn't interested in questions of justice, he was interested in describing the inevitable course of history.

Machan: What then is the role of a good deal of morally laden language in Marxism?

Hook: That morally laden language is, despite Marx's own views, the clue to the dynamic of the Marxist movements. Very few people have been influenced by his theory of...value...or the technicalities of historical materialism. But most human beings in the last century look to the reform of society and recognize in Marxism a movement in that direction.

Machan: Isn't it the case that honoring the laboring masses is one of the most attractive parts of Marxism?

Hook: For Marx the source of all value—economic value—is the amount of socially necessary labor time involved in production. Most economists certainly do not accept this analysis, particularly since he thought of labor as a homogeneous quality and tried to reduce skilled labor, intellectual labor to compound physical labor. And that is inherently unacceptable in terms of any economic or philosophical evidence.

Machan: But in a way it seems to accord more with common sense because most of us as ordinary human beings find it unjust that a person who sweats and labors over something gets paid so much less than a person who does something that comes easy and is a matter of joy or game of the mind.

Hook: Yes that's true. But there's a difference between asserting that unless a person makes a contribution to society he's not entitled to a reward, and asserting that the rewards that one gets should be a function merely of the amount of labor that one engages in. It would be like trying to draw an equation between Shakespeare and 1,000 minor poets—or how would you equate the labor of a scientist, whose discoveries might transform the productive potential of a country, with a laborer—the unskilled labor of someone who is engaged in that physical process of production?

Machan: There are so many versions of Marxism afoot in our time. What is the difficulty with understanding Marx?

Hook: That's not unusual—the fact that there are different interpretations of Marx. If someone told you he believed in Christianity, could you predict the specific doctrines that he held? He might believe—be a follower of St Augustine, Thomas Aquinas, or of Tolstoy. Each age in a sense has reinterpreted Christianity and it is not surprising that Marx's ideas have been reinterpreted from time to time. Now that's partly due to the fact that Marx's own ideas developed when he was a young man. In relation to his time, he expressed revolutionary views. When he was an older man and when suffrage had been introduced into Western Europe he relied more upon the parliamentary process. Now since we always interpret the past from the standpoint of the present, people with different points of view are trying to use Marx for their own specific ends. Nonetheless, despite all these variations in the interpretation of Marx, there is a kernel of thought which most people who call themselves Marxists would admit that Marx held.

Machan: Are there some key ideas that should be identified with that kernel?

Hook: Yes, definitely. I think many people are impressed by Marx's realistic grasp of the role of what he called the mode of economic production, the way in which people earn their living in the life and culture of the society.

Now he said that he meant more than the common idea that in order to live one must eat, that the economic facts play a role in life. Obviously without the economic factor there wouldn't be any life; without oxygen there wouldn't be any life.

But the significant thing about Marxism, as I've understood it, is the way in which he traces in detail the influence of this so-called economic factor, the mode of economic production, on the motivations, the aspirations and the institutions of a society.

Dialectical Materialism

Machan: Now some of Marx's ideas were of course not original. But one of them clearly was—the notion of scientific socialism. And yet he wasn't quite like all the other scientists we are familiar with in the Newtonian era; he wasn't like J. S. Mill who also thought himself to be a scientist. What was it about Marx that made him a different kind of scientist?

Hook: Marx thought of himself as a scientific socialist in contradistinction to utopian socialists, although I think a good case can be made that he was one of the most important utopian socialists who ever lived. When he spoke of himself as a scientific socialist he meant that he was concerned with those conditions that were necessary before socialism could be introduced into society. He was distinct from other thinkers who were under the impression that socialism could be introduced anywhere if there were a number of benevolent people willing to make the first move. So that he was more realistic in his approach, he "hugged the ground," as some historians would say, indicating historical limits on what was possible. You couldn't have socialism, according to Marx, in an economy of scarcity.

Now this is very important because in his very early writings, in the 1840s, he maintained that the attempt to introduce a collectivist economy in a country where scarcity was the rule would do nothing but socialize poverty. It would bring back the classes and class struggles and, in his own words, "all the old trap of previous societies." Now if you take that literally it raises a question whether the Bolshevik revolution of 1917 and the Chinese communist revolution were actually carried out in the light of Marxist principles or in defiance of them—though they all invoke the name of Marx.

Machan: Is there any role in this area for the dialectic? Marx is called a *dialectic* materialist by historians. Does the dialectical mean anything here?

Hook: Well, the term dialectic is a term that has many meanings, and has many meanings in Marx too. Derived from Hegel, when people speak of the dialectic in Marx it depends on the context as to how it's to be interpreted. For one thing dialectic represents the principle of struggle, the principle of negation. The flower is fertilized by the bee that robs it of its honey. Now that act of aggression in relation to the flower has produced positive results.

Marx looked at history as a process in which there was action, reaction, struggle, and in one way what he was maintaining is that anything that occurred in history—no matter how terrible it was— was necessary to the outcome, that the pain of the parts, so to speak, was necessary for the good of the whole.

You might even say this is a sort of secular equivalent of religion since he was trying to find a justification for struggle that would disappear when men would live peacefully together without any struggles.

Machan: So, in a way, this notion of dialectics serves to explain development and growth in human society?

Hook: In general. But Marx would maintain that historical explanation had to be more specific—that if you want to understand the development of the economy you had to start with the nature of a commodity and with the processes of manufacture, the accumulation of capital and thus the dialectical process would be illustrated.

By my own reading of Marx he had a tendency to interpret the dialectic method as more or less equivalent with a scientific method as applied to the social process. And if that's true I don't think there's much illumination in exploring the meaning of the dialectic method, if it is synonymous with scientific method. One can ask a question of a Marxist—is there anything that is scientifically true and dialectically false? Is there anything which is scientifically false and dialectically true? And I think Marx himself would answer negatively to both questions.

Machan: But in a way the whole notion that, for example, in capitalism the two classes, the capitalists and the workers, can't get together and resolve their differences is explained by reference to this dialectic.

Hook: No, it's explained by reference to the fact that a social product has to be divided among those who own the instruments of production, and it's quite clear that the more one has the less the other has. And what Marx prided himself on doing is ensuring that the way in which the economy functioned would result in this conflict, that the workers wouldn't be pauperized by the development of the economy, that the rich would become richer and the poor would become poorer. It didn't turn out that way, but the consequence was a consequence of the economic process rather than this general principle of dialectic.

Machan: One of the things that is often remarked though is that Marx differs from his own age in that, unlike many of his contemporaries who adhered to a more classical mechanistic view of science, he introduced a more biologically oriented scientific model which is expressed in terms of the dialectic—this *developmental* approach. The world is not a static machine, it's a dynamic system of growth, and predictions are not as easy in such a dynamic system.

Hook: I think Marx didn't hesitate to make predictions. It is true that he was concerned with the processes of growth; it is also true that he rejected the view that you could apply the mechanistic principles that you find in physics and chemistry to the phenomenon or the phenomena of growth. He believed that there were social laws which were not reducible to laws of physics or chemistry.

So in that sense he repudiated what is called the mechanistic materialism of the eighteenth century. But a biological scientist would maintain that there was nothing distinctive about this approach to growth—that if you take a scientific approach to growth you are bound by what you find in your material, and the laws of evidence (what's true or false) remain the same regardless of whether you're studying physics or chemistry or biology.

Machan: Yet one of the things that one might say to those who say, "Well, look, Marx's predictions are sort of vague and ambiguous and you can't tell when the revolution will come and the predictions are overturned by history or they lack specificity," is that Marx was not the kind of mechanistic scientist who offered you very precise predictions; he's talking more like a botanist would talk about the growth of a forest or the growth of an individual human being. At any rate the contrast is between those people who offer predictions which say in 1985 or 1986 this will happen, and people who look at it more in a biological way, as in the growth of a human being, for example. Adolescence is reached approximately at this point in history.

Hook: Yes, that's quite true. There are more variables involved in history than in biology, in biology than in physics. And even in physics astronomy is a much more accurate science than is geology—it's a matter of degree.

Nonetheless Marx made predictions about the future of the capitalist society in his own lifetime; every ten years he expected the economic system of capitalism to break down. Well, by the time he published his first volume of *Das Kapital in* 1867—he died in 1883—capitalism took off really and developed in a way which Marx never anticipated. Unless we take his predictions within a time frame, he can never be refuted, no matter what would happen. His statements wouldn't have any empirical content, and that certainly would mean that he was anything but a scientific economist or sociologist.

Machan: But let's give Marx a little bit of help here. Suppose that his eagerness in making predictions about the collapse of capitalism was due mostly to his activism, his political self rather than his theoretical self. If we consider that for a moment, isn't it true that quite possibly capitalism over time was going to meet the fate that Marx said it was going to meet?

Hook: Nowhere does he indicate that to be true. Now, more specifically, he maintained that socialism would first come in those countries which had developed the material presuppositions for it, an expanded economy, a high standard of living, indeed even a high degree of culture, and he maintained that it would come either in England or the United States or Western Europe because the presuppositions were there. But now we discover that those who call themselves Marxists seize power in countries which are backward, and mostly agricultural. This, on the basis of his own theory, is impossible.

So that way we can actually say, regardless of the kind of economy which exists in communist China and the Soviet Union today, that those who seize power in these backward countries in contradistinction to what existed in Western societies, built an economy on the basis of that political power; whereas on Marx's own views the political power always reflects the economic organization of society, a prediction which was not fulfilled.

Machan: One answer might be, "Let's not listen to what they *call* themselves: maybe they are indeed, in Marx's own terms, feudal states. The real transformation is going on in Western societies, with the gradual erosion, for example, of the principle of the private ownership of resources." In Western societies that principle is no longer as strongly held as it was 50 or 100 years ago. And if we ignore the Soviet and Chinese claims to being the proper bearers of the Marxist torch and simply look at Marxist theories, it may still be true that eventually the West is going to reach a kind of socialism that Marx had in mind, sooner than the East will.

Hook: Well that may be, but if we look at the actual development of Western societies, we find that the economic predictions that Marx made which were to be the basis of this transformation have not occurred. The proletariat has not become pauperized, but has become more middle-class. Marx overlooked the influence of politics on economics. By virtue of the existence of democratic political society the economy of Western Europe has changed to a point where we have the emergence of the welfare state. Now Marx never predicted the welfare state as we understand it. He maintained that as capitalism developed there would be a greater accumulation of wealth on one pole, and misery on the other, and that the workers under the whiplash of hunger and need would rise and seize power, but it didn't occur that way.

Machan: But in capitalist societies which are mostly democratic, Marx said that people could achieve the transformation from capitalism to socialism through the ballot box. They would not have to have a violent revolution, but they *would* have a revolution. It is then arguable that in the way in which the West is developing there is an erosion of the base that was necessary for capitalism—for example the institution of private property. And there's a great deal more public participation in the decision-making process over property. For example, factories aren't allowed to be closed by the owners—city councils participate in these decisions and that is something Marx might very much welcome.

Returning to the earlier point, despite the fact that so many people know Marxism as dialectical materialism, is there really anything left of this dialectic worth paying attention to any more?

Hook: In my view, whether Marx's views are accepted or rejected, if they are to be properly understood they have to be understood as an empirical scientific attempt to understand society. From that point of view the term dialectic is superfluous, unnecessary.

Marx and Human Nature

Machan: Does Marx have some definite concept of human nature, or is that concept in evolution throughout history?

Hook: I think Marx had a historical conception of human nature. That is to say, in his own time he was aware of the number of people who'll deny that it was possible to have a socialist society on the grounds that it was against human nature. There are some people who thought that man is inherently evil; there are some who thought that man is inherently good.

Marx would have maintained that human nature is both good and evil, that the nature of human nature must be found in every historical situation. In one place he actually says that human beings by acting upon the external world modify it and by modifying it modify their own nature. I'm inclined to agree with Marx's view of human nature, and to deny that you can rule out anything of behavior on the ground that it's against human nature particularly if history gives illustrations of it.

Machan: Isn't it the case though that at some point this development of human nature is supposed to come to an end, and then we will really have a kind of new man?

Hook: That is where the utopian Marx makes an appearance. At some time in the future where society has been transformed, where the state has allegedly withered away, the modes of human conduct will be different from the modes of human conduct today. As we view the future as he described it very inadequately and imperfectly—we would say he's described a world which we do not know, a world which transcends even the angelic world.

Machan: Is it true that that's why the concept of alienation has figured importantly in his earlier writings? He was saying to us basically that we have not yet reached that part of history where human nature has fully realized itself, so we're at odds with ourselves.

Hook: Now this concept of alienation actually finds its expression in Marxist writings before Marx became a Marxist. You must remember that Marx was not born a Marxist, he was first a Hegelian, then a Feuerbachian and then in 1847, in a book called *The German Ideology*, he developed what I think was a distinctly Marxist point of view.

His early manuscripts were published long after the impact of Marxism on Western Europe and the development of the working-class movement of Western Europe. (It is significant that these early manuscripts in which he speaks of alienation had a great appeal to the French existentialists.) I would maintain that what Marx wrote when he was a beardless youth is not so significant for the impact of his ideas, as what he wrote when he was the mature author of *Das Kapital*.

Machan: Would you say that the concept of species-being—this notion of man as being part of all of society and as the conqueror of nature—was there from the beginning or is that a later development?

Hook: No, that is the early Marx when he was not yet a Marx-ist. If Marx believed that human nature was a historical variable then he would not have maintained that there was an essence of human nature or a species that was independent of history, that was incompatible with Marx's historical approach and even with the Hegelian influence in Marx.

Machan: Yet one can still think of it in the following way. One can conceive of human nature even though one only has its infan-tile versions at one's disposal for study. One can also think about, say, an oak tree, but only have the sapling before one to study and project what the sapling will turn into. I think maybe Marx looked at human beings in capitalism and in feudalism and pro-jected what that would lead to in communism.

Hook: If that were true then Marx would have to be an Aristo-telian who believed that final causes or the goals determine eve-rything that preceded them. This would be incompatible with the whole evolutionary outlook of Marxism. You see, when people speak about human nature at most they're talking about man's biological nature. Marx talked about human nature in terms of what we would today call social psychology, and asserted that the modes that moved human beings are functions of the society in which they live.

Marx was not a follower of Bentham; in fact he disagreed with Bentham. Bentham believed that there was a fixed human nature, that human beings always act on behalf of their own interests, and that motivation is selfish. Now Marx would have said, human beings are sometimes selfish and they're sometimes unselfish. He wasn't concerned with individuals, he was concerned with the pattern of modes that you find in existing societies. And he would say for example, if the economy was in a state of scarcity, if there was great need, then more actions would be self-interested than if the economy were one in which there was plenty, in which case more actions would be concerned with the interests of others.

So that in that sense, to use an analogy, if you were trying to explain marriage systems throughout the world, Marx would deny that you could deduce the marriage system from the biology of sexual reproduction. The marriage system depends on a number of social factors. He thought that economics had a great influence even on the marriage system.

Machan: Human nature may for Marx be relative to the material reality that surrounds human beings. But that material reality is in a state of evolution, so there is some kind of a predictable element in how this human nature will develop because nature around human beings develops predictably. There is a dynamic to it and there is a principle of this dynamic. So while there is a contextual element to what human beings are, it is not entirely flexible. It's not always, "Well it may be one way or the other way." Nature around human beings is one time a feudal system, another time it's a slave system, another time it's capitalism, eventually it's socialism. Human nature moves along with it in a somewhat predictable way, doesn't it, for Marx?

Hook: The prediction was based primarily on the expectation of the kind of society in which human beings would live, and one of the reasons why Marx sketched so inadequately his classless society of the future is that he could hardly anticipate what would develop. But let me put it this way: Marx would be prepared to say that human nature is what human beings are accustomed to, and very often when people say that something is against human nature it turns out that it's against what they are accustomed to.

You are right. Marx was a materialist but for him part of the determining material forces was social. You will recall his contention that men's consciousness does not determine their social existence, but their social existence determines their consciousness. Now that's what he believed, yet that was only partly right. Marx's own social existence certainly didn't determine his consciousness. The leaders of the working class came from other segments of society, so that here you have a situation in which Marx has an insight, but, as with so many of his insights, it is a matter of degree. He doesn't tell you to what extent, and the opposite can be just as true as some of Marx's own assertions.

Machan: But something that puzzles me is that, if the social situation that surrounds us does not happen randomly but follows a pattern of development, then human beings too will be what they have to be on the basis of this pattern of development of the societies they live in.

Hook: Well, in a way Marx would consider that a tautology—human beings would be what they have to be but you can't tell what they'll have to be until you know the society in which they're living. I would assert that, in so far as Marx was taking a scientific approach to human behavior and to social behavior, then the interposition of his own ideals would fall out of the range of acceptability.

Machan: Is it possible to say of Marxism that, at least prior to the achievement of communism, there is in every historical approach at least two kinds of people, members of the two classes which are in conflict with each other?

Hook: I think Marx sometimes says that. But it's obvious that in some societies there are more than two classes. And it is obvious that in some societies the classes conflict with each other more than they do with opposite classes.

Machan: What are the major features of these two classes in terms of the kind of people we should expect to be parts of them?

Hook: The major conflict, class conflict, for Marx is derived from the role people play in the instruments of production. And in the *Manifesto,* as you'll recall, he talks about the slave and the slave owner and the serf and the feudal lord and the worker and the capitalist. He regards these oppositions as flowing primarily from the way in which the social product that is created is distributed. Now one might point out that Marx seemed to be unaware, even though he made allowance for the tremendous productivity of science and technology, that there will never be a time when there's more than enough of everything for everybody.

Machan: But he did seem to believe that exactly! When we talk about this Marxist conception of human nature in practical terms, should we understand by this that a person in the fifth century BC was very different and probably couldn't understand us if we were to have a conversation with him?

Hook: I think it is more plausible to assume that a person in the fifth century BC would not be able to understand our modes of behavior in the twentieth century than that a person in the twentieth century would be unable to understand a person in the fifth century BC. We have the benefit of the continuity of tradition. That is to say we live our lives not only in the twentieth century, but as a result of the vicarious experiences we've had and reading the literature or the poetry acquainting ourselves with past traditions. In that sense the present can understand the past more readily than the past the present.

Machan: But there are some outstanding contrary examples. When one reads a dialogue by Plato one finds ideas expressed that one heard yesterday on the radio or television. There seems to be that kind of transcendence of history which in Marxist terms doesn't seem to match up very well.

Hook: I think that's correct. Marx assumes that the ideas of a period were so unique that they could hardly be grasped in subsequent times unless there was this continuity.

Machan: Is there anything steady in human nature despite this constant evolution as Marx sees it? Is there something essential which we are in some crucial sense?

Hook: As I understand Marx he would have to say, if he was consistent, that perhaps man's biological structure was relatively invariable. But, he would go on to add, the way in which the biological structure functions is sometimes determined or influenced by the social environment. Now this creates a problem of definition. At what point, then, would you say that man becomes something different from what he is? In a sense Marx says man is different today from what he is yesterday; certainly he's different as an adult from what he was as a child or as an infant. Well, as far as human beings are concerned one might say there is less change than Marx sometimes anticipates.

Machan: There is this notion current in our own culture of raising our consciousness. It occurs in the Women's Liberation Movement, in the Black Movement and even in the movements of certain national liberation groups—the idea that one's consciousness is raised. Is that somewhat connected with the Marxist notion that human beings evolve in their awareness and their outlook?

Hook: To some extent. But there is a certain difficulty because Marx's emphasis was on what determines the consciousness, and he himself, as you recall, repeatedly asserted that consciousness does not determine social existence, that social existence determines consciousness. Many of his followers also maintained that the mere existence of a trade union movement by itself is not sufficient for the development of the revolutionary consciousness of a new society, that you need somebody to raise the consciousness of the workers to a point where they are willing to organize and take risks and action.

Machan: And how does a person who is raising everyone's consciousness get his consciousness raised?

Hook: Marx said the educators themselves have to be educated, but he never made clear how they were to be educated. That would have to be explained in terms other than the mode of economic production because that would be common to everybody in a society and therefore wouldn't explain the differences in consciousness.

Machan: At one point Marx does say that communists have a special way of looking at things which allows them to extricate themselves from the condition of merely reacting to their social circumstances.

Hook: Yes, and the implication here is that ideas play a greater role than his own theory of history made allowance for. You must recall that Marx used to distinguish very sharply between the proletariat and the lumpenproletariat, and he held the latter responsible for the fact that they didn't live up to certain measures of behavior which he thought followed from their duties as workers. At one point he goes so far as to say that the working class regards its self-respect as more important than its daily bread and that's very hard to reconcile with his theory of historic materialism.

Machan: Does this have some implication for the way in which today so many people in the working class (if there is such a class) tend to be reactionary in their outlook and wouldn't have anything to do with communism, at least as they understand it?

Hook: It would have a definite bearing on the validity of Marx's view of membership in a class, because, as you have just pointed out, the Tory party in England on occasions has been supported by large sections of the working class.

Machan: And the "hard hats" in America during the late 1960s backed Nixon.

Hook: Now what Marx assumed—and here again his assumption can be challenged—is that conditions would become so bad that these workers could recognize that their overwhelming burden of deprivation and poverty could only be transformed by revolutionary action. But it turned out that conditions have improved, that large sections of the working class have aspirations quite common to members of the middle class.

Machan: You've said this before and I'm puzzled because there is a debate among scholars as to whether this alleged improvement is perhaps a misunderstanding. Some say that although there is a rise in the standard of living of the working class Marx would focus more on the widening of the gap between the rich and the poor. The poor are living a little bit better but relative to the rich they are worse off!

Hook: This is the standard reply to those who maintain that Marx's prediction about the pauperization of the working class was refuted by history. They say that the disparity between those who are rich and those who are less rich grows greater. Now I view that as an absurd response for the following reason.

Suppose we were to give every worker a million dollars, and the standard of living would change on the assumption that those had fixed value, then even if it were true that those who are not workers had a hundred million dollars, or a thousand million dollars, certainly you could not maintain that workers still experienced increasing distress, something Marx described specifically and concretely as hunger, as want, as deprivation.

Machan: I understand. But again let's extend a helping hand to Marx. With hindsight we may say that the anxiety, the psychological stress, now experienced by so many people who are better off than people in the eighteenth century used to be, nevertheless parallel the hunger and deprivation.

Class

Machan: Class conflict is one of the most prominent themes in Marx. Marx is a social analyst—a predictor of the future, a describer of the past. To what extent does this class conflict correspond to actual events in history?

Hook: That's an interesting question. Of course everybody is impressed, and justifiably so, with Marx's emphasis on class and class struggle and the way in which ideologies are reflections of the interests of classes. But one must ask certain fundamental questions: What other classes are there in history and is it true that all history, as Marx proclaims in the *Manifesto, is* the 'history of class struggle'?

Now I believe Marx had a great many insights in relation to class, but one cannot accept the generalization without qualification, e.g. the history of science is part of history but it would be absurd to interpret it as a manifestation of class struggle. There are other classes in the society besides economic classes. There are religious classes, racial classes, national classes. What Marx was saying is that economic class consciousness and the conflict of economic classes override all these other conflicts.

Now sometimes that's true, sometimes it's false. The true believer thinks that this notion of class struggle is the same in all societies, throughout all of history. But I would defy anybody to interpret the history of Ireland or the history of Israel merely in terms of economic class conflicts.

Machan: Do you think that this contradicts the empirical tendencies in Marxist analysis, this insistence on looking at things as a part of a class struggle?

Hook: No, I think it's a fruitful approach, but it must be tested in the analysis of specific events. For example, let's take two illustrations from American history. The adoption of the Wagner Labor Relations Act by the American government actually organized the American working class. Now this could be interpreted as a manifestation of the class struggle, but certainly a very *peculiar* manifestation, since the actual initiative for organizing these workers came from the government, which presumably represents, on another of Marx's views, the interests of the ruling economic class. Or take the impact of prohibition on American history. There's no one who can explain the United States in the twentieth century without reference to prohibition, but I would challenge anybody to interpret the prohibition amendment as a result of the class struggle. It was the result of the activity of the Women's Christian Temperance Union. The Union seized the opportunity of the First World War and the fact that the liquor industry was owned by the Germans to introduce the prohibition amendment.

Machan: Does the class struggle approach nevertheless apply to periods of history such as ancient Greece?

Hook: Certainly. The class struggle approach applies to all periods but the question is, Is that sufficient? How do you measure the impact of religious struggles and the impact of economic struggles? Is it plausible to assume that every religious struggle, every national struggle is reducible to conflict in economic interest?

Here again we must beware of accepting the generalization in its totality, or rejecting it. It's a question of more or less, it's a question of measurement, it's a question of empirical analysis.

Machan: Sometimes Marx seems to suggest that people who defend views other than his own—say the significance and importance of capitalism as an ongoing arrangement in society—are merely expressing the vested interest of the ruling classes. This seems to block debate. It gives an approach to discussing Marx's own ideas so that he can dismiss all criticism as a form of rationalization.

Hook: If one were to take that point of view I think it would be self-refuting because someone could then characterize Marx's own views as an expression of the alienated intellectuals who look forward to a society in which the intellectuals would be the ruling class.

I don't believe that Marx relies on this *argumentum ad hominem* decisively. He believed that his position is one that can be verified in terms of evidence.

It is true that his disciples often resort to this *argumentum ad hominem* in order not to confront the evidence in appraising the validity or the invalidity of the doctrine. But scientifically we have to rule out any attribution of motives. It's like answering a man's arguments against vegetarianism by maintaining that he has interests in a meat-packing plant. But the arguments for or against vegetarianism are independent of what causes a person to believe it.

Machan: Yet that elementary fallacy seems to permeate some of the discussions because it seems as though the words "apologist," "reactionary," "ideologue" are part and parcel of the discussion of the merits of Marxism or its opposing systems.

Hook: Anyone who introduces epithets of that kind has ruled himself out of the realm of scholarship. A scholar is concerned primarily with the evidence and not with the alleged motives behind the assertions that people make.

Machan: It is not however still a fair charge against Marx that by reference to his notion of class consciousness and the narrow framework of members of the classes this line of argumentation is certainly suggested by him?

Hook: I think that's true. But, in terms of his own argument, I'm sure he would repudiate the notion that he himself is speaking only for a certain vested interest or a certain group. I think he presents his point of view as one which he thinks would have a universal appeal to anybody who's prepared to look at the evidence. And I'm prepared to examine the evidence. And I find there's a great deal of Marx which is sound and a great deal which is unsound. To use a phrase that comes from Engels, the proof of the pudding is in the eating, and that means actually that the evidence must decide.

Machan: Let me go back to this notion of class conflict. One of the greatest cataclysmic events in the last few centuries was the American Revolution. It certainly changed the face of geopolitical arrangements in the world. Yet it doesn't seem class conflict had any role in it whatsoever. Is that correct?

Hook: Well, no. I think as far as the American Revolution is concerned there certainly was a class conflict between the merchants in England and the merchants in the United States. That is to say it wasn't so much a conflict between the workers and the employers.

Now Marx certainly recognized that there are conflicts *within* the classes. There's a conflict between those who want to sell tomato juice to the American public and those who want to sell orange juice, but over and above that conflict Marx was saying is the much more fundamental conflict between those who own the instruments of production and those who work for them.

Machan: That's one of the reasons I mentioned the American Revolution because it's such an important event. Presumably if such an important event can't be fully analyzed in terms of economic class conflict then there is a flaw in that analysis.

Hook: Well, to do justice to Marx I think we have to extend his notion of economics to include the conflict of interests among the various sections of the ruling class.

Machan: What about the current conflicts that permeate the geopolitical atmosphere between, say, the Palestinians and the Israelis and the Irish and the English and various hostilities inside the borders of India, the Russians and Afghanistan? Is this all analyzable in class conflict terms?

Hook: I wouldn't deny that economic class conflict and the conflicts of economic interest certainly enter into those antagonisms and operations. But I certainly would deny that any attempt to interpret Irish history or Israeli history exclusively or predominantly in those terms would be satisfactory. Here, as elsewhere, Marx overlooked the importance of other factors.

I think there are two things that account for what has sometimes been called the relative failure of Marxism in the West: the development of nationalism. In the *Manifesto* Marx actually maintains that the workers of the world have no homeland. But this has been systematically disproved by the occurrence of the First and Second World Wars.

After all, in the First the war was fought by the working classes of the various nations and they were very enthusiastic, which indicates again that we must qualify Marx's generalizations. All history is not the history of class struggle. Sometimes it's the history of class collaboration, sometimes it's the history of class cooperation, e.g. when a community is threatened by disaster.

I think one must approach this whole problem of class analysis case by case, and ask oneself how does one measure the relative strength of economic class consciousness over national class consciousness or religious class consciousness. I would maintain that on some crucial occasions economic class consciousness would be overriding, but on other occasions that's not true.

Machan: So in a way this usefulness of economic class analysis both for purposes of understanding a past and for purposes of anticipating the future is somewhat limited in your view?

Hook: It is limited but I think Marx made a major contribution in calling attention to the importance of these class conflicts because until his time, with the exception of some French historians, people had interpreted history merely in political terms. But it was Marx who maintained that actually if you examine the struggles of political power you will very often find that economic interests are at stake, that property itself—property in things—is a form of power over human beings. What kind of things? Property in the social instruments of production.

Marx has no objection to personal property, property in one's clothing, home, utensils, etc. He was interested however in the social instruments of production and he tried to show that that had been neglected until his time, that property in this area entailed a very real power over the lives of human beings. The analysis is quite simple after all.

How do we know that we have property in anything? Not in terms of the right to use it—if you can't use it society would enforce it. You know it only in terms of your right to deny access to others. Now then, if you own land, since human beings have to use land in order to live, the power to exclude from such land as they need gives you power over their lives. And Marx seemed to recognize that that was true even if this land was owned by the community. There would still be power over the people who could be excluded from it. But he was hostile to the private ownership of the social instruments of production because he thought that the exercise of that power wasn't being responsibly carried out.

Machan: Marx writes a great deal about exploitation—it is probably one of his ideas that has consciously or unconsciously been accepted within the wider community. People who are not Marxists talk about the exploitation of the working classes, of those in the Third World and the like. Exploitation is a class phenomenon, isn't it?

Hook: Yes, going into his analysis, in every class society the very fact that one group owns the instruments of production and the other has to work them entails a conflict over the distribution of the social product.

Machan: Do class conflict and exploitation go hand-in-hand or does this occur only in capitalism?

Hook: I think he would insist that exploitation took place obviously under slavery and under feudalism, and he prided himself on claiming that he had solved the mystery of how profit is achieved in a free enterprise society.

Machan: Private profit I take it—because there's a surplus even in socialism and communism according to Marx.

Hook: That's true, that's true. And indeed his emphasis on exploitation in a capitalist society followed from his theory of value. Now most economists have rejected his theory of value because of internal difficulties. The actual rate of exploitation in an industry which is carried on by intensive labor would, on his analysis, lead to more profit than the profit that you get in an industry which is carried on mostly by constant capital or its own machinery. But it turns out that the rate of profit is independent of the amount of labor or labor power involved.

Now that's a contradiction that occurred in the first volume, and Marx published that in 1867. For 19 years he didn't publish any other books and Engels tried to solve this contradiction when he published volumes 2 and 3, but most economists have rejected his theory of value. There's also no clue to the variations of the business cycle in it.

So I think that in the last analysis Marx uses the term exploitation to indicate that distribution of the social product is not done equitably or democratically.

Machan: It is then a morally laden term in this sense?

Hook: I regard it as such although Marx himself claimed that it was not a moral term; it was merely a descriptive term.

Machan: Isn't exploitation basically the phenomenon of the capitalist hiring the worker, the worker actually producing the product from which the capitalist gains an enormous benefit but pays to the worker only a very small portion of it, and the rest of it is free of charge—a benefit to the capitalist?

Hook: Marx regards that obviously as wrong. But at the same time in *Das Kapital* he maintains that there's nothing immoral or illegal about it all.

Machan: That's exactly right. He says, roughly, "I paint a capitalist by no means *couleur de rose* but you should not misunderstand me. I am a natural historian." Yet does not exploitation become one of the immediate causes of a revolution—eventually, through the business cycle, through dislocation in the labor market—by people losing their jobs and then regrouping and finding new jobs, and this happening over and over again, so eventually they get so disenchanted with the process that they abolish the system under which this occurs?

Hook: Yes, but let's be more specific. It's not by virtue of the exploitation that revolution occurs, because even when there's prosperity, according to Marx, the worker is being exploited. So long as there is prosperity, so long as capitalism is a going concern, there will be no revolution. But Marx predicted that capitalism would break down and that the misery of the workers would be so intense that they would rise up, socialize the instruments of production in order to get the processes of production going again.

Machan: So it's not just a dislocation in the labor market that precipitates a revolution, it's the actual *immiseration* of the working class.

Hook: Yes. But, to do justice to Marx, he maintained that the reason why there was this accumulated misery in the capitalist system was that the worker was not receiving everything that he had produced. Marx refers to the "inherent contradictions" of the capitalist system that result in this breakdown and this increasing misery.

But empirically the capitalist system has been modified in consequence of the democratic process (which Marx welcomed). But he didn't anticipate that the reciprocal influence of politics on economics would result in a more equitable distribution of the social product.

Machan: Do you think that Marx anticipated the kind of distribution of property that occurs through something like the stock market, pension plans, investments and retirement programs such that now some of the people who are the workers in his terms own large sums of property through this mechanism?

Hook: I doubt whether he anticipated that. But I think he would argue that the actual power decisions in the situation are not made by people who own stocks or whose pension funds are invested in the stocks.

Machan: Do you think that's correct?

Hook: Well, I actually think that the managerial function is exercised with relative independence of the decisions of the stockholders. They tend to judge the wisdom of their investment merely by their return.

Machan: Why doesn't the labor force, the workers who own these stocks, revolt because of that?

Hook: Because it is not accompanied by deprivation. So long as their stocks return a high investment and so long as their mode of living is improved as a result of the applications of science and technology through the economy, they haven't got the impulse.

Machan: Then the managers are doing what the workers want them to do?

Hook: One could argue that under the democratic process that's true, and that if the workers were dissatisfied they would organize their own political parties and, as they have in some countries of Western Europe, via the social democratic or labor parties, control industry. But the interesting thing is that, even when they have done that, they have discovered that the same economic problems exist independently of who owns the instruments of production, whether it is the state or whether the individuals.

Machan: I'd like to look into this transitional period, what one ordinarily refers to as the socialist phase of humanity's development. What would that be like if Marx's theories were actually to hold water—if they were valid? In other words, there's what's called the socialist phase of the development called communism. If it were a valid theory, what would that be characterized by, what would that look like?

Hook: Well, Marx actually assumed that, in this so-called transition stage which he called socialism, the worker would still be paid the same wages, it would be a gradual process. But because of historical developments I must point out that when Marx uses the phrase "the dictatorship of the proletariat," he's really referring to the economic contents in direction of the decisions made during that period. Nowhere, but nowhere, does he identify the dictatorship of the proletariat with the dictatorship of a minority party over the proletariat and over all the other classes as well.

Machan: Doesn't that kind of elite dictatorship still follow from his belief that at the time that capitalism collapses the working classes will still not have the vision that is necessary for them to take up the challenge of leading toward communism?

Hook: No. He thinks the working class will have the vision, he has a certain belief in the spontaneity of the workers' revolt and resistance. The vision is supplied by people like himself—actually people who as the *Manifesto* points out are members of the dominant classes or the middle classes.

But he does not speak of a dictatorship! He refers to the Paris Commune as an illustration of the dictatorship of the proletariat. It's very interesting that in the Paris Commune his political group was not represented in the leadership. And, secondly, one could point out that there is more socialism in England and the United States today than existed in the Paris Commune.

Machan: Wasn't he however disappointed in the ability of the

Paris Commune to sustain itself, to sustain the vision and the revolutionary leadership? Didn't he then become a bit despondent about this and so some of the disciples later on thought that maybe we cannot trust the working class alone to carry on with the revolution?

Hook: Well, those who came to the conclusion they couldn't trust the working class would be repudiating a central contention of Marx, who asserted that the liberation of the working class can only be achieved by the liberating class itself and not by any political party which calls itself the vanguard. It is true that Marx was not in favor of establishing the Paris Commune; he thought it wouldn't succeed.

Machan: Do you think there is anything then to the claim that Marxism—in some ways, if not completely, at least significantly—provided the intellectual foundation for the subsequent Leninist versions now in circulation?

Hook: No, but on the other hand I doubt whether he would have accepted Engels's view that if any great man had not appeared in history someone else would have appeared to do his work. This seems to me to be really an absurd view, incompatible with all of the evidence we have of the role of men like Caesar and Napoleon and Lenin himself.

Machan: Let me just turn back a little bit more to revolution. Just because we don't see a cataclysmic development toward socialism and eventually communism, isn't it at least arguable that some of the legal trends of the past few decades, whereby the ideal of private property is hardly in force any longer even in the United States—where almost every use of private property must go through an extensive "democratic" process of permission granting by commissions deciding over it and so on—the kind of revolution from capitalism to at least socialism that Marx was talking about nevertheless has occurred in a small, perhaps not so perceptible, way as we might anticipate?

Hook: Well, it's a matter of degree but you're assuming that there was time when you had really a free enterprise economy in a pure form. I don't believe there ever was such a time. The rights of property were always subject to some kind of control. And, with the development of society and more complex developments, more and more controls came.

But certainly despite the existence of all of these controls there's a difference between the kind of society that you find in Western Europe and the United States and the kind of society that you will find in the Soviet Union and communist China.

Machan: Are you saying that, at least in terms of its laws, the Soviet Union and communist China more closely resemble the socialist period that Marx was talking about—not in terms of its abundance but in terms of the legal mechanism?

Hook: Yes, in terms of the legal mechanism. And, as a result of what occurs in those countries, social democratic parties of Western Europe have modified their economic program and no longer look to nationalization or socialization of industry as a cure-all for economic difficulties. More and more you're reaching a situation where the choice is not between capitalism or socialism, but more or less of either, depending on the fruits of the consequence.

Liberty

Machan: There's this persistent puzzle in discussions of Marxism versus the philosophical (or the ideological or political) traditions in the West concerning the notion of liberty. Marxists are for the liberation of the workers, they are for the liberation of the downtrodden. But of course the American Revolution and the American political system proudly announce their alliance to liberty and freedom. And yet these two outlooks seem to be at diametrically opposite ends in matters of policy. Perhaps we need to discuss what they mean by freedom. They surely don't mean the same thing—or do they?

Hook: Well, I think Marx certainly heralded the freedoms of the American Revolution and the French Revolution as a basis for other freedoms. That is to say, he certainly would accept the justification of government based on consent. And now if you take political freedom—being defined that way—he would argue that all social institutions that affected human beings should be determined by the consent of those who were affected. What he was trying to do, as I understand it, was to extend this area of democratic self-determination to other institutions of society, especially economic institutions. Just as he was opposed to political monopoly he was opposed to excess of economic power as undermining the operation of a political freedom.

Machan: But the kind of freedom that Marx is talking about here is not the freedom of free enterprise where individuals are autonomous or sovereign in the decisions as to how they will contribute to the productive process.

Hook: I don't think that in any system individuals can be autonomous in determining what they're going to produce or when or how. In the heyday of free enterprise there were all sorts of restrictions on the freedom of enterprise; there are certain things that you cannot produce.

Machan: We know that some of these views depart from reality. Yet at least the ideal of a free market capitalist system is one in which the primary ingredient is that other people—including other groups, one's neighbors, one's political community—do not determine what one does with one's labor and one's belongings. Whereas in Marx one's labor and one's belongings become socialized. They become part of the entire community and so any sort of independent judgment concerning the allocations of these flies out of the window.

Hook: Well, Marx would assert that even in the free enterprise system, as you've described it, its operation often interferes with the freedom of others. In the emergence of monopolies certainly the freedom of people to compete is affected. He would argue against the notion that freedom is absolute.

I would point to the fact that in all situations there are conflicts of freedoms and you have to resolve these conflicts of freedoms. Then he would maintain that you resolve them in such a way as to preserve the maximum structure of freedoms. No particular freedom could be absolute, even in our own system.

Machan: Well, when I interpret Marx I think his conception of freedom is more in the tradition where you are free to grow to your full potential. And that means that you must be provided with the necessities for this growth. Whereas in the system that seems to be opposed to Marx—say the Lockean system—the provision of your growth is supposed to be achieved by yourself via your interaction with nature and your consenting fellow human beings. No such provision is supposed to be established politically. That boils down to the negative conception of freedom of the American political tradition, as distinct from the positive conception of freedom of Hegel, Marx, T .H. Green and some others.

Hook: Well, I think Marx's view actually transcends that opposition between negative and positive freedom. Marx certainly would not have accepted the Lockean rule that any freedom is absolute, that there could be absolute right to property, regardless of its consequences.

Machan: But I don't think that is the issue here. The issue is not absolute versus relative, it's the emphasis.

The Lockean notion of freedom I think emphasizes one person's freedom *from* the intrusion of another person; the Marxist notion of freedom I think emphasizes one person's freedom *to* pursue ends for which it may be necessary to supply various means that are produced or thought of by other people. For example, if I am unhealthy I am not free to do what I want to do, and in order to make me free doctors have to provide me with medical care. This is a limitation on the Lockean freedom in order to secure for me the Marxist freedom.

Hook: Yes, that would be a correct interpretation of Marx and Marx would justify it on the ground that freedom of this kind can only be achieved by the preservation of political freedom and a political democracy and the structures that you build on that.

Machan: You see, this is the difficulty: if you socialize property—if you socialize the most fundamental means of production, which is labor—democracy then cannot be upheld. Democracy requires that the voter is independent of the larger arena of political operations so he can withdraw from it, so he's not always beholden to it. How can he retain this independence of thought, which is a prerequisite of the democratic process, when he's in fact part of the whole and he doesn't have any material independence?

Hook: Marx's view I think would stress the fact that in such a situation whenever you have a conflict of values, and you have to make a choice, you cannot regard any one value as always absolute. In terms of our own constitutional system, certainly it couldn't function without freedom of speech, and we know that freedom of speech doesn't mean the right to incite a lynch mob to take a person's life. Our system depends on freedom of the press but sometimes the freedom of the press will interfere with a man's right to a fair trial.

Now in these conflicts of freedom there has to be a collective decision in a democracy, and what Marx is saying is, when there are these conflicts of freedom through the democratic process, we make a decision that we can control which freedom we pursue and to what extent. Otherwise you will have a view which I don't think is tenable; you can't believe in absolute freedom if there's more than one freedom.

Machan: The trouble with that is that the decision-making process then becomes arbitrary.

Hook: No, why is it arbitrary? The decision-making process depends on exploring the consequence of furthering one right as contrasted with another.

Machan: Then we're utilitarians talking not about some right to freedom or self-expression or property. We're talking about maximizing wealth and maximizing satisfaction.

Hook: No, maximizing freedoms! Maximizing freedoms even when they're in conflict. Now this is my own interpretation of Marx's influence. I would say on this view intelligence is about the nearest approach we get to an absolute right. And we make a choice when freedoms conflict as to which freedom we give priority. Sometimes we give priority to one rather than to another.

Machan: On what basis?

Hook: Again on the basis of an assessment of the consequences of one mode of action over another. For example in Great Britain greater emphasis is placed on the right of a man to a fair trial than the right of the free press if that conflicts.

Machan: Are they right or wrong or are we right?

Hook: Again, that would depend on the situation. I agree with the English system in that a man's right to a fair trial should have priority, but I can conceive of situations in which that wouldn't be the case. You can't legislate in advance all decisions you make when there are conflicts of freedoms. All that you know is that you're committed to maximizing these freedoms, just as our constitution tries to do.

Machan: But on that basis the suppression of the voices of dissidents in the Soviet Union can be justified.

Hook: No, you have no democracy there. Put it this way, Marx does not believe that the majority could be unenlightened and he has always been criticizing unenlightened majorities. But I think he would say that the appeal for an unenlightened majority had to be made to an enlightened majority and not to an enlightened minority, certainly not the party holders or bureaucrats or what not.

In that sense, you see, Marx really was a democrat and in the *Manifesto* he says the first thing that the communists would do if they come to power is introduce democracy. Now to be sure one must remember to take Marx's writings in their times. When he wrote *The Communist Manifesto* the working class of Western Europe did not have suffrage. They weren't in a position to remedy abuses through the democratic political process. Toward the end of his life where the extension of the democratic process had made suffrage universal, he then anticipated that a better society could be introduced through parliamentary means.

Machan: But you yourself maintained earlier that one of the failures of Marxist thinking may have been that he did not anticipate the political consequences of his revolutionary doctrine, and what I'm pointing out is that one of the political consequences of economic socialism and communism is that the independence of the democratic process has been obliterated.

Hook: I would agree with you that Marx did not stress sufficiently the relative independence of the democratic process, and he failed to anticipate the consequences of the democratic political process on the economic system. After all even taxation represents a political process by which you redistribute wealth. And he failed to take note of the modifications in the economic system that were produced in consequence of the extension of democratic rule.

Machan: Now we come to What is communism? What are those renaissance men and women? Where do they come from? How did Marx imagine that people could do away with the ordinary toils and chores of their ordinary lives as we know them, and catapult themselves into a state of simple luxurious living—thinking and creative artistic activity—and live a very productive, not profit-seeking, life?

Hook: I think Marx assumed that science would open the doors to infinite plenitude. And in a way he was right. If we recall that the vision of space travel was formulated in the middle of the last century, his anticipation of the applications of science and technology to society seemed quite on the mark.

Machan: Washing machines, gadgets—things like that that eliminate chores?

Hook: Two things one must bear in mind. First, he overlooked the possibility that science could develop to a point that would destroy the world; secondly, he overlooked the fact I mentioned earlier, that there are certain problems of distribution that would remain in any society.

The utopian aspect of Marxist thought arises from his view that actually the state and all authority—instruments of coercion—would disappear when we had a plenitude of material things. In one sense he had the same point of view as James Madison. Number 10 of the *Federalist Papers* restates in some form Marx's economic theory of history. Madison somewhere says if men were angels they would have no need of government! Now, if government includes the state, Marx assumed that if there were enough material opportunities and resources in the world they would have no need of government. I think that's a profound error.

Machan: You don't think then that there will ever be enough so that there will be no need for competition, that conflicts will get eliminated and there will be a commune—a large commune where everyone would have what he or she wants?

Hook: No, there wouldn't be enough. And there would be other kinds of conflicts—you forgot the story of Lucifer. After all Madison was wrong when he said if men were angels they would have no need of government. Heaven is very well organized and there is a definite order in the dominions and powers...

Machan: Some people say that there would be an administrative kind of government still under communism.

Hook: But what would happen if the administration wasn't obeyed? It presupposes then that human beings have been transformed. But it's rather unlikely that they'll be so transformed. You might say, after all, you need a traffic system even in a communist society!

Machan: It would be an honor system.

Hook: Yes, but suppose that someone didn't obey the traffic signals!

Machan: But, you see, this is why I think it's vital that Marx has an integrated point of view, internally consistent. You see then that the "new man" is a necessary ingredient of the vision of the new society.

Hook: The new man is carried beyond our ordinary conceptions at the present time! Even angels compete with angels, disputing with each other, envious of each other. So even angels are under some kind of an order.

Machan: Take the division of labor. It is a prerequisite of the development of specialized skills. But if we take Marx to be saying that such development would no longer be necessary in communism because we can live an enriched life—not only a life of production and chores and labor and hustle—then maybe it's perfectly OK to abolish the division of labor on behalf of this more enriched, less economically oriented life.

Hook: You must remember that Marx maintained that in his ideal society of the future work would become a prime necessity for man. And by work here he didn't mean labor that is a chore, but work which represented a kind of fulfillment of man's creative impulse!

Machan: Like musical composition?

Hook: Musical composition or hunting to some extent!

Machan: There is an aristocratic view of work.

Hook: Yes, the Greek view of all-round development. Now I don't think that can be taken literally but there is a positive insight here. I myself can't conceive of a society in which people will find fulfillment on the assembly line. But it is conceivable that somebody may find fulfillment not in creative work but in the work of consumption. I would fault Marx in assuming that everybody had this desire to do creative work and a capacity to do it, that in a sense everybody was a potential Leonardo.

Machan: But that *was* his whole idea of the new man!

Hook: That would be so, but it isn't necessary to take that literally. Looking at our society today I think you can use Marx's vision in trying to organize it in such a way that more and more human beings would be living their life as they earn their living. Today for most people, earning their living is not part of living their life. Living their life begins for them after hours so to speak, or in enjoyment when they get away from the burden of daily labor. I think what Marx was doing was projecting the ideal of a creative intellectual and generalizing it for everybody in the society.

Now it is true that the writer, the artist, the teacher finds fulfillment in his creative task. With that anybody could find fulfillment in his task; I'm prepared to admit that, unless a human being has a center around which to organize his own experiences, he's not fulfilled, he doesn't find himself at the top of his energy. But in being prepared to recognize a world without striving to improve it, in which people voluntarily select their own centers round which to organize their experience, one doesn't have to conceive of a life of creation alone; it might also be a life of appreciation. Even theoretically I can find it possible that a man would find fulfillment even in being a taxi-driver.

Machan: That is more of a Platonic view than a Marxist view. In Plato's ideal order everybody does find his "self" in a specialization, whereas in Marx's ideal order everyone must be a general worker. That, I think, comes from his materialism. That's why he stresses labor so much; however elevated that labor is it has something to do with man's material nature.

Hook: No, I think one could maintain that it's really derivative from the Judeo-Christian tradition, in which creation is the mark of divinity. In the Greek tradition creation is a mark of lack of perfection; the gods don't create because that would indicate they had some kind of a lack.

So what man shares with divinity is a power to create. But I would like to keep the freedom to determine one's own mode of life as much as possible, and I could admire the creative genius of Leonardo without feeling obliged to imitate it or to institutionalize that in society. I want to pluralize the different modes of life.

Machan: What do you think about this image for communism as Marx would have liked to have seen it?—I model it on the jam session of a jazz band, when nobody's paying for them to play a certain kind of music but they're just blowing their own stuff. Nobody wants them to do it; *they* want to do it. They're working very hard and they're sweating and they're very involved in it, and yet it is their true fulfillment. Hard work is really satisfying work.

Hook: But not mine—that's my conception of hell.

Machan: Well, but I'm saying: as Marx saw it, Marx wanted these people to be dedicated to their work and not worry about incentives. For example, he would not be a good supply-side economist.

Hook: Yes, that's true and that's for every great artist who feels his own compulsion to create—there is no problem of incentive.

Socialism as practiced in Western Europe and elsewhere has broken down, I think, because it didn't solve the problem of incentives. And Marx, like so many other intellectuals, took the problem of incentives for granted since there was always an incentive for him to do the work for which he felt he must find commitment.

Machan: You think that this is what accounts for Marxist utopianism, despite his self-proclaimed adherence to science?

Hook: There's one aspect of his utopianism here. The other aspect of it is belief that the state would wither away and that there will at some time be no need for authority and coercion in human life. Now possibly that could come into existence but since it's not true for the angelic community it's beyond the compass of my understanding.

Machan: Do you think this phenomenon of Solidarity, in Poland—where part of the working people is pitted against the government—is a big embarrassment for the claim that in socialism the government represents the interests of the workers?

Hook: Well, obviously in Poland it doesn't, and the best test of whether a government represents the interests of the workers is to let the workers decide who is going to represent them. But in a country like Poland there isn't an opportunity for the workers to decide who will be their governors. That's why, as I interpret Marx, the democracy he was going to introduce when they came to power was a political democracy on the basis of which all the forms of democracy are erected. And I would maintain that, although political democracy by itself may be incomplete, because it doesn't extend to other areas the principle of consent—to operate democratically without political democracy is impossible.

Machan: Do you believe that for Marx democracy was more important than the utopia of communism? Or were they inseparable? It seems that they are separate notions. You seem to emphasize the democratic in Marx. Most of us, including those who are self-proclaimed Marxists—say people in the Soviet Union, Soviet Marxists—emphasize the drive toward communism.

Hook: It seems to me an obvious abuse of language to characterize the system that exists in the Soviet Union as a democracy.

Machan: No, no, I am not talking about that. I'm talking about what they pulled out from Marx. You have been stressing the democratic element of Marxist thought—his loyalty to democracy which you think overrides some other aspects of his thought. There are those who stress the end goal, the final communist state, as the major element of Marxism—something to which they are probably even willing to sacrifice the democratic element. What are the reasons for thinking that your position is more correct than those who stress this communist goal?

Hook: One of the reasons is that it makes sense of Marx's lifetime activity in trying to extend the area of working-class consciousness and power.

One of the reasons that Marx scorned the utopians was their attempt to describe in detail what the future would be, and he shied away from that. And in a sense those who keep their eyes focused on the future, which can only be described in very general terms, offer a religious solution to human difficulties. Marx was very much a creature of his time. In every class struggle that was going on, Marx was trying to improve the lot of the workers. And in very significant passages in *Das Kapital* he talks about the future—he says, the first step toward it was the introduction of the ten-hour day. He was very reluctant to attempt to describe in detail this ultimate goal.

Machan: Wasn't that because he thought that the new man who would be populating this new society will have thoughts, aspirations, goals, concepts and images which we cannot even comprehend as yet?

Hook: Well, he did make some attempt to describe what the new man would do. That passage where he says he was going to be hunting in the morning and write musical criticism in the afternoon seemed to suggest a kind of society which treats achievement as primary. And I think there's a great deal of insight in that but he carries it too far—as I said earlier, he does recognize the importance of a core in human life. But from my point of view he defined working too narrowly as the life of the intellectual and the creative intellectual. Somewhere he says in his future society there won't be a painter, there'll be men who paint. There is always the emphasis on the whole man doing almost everything.

I think that's a worthy idea for some but it is an unreasonable expectation for all human beings. A man can find fulfillment in becoming an expert on who the best athletes are and enjoy that! And for me I'm not prepared to impose a hierarchy here, so long as the various alternatives are freely chosen.

Machan: But as far as Marx is concerned—he may have been wrong—I think it's safe to say that he had to look at the new man in this light because his idea of man as a conscious producer didn't leave him any other alternative for a fully developed conception of human nature. Human beings, when they're truly fully developed, will have achieved this conscious productive aspect of them as the central part of their lives.

Hook: My point is, a man can be a conscious producer, but it doesn't necessarily follow that that's the center of his experience. I mean some people, yes, but it doesn't have to be true for others—where will you get your audience from?

Machan: We'll just love to do it for its own sake. Virtue for itself—the labor for its own sake, not for any rewards, not for applause, not for adulation, just for the sake of doing it. The reward of doing it is the doing it itself.

Hook: And if that's true for the man who does, it should be true for the man who also appreciates, for the man who applauds.

Machan: But we can appreciate *and* do.

Hook: One can, if you can do it all—very well, but suppose you can't? What I'm resisting is the imposition of one form of life as the highest or the best for all human beings.

Machan: But then you're resisting Marx!

Hook: It may be. I don't think he had a monopoly of the truth and I think he would have modified some of his views in the light of historical experience.

Machan: "I am not a Marxist," said Marx. Who are the Marxists?

Hook: He said that in reference to some alleged French followers who probably were more influenced by Lafarge or one of his sons-in-law. He would probably refer to sectarians who used his formulations mechanically to solve problems, and who emphasized the orthodoxy rather than specific concrete organizations' work among the workers. He was rather critical of an American group that regarded itself as Marxist for not engaging in organizational work. Any movement towards dissociation of a pure sect in contradistinction to the broad movement of the working masses is sure to lead to shipwreck rather than to social progress.

Machan: Is it true that perhaps even Engels contributed some-what to this distortion of Marxism.? Did he move away from the empirical stress of a Marxist way of thinking?

Hook: In some respects. I must point out there are some peo-ple who call themselves Marxists who do not distinguish be-tween Marx and Engels.

Machan: Is Engels perhaps one of those who already, in Marx's own lifetime, began to distort Marxism?

Hook: In my view Engels presented an ontology and cosmol-ogy of the world on the basis of Marxist principles, for which I can find no justification in Marx's own writings—particularly for Engels's theory of knowledge according to which a true idea is an image of events or things. He subscribed to a very crude corre-spondence theory of truth which had already been rejected by Hegel, whereas Marx stressed the dynamic aspects of ideas.

So that, as I read Engels, he introduced notions into Marxism that had a great influence on latter-day Marxists which are not justified in the corpus of Marx's own writings. On the other hand it is true that Marx never repudiated what Engels wrote, and ac-tually wrote a chapter in one of Engels's works. But since Marx was dependent on Engels in every way and couldn't survive without him, I doubt whether even if he disagreed with Engels he would have made him the subject of his withering contempt in the way in which he treated others who disagreed with him.

Machan: Moving on to Lenin, he is the most significant self-proclaimed Marxist in our century.

Hook: Yes, I regard Lenin as the chief revisionist of Marx, be-cause it was Lenin who, seizing on the few occasions when Marx used the word dictatorship of the proletariat, went on to identify the dictatorship with the proletariat, or the dictatorship of the mi-nority communist party, and in that way betrayed the whole de-mocratic tradition of the Marxist movement.

Machan: Do you think that he nevertheless understood Marx-ism as it applied to foreign affairs, to imperialism, for example?

Hook: It is an open question whether Engels developed a the-ory of imperialism which later was touted by Lenin. But I should say in justice to Engels that at no time did he identify the dictatorship of the proletariat with the dictatorship of a political party, and in fact, before he died, Engels asserted that a dictatorship of the proletariat could be exercised through the form of a parliamentary democracy.

Machan: I may have mis-stated myself. I was interested in this point of how Marxism got to be such an important methodological device for understanding the relationship of capitalist societies to other societies throughout the world. The notion of imperialism was of central concern to Lenin.

Hook: There are other Marxist thinkers who had views of a similar character: Rosa Luxembourg, for example. And there is implicit in Marx's economic doctrines a view that capitalism sustained its life by expanding the area of its operation to other segments of the world.

So it's an open question to what extent Lenin's theory of imperialism can be derived from Marx's views. Of course, Lenin also adopted views that were held by J. A. Hobson who, I do not believe, can be considered a Marxist, who likewise developed the twentieth century notion of imperialism.

Machan: Just as a slight detour, isn't it the case that Marx thought of colonialism as a good thing rather than as some sort of a defect or a liability?

Hook: In Marx's view of history, colonialism would have to be regarded as part of the inevitable extension of the productive process, and therefore could hardly be condemned. Indeed, writing about India in a passage which I don't think has been made available in the Soviet Union, Marx maintained that the English were responsible for the first social revolution in India in 1,500 years. Although he did not approve of the way in which they extended their rule, he regarded their rule as certainly much more progressive than the rule of the local despots whom the English replaced.

Machan: Marx even went so far as to say that some segments of humanity were a regressive strain, like Negroes and Slavs.

Hook: I don't know whether Marx said that, but I think Engels somewhere said that ...

Machan: Well, there is correspondence in which they discussed this in connection with the writings of the French biologist, Pierre Tremaux, of whom Marx heartily approved.

Hook: Yes, there is no doubt that Marx had views which present-day Marxists would be embarrassed to defend. He also was not free from certain anti-Semitic prejudices, particularly in his references to Lassalle and in the essay "On the Jewish Question," which could have been used, at least parts of it, by the Nazis.

Machan: What about Stalin? The big question is: does Stalin owe any debts to Marx or is he a total fraud?

Hook: I myself think that Stalin was Lenin's heir, not as intelligent as Lenin. I don't think that what took place in the Soviet Union would have taken place to the same degree if Lenin had lived on. But the system which Lenin established in the Soviet Union is what made Stalin possible. Even though Stalin's days are gone, the system which made him possible still exists. And here we must take into account factors which Marx ignored, like the role of personality. As I said earlier, Marx's theory of history cannot account for the heroic role of Lenin in the birth of the Soviet state, in the October Revolution. Trotsky, in his story of the Russian Revolution, raises the question whether that revolution would have taken place if Lenin had not been on the scene, and he seems to suggest that it might not. Perhaps he could have led it, but before he died he admitted that the October Revolution in Russia could not have occurred without Lenin.

Now that's an admission which runs counter to the basic thesis of historical materialism. The twentieth century would have been profoundly different if there hadn't been an October Revolution. I do not believe that anybody who has studied the evidence could claim that it was inevitable. Lenin himself said that it was a fluke, that the victory was a fluke, that staying in power required a great amount of foresight and skill. He said the power was lying in the street, and we picked it up.

Machan: Apart from yourself, would you credit anyone else with a correct understanding of Marxism?

Hook: Oh yes. I think many people have understood Marx in the way I have understood him. But you must remember that although in 19331 published my *Towards the Understanding of Karl Marx*—the book appeared during a bank holiday—which seemed to confirm Marx's analysis of the capitalist system, I regarded myself as a critical Marxist. As events developed, I came to the conclusion that Marx's historical predictions had been disconfirmed by history. So I no longer regard myself as a Marxist, although I believe my understanding of Marx's views, based on my analysis, is sound.

Machan: Are there any self-proclaimed Marxists whom you would credit with a fairly good understanding of Marxism in our own time?

Hook: Self-proclaimed Marxists? Most of the self-proclaimed Marxists with whom I'm acquainted I think are Leninists rather than Marxists.

Machan: I see.

Hook: And here I wouldn't venture any characterization. Leszek Kolakowski was a Marxist, of a critical vein in which I was once, but he too no longer regards himself as a Marxist. I was a pluralistic Marxist. I attempted to interpret Marx empirically, scientifically, in the light of the evidence. I thought that his views were ambiguous, indeterminate. He would ask what was *the* most important factor in society. And I would say one can't ask a question like that. He refers—in one of his analogies—to the economics of the political anatomy of society. Well, the political anatomy is most parts of the body. There's no scientific position in answer to the question. It's only when you have a problem what is most important for the solution of this problem is that we can look for a center. But you can't say what's most important for the functioning of the body!

Machan: But is this not somewhat reminiscent of the influence of pragmatism on your thinking?

Hook: I think there are pragmatic elements in Marx's philosophy which he didn't develop. And again in my early days I thought that these had been extensively developed by John Dewey.

I'm prepared to admit that the dominant interpretation of Marx is quite different from my own. I want to call attention again to another important metaphor in Marx. When trying to explain the significance of the economy in history, he says it is the foundation on which the superstructure is built. But he also recognizes what he called the reciprocal influence of the superstructure on the foundation. Well, how can you do that? And first of all, even if you have a foundation, that doesn't determine altogether how high the building is; what a foundation does is to exclude possibilities but it doesn't determine what's going to happen. And while you have a foundation of a building, what about its style, what about its ornaments, what about the things which make the building livable? That can't be derived from the foundation alone.

Machan: Yet we do go back to the undeniable fact that Marxism is prominent in our intellectual environment, that if you go to any university bookstore you will see book after book on Marx by Marx around Marx, and sometimes, rarely, critical of Marx. Every other social problem is analyzed from a Marxist perspective—women's liberation, the drug problem, race relations, etc.

Humanism

Machan: In our particular times there are certain kinds of controversies that appear on the cultural scene, one of which is the conflict between a religious understanding of American history and a more secular humanist understanding of American history. Some people claim—they have even taken this to court now and then in the case of the scrutiny of high school textbooks—that there's been an extraordinary influence of secular humanism on our way of understanding our past. Is this secular humanism the humanism that some people mention in connection with Marxism?

Hook: Not as I understand it. I think secular humanism is an indigenous American development that flows from the erosion of religious belief, and the discovery of a conclusion that moral judgment is autonomous, independent of religion. What makes an event or an action good or bad, or right or wrong, is not a supernatural command from on high, but an intrinsic character of that action or the consequences of that action.

So secular humanists may be Marxists or they can be anti-Marxists. After all, one of the leading secular humanists in the U.S., Ralph Ingersoll, was certainly no Marxist. So I myself think that it would be a great error to try to interpret secular humanism as manifesting any influence of Marxism whatsoever.

Machan: So what is it that Marx has influenced in our culture? How does it relate to our culture? There's a great deal of concern about Marxism; there's a great deal of worry about him—some people think of him as the worst part of human history and they're fearing him and denouncing him, other people are admirers of Marx and many people of the intellectual centers of our culture are very respectful of Marx's ideas. Where is the actual impact of Marxism in our society?

Hook: Let's face it—most people who think of Marxism today tend to identify it unfortunately with the theory and practice of the Soviet Union—communism. And most people are unaware that some of the leading Marxists of the twentieth century, for example Karl Kautsky, the German Social Democrats, etc., were bitterly opposed to the communists who actually held them responsible for the failure of the Western countries to introduce any socialist revolutions.

In fact when the communists seized power in Russia and after they called a meeting of the constituent assembly where they had polled only 19 per cent of the vote, they seized power in the expectation that there would be a socialist revolution in the West. They didn't expect to hold on to power.

Marx thought of socialism as international, not as national. It didn't come, and so under Stalin they dedicated themselves to building socialism, and undermining the regimes of all other countries. And this of course has produced natural resentment and fear so that very few people are prepared to look at Marx's doctrines independently of the way in which Lenin and his followers have interpreted Marx.

Machan: Suppose we do that for a moment. Let's assume that we should not think of the Soviets and of Marx in the same light.

Now, if we have understood Marx correctly, what is it about our culture that owes something to him? What is it about our culture, in turn, that definitely repudiates him?—let's judge by *The Communist Manifesto's* several points of what must be accomplished by the revolutionary movement.

Hook: Many of the things that were demanded by *The Communist Manifesto* have already been realized under our existing system. I believe what is impressive about Marx, as I pointed out earlier, is his stress on the influence of the mode of economic production, the way in which property affects personality and all other aspects of culture. Now he exaggerated. It's a matter of degree, and one can use Marxism as a heuristic method, as a method of inquiry to broaden one's understanding of the past. I think one will have to reject Marx's generalizations on the basis of the evidence, and part of the evidence which will lead one to the rejection of the Marxist theory of history is actually what the communists have done in the Soviet Union and elsewhere. In Marx's view, for example, war was a consequence of capitalism. But here you have socialist countries going to war, here you had the Soviet Union threatening to use atom bombs against communist China. So certainly that explodes this notion that war is a consequence of the capitalist system in its struggle for markets and things of that sort.

Machan: Do you think that there's a legacy of Marxist ways of understanding, for example, poverty, and its influence on crime, poverty and its influence on the development of children to reach some sort of successful stage in our society? Do these derive from Marx's ideas? Or are they so general that you cannot really credit Marx with them?

Hook: I believe that these views derived from other sources primarily. After all, the whole sociological approach to society beginning with Kant, whom Marx has criticized rather unsympathetically, stressed the social factors. That is to say the emphasis on nurture, in the nature/nurture controversy, goes back before Marx. Those who are influenced by Marx have a tendency to try to interpret the social influence in economic terms. A Marxist environmentalist tends to be narrower in his view of the environment. It's perfectly possible for an individual to believe in social reform and social progress, and yet not be a Marxist.

Machan: So in a way you are saying that Western, and especially American, culture today is really free of a significant dose of Marxist influence?

Hook: I think it would be true to say that there's no evidence of a pervasive influence of Marxism on American life. Even the American labor movement has never been sympathetic to explicitly organized socialist political parties.

Machan: In contrast to the British labor movement?

Hook: In contrast to the British labor movement, in contrast to the German labor movement, the French labor movement, the Italian labor movement. There's a standing problem as to why the American labor movement is not socialist in its orientation or its aspiration.

Machan: But isn't it the case that that pervasive contrast between labor and capital that has entered into our culture has outstripped its usefulness because of the Marxist frame of reference to which it owes some debt?

Hook: The odd thing about it is that the intensity of the labor/capital conflict in the United States was fiercer here than in Europe and, despite the intensity of that conflict where strikes were almost occasions of civil war, there was no political expression of that. And with the emergence of the New Deal, the American labor movement organized its support on behalf of the New Deal.

Machan: The democratic aspect of Marxism would indicate that it is really in this country, which is more responsive to democratic pressures, that a certain kind of socialism is emerging. A kind of homage to Marx is emerging here that the Soviet Union is a fraudulent Marxism. The growing socialization of property in America may be the genuine Marxist expression.

Hook: I think a case could be made for that. It would require some thoughtful analysis to qualify it. But I can imagine someone maintaining that the unfinished task of democracy in the United States is being fulfilled along democratic Marxist lines. I don't think that's altogether true because the economic class struggle in this country is overlaid with other struggles, religious, racial, regional and they can't be reduced merely to economic struggles. So that you have a skein of many different colors and tendencies.

What is unique about the American culture is that the operation of economic forces in Western Europe takes place here without any feudal traditions, in an atmosphere where there's no sense of class, where it can be argued, as the young Leon Sampson once argued, the whole notion of Americanism has replaced traditional forms of socialism.

I still remember a time in this country where if you got up and said that we live in a class society that would be regarded as subversive. Whereas in Europe if you got up and said, you live in a classless society, that would be regarded as subversive. The notion of class and belonging to class is taken for granted in Europe in terms of the heritage of feudalism and what followed it. But in the United States the notion of class and identification of class is relatively new. There have always been classes here, there have been class struggles, but there has been reluctance to recognize the polarizing and differentiating factors in the light of the belief that "a man's a man for that," and he has an opportunity to improve himself. There was a period when you had unlimited land, and you could go out and carve a career for yourself and that came to an end of course in the twentieth century. But the ideology—some people say the mythology—of the past still plays a role.

When I was young, I was asked what I wanted to do when I grew up. Well, I wanted to be President of the United States. Now practically every boy on the block in the slum in which I was brought up, if asked the same question, would have said, "I want to be President." That consciousness played a role which is absent in Europe because—maybe I'm mistaken but—I can't think of a country in Europe where the children of the proletariat, when asked about their future, would respond in this way.

Machan: Is it fair to claim that the rhetoric of Marxism in many societies, especially in the Soviet Union and where it has great influence, is a cover for a renewal of a certain feudalist type regime—something that isn't substantially different from what feudalism was except in some of its ornamentations and some of its inessentials?

Hook: Well, it was Oscar Lange, a Polish economist, who referred to the Soviet Union as a form of industrial serfdom. But whether that can technically hold water or not there is no doubt that there are classes in the Soviet Union, comparable with the power that various classes had in other parts of the world in other periods of history.

Machan: Let me just ask one final question about this. Quite apart from whether the Soviet Union authentically latches on to this label "Marxist" for itself, are there particular worries that we in the West ought to have about the Soviets because they have chosen Marxism as their cover, as their official ideology? Because of that alone, is there some particular worry that we should pay attention to?

Hook: I believe that what we have to worry about is not so much their Marxist beliefs, but their aggressive actions. It's their paratroopers more than their theoreticians who constitute a danger to the democratic West. I believe myself that, if Marx's works were available in uncensored form to individuals in the Soviet Union, they would see the disparity between the kind of society Marx urged on mankind and the kind of society under which they live.

References

Acton, H.B., *Morals and Markets*, London: Longman, 1971.

Acton, H. B., *What Marx Really Said*, Atlantic-Heights, NJ: Humanities Books, 1967.

Becker, G., *The Economic Approach to Human Behavior*, Chicago: University of Chicago Press, 1976.

Bellah, R. *et al.*, *Habits of the Heart: Individualism and Commitment in American Life*, New York: Harper and Row, 1984.

Bolton, J. D. P., *Jest and Riddle: A Study of the Growth of Individualism from Homer to Christianity*, NY: Barnes and Noble, 1973.

Campbell, T., *The Left and Rights*, London: Routledge & Kegan Paul, 1983.

Christian, S., *The Atlantic*, August 1983.

Conway, D., *A Farewell to Marx*, New York: Penguin, 1987.

Davis, P., *Where is Nicaragua?* New York: Simon and Schuster, 1986.

Easton, L. D. and Guddat, K. H. eds. and trans., *Writing of the Young Marx on Philosophy and Society*, Garden City, NY: Anchor Books, 1967.

Engels, F., *The Dialectics of Nature*, NY: International Publishers, 1945.

Friedman, M., "The Line We Dare Not Cross," *Encounter*, November 1976.

Hayek, F.A. (Ed.), *Capitalism and the Historians*, Chicago: University of Chicago Press, 1960.

Heller, A., "Toward a Marxian Theory of Value," *Kinesis*, Fall 1972.

Machan, T. R., *Human Rights and Human Liberties*, Chicago: Nelson-Hall, 1975.

Machan, T. R., *Individuals and their Rights*, Chicago: Open Court Publishing Company, 1989.

Machan, T. R., *Capitalism and Individualism: Reframing the Argument for the Free Society*, NY: St. Martin's Press, 1989.

Machan, T. R., *Classical Individualism: The Supreme Importance of each Human Being*, London: Routledge, 1998.

MacIntyre, A., *After Virtue*, Notre Dame, IN: University of Notre Dame Press, 1984.

Marx, K., *The German Ideology*, NY: International Publishers, 1939.

McKenzie, R., *The Limits of Economic Science*, Boston: Kluwer-Nijhoff, 1983.

McLellan, D. ed. & trans., *The Grundrisse of Karl Marx*, NY: Harper Torchbook, 1971.

McLellan, D. ed., *Karl Marx. Selected Writings*, NY: Oxford University Press, 1977.

Meyer, A. G., *Communism*, NY: Random House, 1967.

Morris, C., *The Discovery of the Individual 1050-1200*, NY: Harper and Row, 1972.

Norton, D. L., *Personal Destinies, A Philosophy of Ethical Individualism*, Princeton, NJ: Princeton University Press, 1976.

O'Brien, J.C., "Marxism and the Instauration of Man: A Second Glance," in Engelhardt, W. W. and Thiemeyer, T. (eds.), *Gesellschaft, Wirtschaft, Wohnugswirtschaft. Festschrift für Helmut Jenkis*, Duncker and Humblot, 1987.

Pelczynski, Z. A. ed., *Hegel's Political Philosophy: Problems and Perspectives*, Cambridge, UK: Cambridge University Press, 1971.

Roberts, P. C. and Stephenson, M., *Marx's Theory of Exchange, Alienation and Crisis*, Stanford: Hoover Institution Press, 1979.

Smith, A., *The Wealth of Nations*, NY: Modern Library, 1939.
Sowell, T., *Marxism: Philosophy and Economics*, NY: Morrow, 1985.
Weaver, P., *The Suicidal Corporation*, NY: Simon and Schuster, 1988.

Index